Computer Science and Engineering Education for Pre-Collegiate Students and Teachers

Computer Science and Engineering Education for Pre-Collegiate Students and Teachers

Special Issue Editor

Andrea C. Burrows

MDPI • Basel • Beijing • Wuhan • Barcelona • Belgrade

MDPI

Special Issue Editor
Andrea C. Burrows
University of Wyoming
USA

Editorial Office
MDPI
St. Alban-Anlage 66
4052 Basel, Switzerland

This is a reprint of articles from the Special Issue published online in the open access journal *Education Sciences* (ISSN 2227-7102) in 2019 (available at: https://www.mdpi.com/journal/education/special_issues/Computer_Science_and_Engineering_Education)

For citation purposes, cite each article independently as indicated on the article page online and as indicated below:

LastName, A.A.; LastName, B.B.; LastName, C.C. Article Title. *Journal Name* **Year**, *Article Number*, Page Range.

ISBN 978-3-03897-940-1 (Pbk)
ISBN 978-3-03897-941-8 (PDF)

Contents

About the Special Issue Editor

Andrea C. Burrows is an Associate Professor at the University of Wyoming (UW) in the College of Education's (CoEd) School of Teacher Education. She received her doctorate degree from the University of Cincinnati in 2011. She was awarded the UW CoEd Early Career Fellowship (2013), the UW CoEd Faculty Award for Outstanding Research & Scholarship (2015), the UW CoEd Faculty Award for Outstanding Service to the Education Profession (2016), and the UW CoEd Honored Fall Convocation Faculty (2017). Since beginning at UW, Burrows has written, implemented, or evaluated over 50 unique grants. The core of her research agenda is to deepen science, mathematics, engineering, and technology (STEM) partnership involvement and understanding through STEM discipline integration (often regarded as iSTEM) with in-service teacher professional development (PD) and pre-service teacher coursework. Her research agenda is composed of a unified STEM education partnership structure and connects educational research to real-world practices. Burrows' many publications appear in leading journals. She is the Co-Editor of CITE-Journal Science (www.citejournal.org). She is active and presents in several organizations such as AERA, ASEE, ASTE, NSTA, and SITE. Before beginning her work in higher education, she taught secondary school science for 12 years in Florida and Virginia (USA).

Preface to "Computer Science and Engineering Education for Pre-collegiate Students and Teachers"

There was a call put out in Fall 2018 requesting articles regarding the current hot topics in computer science and engineering education for pre-collegiate students and teachers. The following is a summary of that call.

There are widespread areas to explore in both engineering education and computer science education. While computer science has roots in mathematics and is often seen as a branch of engineering, based on Johri and Olds' Cambridge Handbook of Engineering Education Research (2014) and Kadijevich, Angeli, and Schulte's Improving Computer Science Education (2013), the exploration of computer science and engineering education offers a rich field of study. This Special Issue "Computer Science and Engineering Education for Pre-Collegiate Students and Teachers" is a mechanism to advance and capture the current conversation about computer science and engineering education in pre-collegiate schools—worldwide—by using current research studies in the area. Quantitative, qualitative, mixed methods, and action research methodologies are welcome for this Special Issue. A clear problem and research questions, appropriate theoretical framework, literature review, methodology and methods, analysis, conclusions, and limitations are expected for all submitted articles. Additionally, there are many resources that this Special Issue could highlight and bring to the forefront of computer science education. Authors of potential articles should consider including a successful lesson or professional development activity as exemplars of "ideas to try". A Special Issue in computer science and engineering education also warrants connection to other disciplines (science, technology, engineering, mathematics, among others) in order to highlight how current teachers (and students) can enhance what they are already considering or implementing in pre-collegiate classrooms (that might even seem distant from these research areas). Engineering, technology, and computer science standards from states, countries, and organizations are also welcome and encouraged as a piece of the research studies.

Questions to consider when writing about pre-collegiate computer science and engineering research studies: (1) What courses are offered at the pre-collegiate level in computer science and/or engineering in the geographic area of the study? (2) Are the courses offered in isolation or combined with another subject? (3) Who (teacher and/or student) has access to the computer science and engineering courses? (4) What approaches are used in the computer science and engineering courses? (5) What professional development learning opportunities are available for teachers delivering computer science and engineering course content? (6) What standards do teachers and students use in computer science and engineering courses? (7) What is needed to move pre-collegiate computer science and engineering education forward as a field? (8) What collaborative partnerships have enabled the successful adoption of computer science and engineering education in pre-collegiate environments? and (9) other questions related to context, successes, and challenges in pre-collegiate computer science and engineering education. Finally, consider this: How close are we as a global community to the vision set forth for 2020 in Greening's Computer Science Education in the 21st Century (2000)? Keywords for articles could include: engineering education; computer science; pre-collegiate teachers; pre-collegiate students; K–12; NGSS.

All papers were peer-reviewed, and the accepted six papers were published in the journal together on the Special Issue website (and found in this book). Research articles, review articles, as well as short communications were invited.

Andrea C. Burrows
Special Issue Editor

education sciences

MDPI

Article

A Systematic Review Exploring the Differences in Reported Data for Pre-College Educational Activities for Computer Science, Engineering, and Other STEM Disciplines

Adrienne Decker [1,*] and Monica M. McGill [2]

[1] Department of Engineering Education, University at Buffalo, Buffalo, NY 14260, USA
[2] Department of Computer Science, Knox College, Galesburg, IL 61401, USA; mmmcgill@knox.edu
* Correspondence: adrienne@buffalo.edu

Received: 31 January 2019; Accepted: 28 March 2019; Published: 30 March 2019

check for updates

Abstract: There has been considerable investment in pre-college educational interventions for all areas of STEM (including computer science). The goal of many of these initiatives is to engage and interest students early in their educational career. In this study, a systematic literature review was undertaken to determine the demographic and program data collected and reported for the field of computing education and for other STEM disciplines for activities that were not designed as part of the formal in-class curriculum (e.g., outreach activities). A comparison-contrast analysis of the resulting 342 articles found similarities and key differences in the reporting of this data as well as overarching characteristics of missing or incomplete reporting across disciplines. Authors from both fields reported equally well in the four categories studied: information about evaluation, participant gender, participant race and/or ethnicity, and activity demographics. However, the computing education articles were more likely to have clearly stated research questions and comparative analysis based on demographic characteristics. They were less likely to include the number of participants in the study, participant age/grade level, socioeconomic status, disability information, location of intervention, and instructor demographics. Through this analysis, it was determined that reporting can be improved across all disciplines to improve the quantity of data needed to replicate studies and to provide complete data sets that provide for the comparison of collected data.

Keywords: pre-college computing activities; pre-college engineering activities; pre-college STEM activities; K–12; literature review; computing outreach; engineering outreach; STEM outreach

1. Introduction

When President Obama publicly announced the Computer Science for All initiative in January 2016 [1], it consolidated a growing movement within the computing education community in the United States (U.S.) to bring computing into schools prior to university [2]. Since that time, there has been a growth in the number of states in the U.S. adopting standards for computing education in primary and secondary (K–12) schools, with all but six states having adopted some sort of computing policy or standards as of the *2018 State of Computer Science Education* report compiled by Code.org [3]. Organizations such as the Computer Science Teachers Association (CSTA) and ISTE have released standards for learning not just about technology, but about computing and computational thinking at the K–12 level [4,5]. This effort is not localized to the U.S., and there are examples of organizations and standards in other parts of the world that mirror these efforts [6–8].

However, prior to and even when standards are approved and adopted, there is a wide variety of ways in which the content is being delivered, including activities both within and outside the classroom [9–12]. It remains unclear from the computing education literature what the most effective practices are for engaging students with this material as well as the long-term effectiveness of these activities, particularly with regard to claims of fostering student interest in the discipline [13,14]. With increasing effort, time, money, and resources being invested in pre-college computing education, being able to determine empirically the best interventions for a specific target demographic or environment can be valuable to the community.

Further, credible research and findings rely on two important indicators—replication and generalizability. Replication is needed in order to determine whether the results of a study are robust or whether they were merely an anomaly [15]. Due to the newness of computing education, replication studies in educational research are still lacking and the data that are reported are incomplete [14,16,17]. However, other STEM education fields (e.g., chemistry, medicine, and psychology) have similar issues with lack of replication [18–20]. This limits how confident researchers can be about the results of educational research studies, with the U.S. National Science Foundation recognizing this and publishing Companion Guidelines for Replication and Reproducibility in Education Research in November 2018 [21]. In it, there is a call for more transparency in research, open data access policies, and full documentation of the features of the study, including population, context, and fidelity of implementation. Interventions and populations need to be reported in a consistent manner to allow for better comparison amongst the findings and allow for better replication of the studies, providing researchers with the critical empirical evidence needed to identify best practices among various demographic groups of learners.

Unlike computing, most of the other STEM fields, including their many subdisciplines, have a long-standing and strong presence in the formal pre-college curriculum. While computing is just starting to become part of state standards of education, other disciplines have been part of the standards for decades. Based on previous research showing a deficiency of reporting on many important variables in computing education and the need to report elements of a study design adequately for replication, the researchers considered whether more established STEM fields reported data from pre-college educational activities more holistically in educational research and whether insight could be gained from the reporting of data in these fields [13,14,16]. Therefore, the following research questions guide this part of the work:

- [R1] What type of longitudinal and sequential data collection techniques have been used in the formal, peer-reviewed research that has been conducted on pre-college computing activities for the years 2014–2016?
- [R2] What type of longitudinal and sequential data collection techniques have been used in the formal, peer-reviewed research that has been conducted on STEM activities for the years 2014–2016?
- [R3] What are the similarities and differences between the reporting of pre-college computing activities and other STEM disciplines?

This work is important for K–12 education researchers in computing, K–12 education researchers in STEM fields, K–12 education evaluators, and other stakeholders invested in improving computing education as the K–12 community starts teaching computing to a wide variety of students. It is also important in identifying best practices and is, therefore, impactful on the work being performed by curriculum designers to bring computing into K–12 classrooms. Other stakeholders are institutions such as the U.S. National Science Foundation, Department of Education, and other policymakers who are recognizing the need for more replication of education research to increase the confidence of research findings that inform best practices.

The remainder of this paper is organized as follows. Section 2 discusses the framework and steps undertaken to conduct the systematic literature reviews. Section 3 describes the study results, including demographic information as well as data reported on the activities. Section 4 is a discussion of these results put into the context of previous research. Section 5 provides a high-level overview and its potential impact on future work.

2. Materials and Methods

To answer the research questions, the researchers undertook a systematic literature review following the framework developed by Khan, Kunz, Kleijnen, and Antes [22]. The framework has five foundational steps: frame the question, identify relevant work, assess the quality of the studies, summarize the evidence, and interpret the findings.

Although there was not a protocol pre-registered for this study, Figure 1 shows the Preferred Reporting Items for Systematic Reviews and Meta-Analyses (PRISMA) 2009 flow diagram of the process. It is referenced throughout the discussion of the methods when describing how the initial set of 5917 articles was reduced to 342 articles for inclusion in this study via the five steps of the systematic literature review.

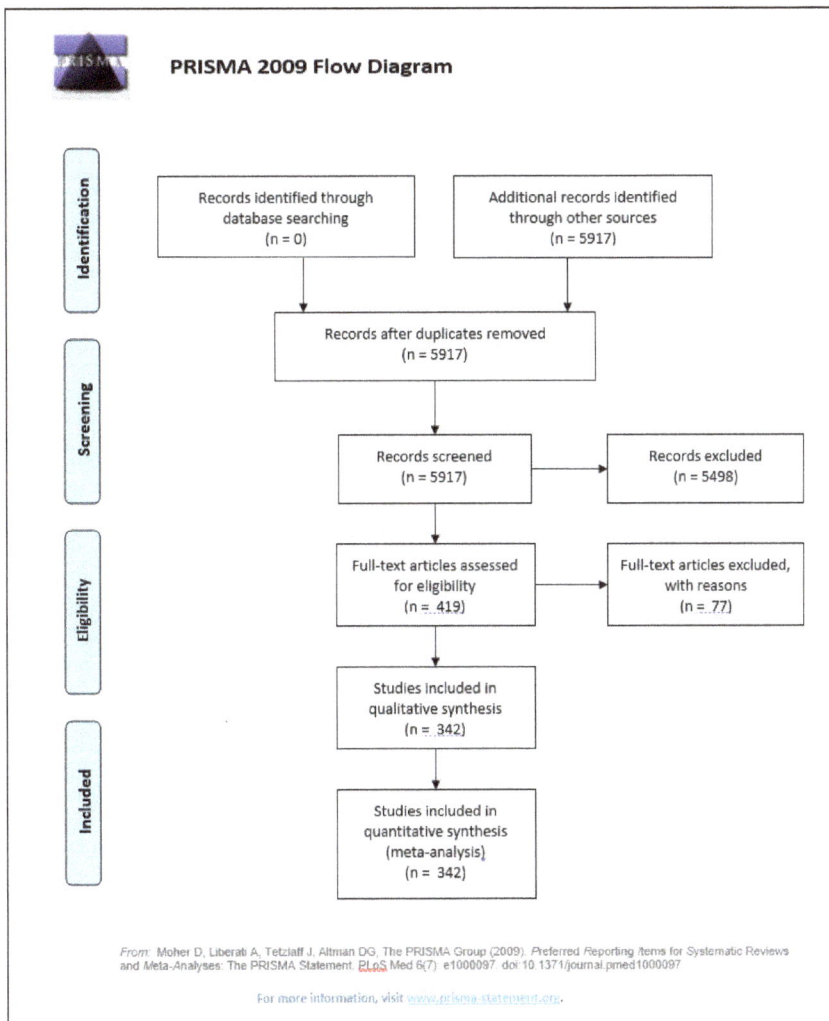

PRISMA 2009 Flow Diagram

Identification

Records identified through database searching
(n = 0)

Additional records identified through other sources
(n = 5917)

Screening

Records after duplicates removed
(n = 5917)

Records screened
(n = 5917)

Records excluded
(n = 5498)

Eligibility

Full-text articles assessed for eligibility
(n = 419)

Full-text articles excluded, with reasons
(n = 77)

Included

Studies included in qualitative synthesis
(n = 342)

Studies included in quantitative synthesis (meta-analysis)
(n = 342)

From: Moher D, Liberati A, Tetzlaff J, Altman DG, The PRISMA Group (2009). Preferred Reporting Items for Systematic Reviews and Meta-Analyses: The PRISMA Statement. PLoS Med 6(7): e1000097. doi:10.1371/journal.pmed1000097

For more information, visit www.prisma-statement.org.

Figure 1. PRISMA flow diagram of this literature review.

2.1. Framing the Question

While the research questions guide this work overall, it is important to further define some of the aspects of this work and the guiding principles for determining what type of educational activity qualifies for this analysis. For this analysis, only activities that are created and administered outside of the formal in-class curriculum are considered. For purposes of this work, the formal in-class curriculum refers to curricula that fulfill state/national education requirements and/or content that is offered as part of a school's required or elective course or module. Some examples of the types of activities that are not part of the formal in-class curriculum include outreach activities, summer camps, and after school programs. Also, since the research questions are looking for data collection techniques and reporting, the articles must provide the data collected and the analysis or evaluation of the educational activity.

To summarize, the following criteria was used for inclusion:

- Computing or STEM activity
- Designed for K–12 participants (students or teachers)
- Designed to teach computing, computational thinking, STEM concepts
- Outside of standardized curriculum or courses
- Provides information about participants, data collected, assessment and/or evaluation

2.2. Identifying Relevant Work

This section, explains how the sources were identified for both computing and STEM research venues for this study as well as how the articles were subsequently identified within these venues.

2.2.1. Venue Identification Procedures

Since there were two sets of data collected, one on computing activities and one on STEM activities, this methodology for identifying relevant educational research is presented in separate sections.

Computing Education

In the academic discipline of computing (or computer science), publishing in journals is not as common as publishing in conference proceedings. The Association for Computing Machinery (ACM) and Institute of Electrical and Electronics Engineers (IEEE) are the premier international associations for publishing computing education research. Both sponsor conference and journal publications that are considered the most reliable sources for formal, blind, peer-reviewed computing education research. Also included in the set of sources are any additional venues (conferences or journals) from outside of those two organizations that are recognized within the computing education community as presenting relevant and high-quality work. Table 1 shows the final list of venues for inclusion in this literature review.

Table 1. Table of venues for computing education literature.

Sponsor	Title	Type
ACM	International Computing Education Research (ICER)	Conference
ACM	Innovation and Technology in Computer Science Education (ITiCSE)	Conference
ACM	Technical Symposium on Computer Science Education (SIGCSE)	Conference
ACM	Transactions on Computing Education (TOCE)	Journal
Taylor and Francis	Computer Science Education (CSE)	Journal
IEEE	IEEE Global Engineering Education Conference (EDUCON)	Conference
IEEE	Frontiers in Education (FIE)	Conference
IEEE	Transactions on Education (TOE)	Journal
Sage	Journal of Educational Computing Research (JECR)	Journal
	Koli Calling International Conference on Computing Education Research (Koli)	Conference

Closely Related STEM Disciplines

In order to identify relevant work in closely related STEM areas, a working definition of STEM is needed. In *Science, Technology, Engineering, and Mathematics (STEM) Education: A Primer* STEM is defined as "Some federal agencies, such as the NSF, use a broader definition of STEM that includes psychology and the social sciences (e.g., political science, economics) as well as the so-called core sciences and engineering (e.g., physics, chemistry, mathematics). Others, including the Department of Homeland Security (DHS), U.S. Immigration and Customs Enforcement (ICE), use a narrower definition that generally excludes social sciences and focuses on mathematics, chemistry, physics, computer and information sciences, and engineering. Some analysts argue that field-specific definitions such as these are too static and that definitions of STEM should focus on "an assemblage of practices and processes that transcend disciplinary lines and from which knowledge and learning of a particular kind emerges." [23] (p. 2)

Further analysis led to an article by Freeman et al. [24] which indicates that in their literature review "We used four approaches (35) to find articles for consideration: hand-searching every issue in 55 STEM education journals from June 1, 1998 to January 1, 2010 ... searching seven online databases using an array of terms, mining reviews and bibliographies (SI Materials and Methods), and "snowballing" from references in articles admitted to the study (SI Materials and Methods)." (p. 8414). The researchers chose to adopt the 55 journals listed in Table S3 of [24], which mirrored the process undertaken to define computing venues. Of these 55 journals, journals that focused on undergraduate education as noted by its title, aim, and/or scope were removed (*Journal of Undergraduate Neuroscience Education, Research in Collegiate Mathematics Education, Chemistry Education: Research and Practice (UnivChemEdu), Journal of College Science Teaching, Active Learning in Higher Education, Advances in Engineering Education, Chemical Engineering Education, International Journal of Electrical Engineering Education, International Journal of Mechanical Engineering Education, American Journal of Physics*).

Then, journals that focused on computing education and/or were already evaluated were removed: *ACM SIGCSE Bulletin, Computer Science Education,* and *Journal of Educational Computing Research*.

Next, the description of each journal along with the titles and abstracts of the articles in the most current issue were evaluated. If these appeared to be focused on post-secondary education, they were then removed from the list (*Advances in Physiology Education, Bioscience, Journal of Food Science Education, Journal of Microbiology and Biology Education, International Journal of Engineering Education*).

Additional journals were removed due to the lack of a focus on education (*BioScience* (only one education related article in Jan–April 2017)), no articles during the 2014–2016 time period (*Chemical Education International, Engineering Science and Education Journal, Mathematics Education Review, Astronomy Education Review*), or for being solely curriculum and activity focused (with no assessment/evaluations or data about the activity provided) (*Physics Education*).

After these journals were removed, 31 journals remained. The size of this set was three times the size of the set of computing venues. To create a set of venues of similar size to the number of computing venues, sampling was needed. Looking at the number of venues for each subdiscipline for those that were over-represented, a systematic sampling technique, where every n^{th} sample from a list is included was used [25].

The first aim of the sampling was to create an almost equivalent number of venues focused on each of the subdisciplines of STEM to not have one subdiscipline dominate the results. Chemistry, Geology, and Psychology each had one venue. Engineering had two venues that encompassed all of the subdisciplines of engineering, which the researchers considered to be an appropriate number in relation to the others. Biology had three venues, which were also deemed an acceptable number. Physics had four venues, which would cause it to be the largest sample in the sciences. To bring this number in alignment with Biology, one venue needed to be removed. A random number generator was used to determine which of the venues (1–4) should be eliminated. The number three was chosen and the third venue was eliminated.

For Mathematics, there were ten venues. A systematic sampling of every other would yield five venues which may have over-skewed the sample to mathematics education. A systematic sampling of every third would yield four venues. While this is higher than the other subdisciplines, mathematics is taught more broadly than the specific sciences in the pre-college curriculum and this was deemed acceptable by the researchers for the sample. There were also ten General STEM venues and a systematic sampling of every other venue would yield five venues. Since these were general STEM venues encompassing any part of STEM, five seemed reasonable. This systematic sampling yielded 19 venues, which was still almost double the amount of computing venues, but seemed to accurately represent the subdisciplines of STEM. The included and excluded venues are shown in Table 2.

Table 2. Table of venues for STEM literature.

Discipline	Journal Name [1]
Biology	Biochemistry and Molecular Biology Education (Biochem Ed)
	CBE—Life Sciences Education
	Journal of Natural Resources and Life Sciences Education
Chemistry	Journal of Chemical Education
Engineering	European Journal of Engineering Education
	Journal of Engineering Education
General STEM	Electronic Journal of Science Education
	International Journal of Science and Mathematics Education
	International Journal of Science Education
	Journal of Research in Science Teaching
	Journal of Science Education and Technology
	Journal of STEM Education
	Research in Science Education
	Research in Science and Technological Education
	Science Education
	Science Educator
Geology	Journal of Geoscience Education
Math, Statistics, CS	Educational Studies in Mathematics
	Electronic Journal of Mathematics and Technology
	Eurasia Journal of Mathematics, Science, and Technology Education
	International Electronic Journal of Mathematics Education
	Journal for Research in Mathematics Education
	Journal of Statistics Education
	Mathematics Education Research Journal
	Primus
	Research in Mathematics Education
	Statistics Education Research Journal
Physics and Astronomy	Physical Review—Physics Education Research
	Physics & Astronomy
	Physics Education
	The Physics Teacher
Psychology	Teaching of Psychology

[1] Shaded rows indicate journals not included in this analysis.

Additionally, some of the venues that were identified for computing education also had articles relating to general STEM education and in the review process, articles from those venues were also included in the STEM set of articles as they were found. Additional STEM articles were found in IEEE EDUCON, IEEE FIE, IEEE TOE, and JECR.

2.2.2. Article Identification Procedures

The next step in the process was to determine which articles in each publication should be included in the literature review. To do this, a manual reading of each abstract was conducted to determine whether the content of the studies reflected in each article contained the following characteristics:

- Designed for K–12 participants or teachers
- STEM/Computing educational activity or process
- Outside of standardized curriculum or courses

- Provided information about participants, data collected, assessment and/or evaluation
- Categorized as computing if designed to teach exclusively computer science or computational thinking
- Categorized as STEM if designed to teach one or more categories in STEM other than computing

Because the process of reading each abstract does not rely on search terms or automation, the search has been limited to a range of three full calendar years, 2014–2016, which encompass the reporting of activities just prior to the announcement of major U.S. government funding for pre-college computing education. For the venues in that time, there were 2566 computing articles and 3351 STEM articles published, resulting in 5917 articles (as shown in the PRISMA chart in Figure 1). A spreadsheet was created so that each row of the spreadsheet represented an article published in each of the venues for the years 2014–2016 inclusive. For each article, relevant bibliographic information was captured (e.g., title, author, venue, page numbers) including a hyperlink to the article for viewing. Most importantly, the article abstract was captured for each article as a key part of the first phase of this analysis.

The inclusion of an article for the final thorough review was a two-phase process. The first phase involved two independent coders reading each abstract and coding the article as relevant or not to the review. Relevance was determined by each coder by rating the information in the abstract against the criterion above. After the two coders independently coded the article abstracts, their results were compared and discrepancies were resolved through discussion. Inter-rater reliability on the coding of the abstracts for computing articles was 96.5% and for STEM articles was 96.4%. At this point, all identified articles (419) were moved onto the next stage of the process. The reading of the abstracts (or screening as indicated in Figure 1) eliminated 5,498 articles.

2.3. Data Collection Process

The next stage involved a careful read of the 419 included articles to extract data for the previously identified program elements. The process that determined the program elements is described more fully in [16]; to summarize, a random subset of 10 articles were read and notes were created about the types of information the articles reported about the research studies. After the initial set of articles were read, a set of 13 article/study characteristics and 24 program elements were created that represented the type of information that was being reported by the studies. Table 3 gives the list of article/study characteristics while Table 4 gives a listing of the program elements.

Table 3. Research/study characteristics coded during the literature review.

Characteristics	Codes
Type of article	Research article, experience report, literature review
Focus area	Activity, curriculum, evaluation instrument, professional development
Basic study design	Cross-sectional, longitudinal, meta-study, retrospective, not applicable
Research approach	Mixed methods, qualitative, quantitative, unspecified
Research questions/hypotheses	Actual questions/hypotheses recorded
Experience Report summary	Actual text of summary recorded
Time period for study	Actual amount of time recorded
Analysis based on gender	Yes/no
Analysis based on race/ethnicity	Yes/no
Analysis based on socioeconomic status	Yes/no
What was measured	Freeform text about what was evaluated
Measurement frequency	Longitudinal, mid-intervention, post-intervention, pre-intervention, retrospective (can code to more than one)
Measurement type	Freeform text
Instrument name	Freeform text

Table 4. Program elements coded during the literature review (all freeform text).

Student Demographics	Instructor Demographics	Activity Components
Number of participants	Who was the instructor (e.g., researcher,	Type of activity (e.g., camp, field trip, workshop)
Age	classroom teacher)	Learning objectives
Grade level	Number of instructors	Required or elective
Gender	Gender	Curriculum used
Race/ethnicity	Race/ethnicity	Teaching method (lecture, lab, PBL)
Socioeconomic status	Prior experience of instructors	Tool/language used
Disability data		When activity was offered (camp, class)
Prior education and experience		Duration of activity, including contact hours
Location		Average number of students per session (if multiple sessions)

As the researchers progressed through the reading of each of the candidate articles, 29 computing articles and 48 STEM articles were removed from further analysis because upon reading the articles, they did not provide any formal evaluation or data about the intervention described. The articles may have fulfilled many or all of the other criteria (pre-college and outside formal curriculum), but did not present evidence of assessment or efficacy. These articles simply described the educational process or intervention.

After these articles were removed, 199 computing articles and 143 STEM articles were analyzed and the program elements were recorded. Both reserachers participated in the coding process. For the computing articles, a two-level review system was adopted. An initial coder categorized the elements from the articles listed in Tables 3 and 4, and a second coder verified those categorizations. Roles were reversed frequently and discrepancies were discussed throughout the process. It is important to note that every attempt was made to capture the information as the authors published it and to not infer or interpret the information given in the articles. For this review, investigators or article authors were not contacted to provide missing information. The data for the STEM articles were coded by one of the researchers based on experience of coding the data in the computing articles. The coded data for the computing articles are housed on https://csedresearch.org [26]. The coded data for STEM articles are available from the authors upon request.

2.4. Synthesis of Results, Study Bias, Limitations

For this review, only descriptive statistics were calculated and reported. Counts and percentages of the data recorded are reported, but no further analysis of the data was conducted. Issues of bias of individual studies were not considered by this review. No codes were assigned to articles about the discussion of limitations or bias of the intervention and/or evaluation. However, it is recognized that this may be an interesting factor to look at in the future.

In terms of the aggregate bias for the entire study, there is a selection bias present in terms of the venues that have been chosen. For the computing venues, the set of venues was determined based on researcher experience as active members in this research community, previously published literature reviews in computing education on this topic, and information gathered from a focus group [13,14,27]. There may be other venues publishing computing education research that would be relevant to this search.

For the STEM venues, it is outside the researchers' domain of expertise and, thus, the search began using another literature review published in a highly respected venue (Proceedings of the National Academy of Science) to guide the identification of appropriate venues [24]. From there, the venues were narrowed down to those focused in the pre-college domain and then a systematic sampling was conducted to create a more even distribution of the STEM disciplines. This process may have introduced bias into the sample. However, no additional venues were included in the set as the reserachers did not feel they had the expertise to judge the quality of the venue in the STEM domain. There may be other venues that publish STEM education-related articles that could be considered in this literature review. One example that was brought up during the review process was the American Society of Engineering Education (ASEE) which has an associated conference about topics in engineering education. There may be other additional venues not considered on the STEM side.

In terms of other larger systemic bias of the sample studied and the overall analysis, care was taken to report the data collected based on what the authors of the articles reported. Success of interventions was not considered, but rather whether or not the authors reported certain information about their study and participants. Thus, it is believed that the risk of bias in the recording of the data was low. There was no coding for impact on the academic achievement of the participants of the studies.

3. Results

This section will present the results of the analyses of the comparison of the data extracted from the articles considered. This corresponds to step 4, Summarize the Results, of the Khan, et al., framework [22] that is being followed for this systematic literature review.

3.1. Report Type

Table 5 shows the report type for each article analyzed. Articles were coded as research, experience report, or literature review. An experience report is a common format in computing education conferences and contains information about an educational intervention and reports about its success or failure, but does not report the results of an actual research study. For computing articles, there is almost an even split between the number of articles that qualify as experience reports versus those that qualify as pure research. However, STEM articles are dominated by research reports. This is most likely due to the nature of the venues for the two categories of articles. For computing education conferences, experience reports are considered valuable and important, and are encouraged, accepted and presented at a similar rate as research articles. Journals in computing education tend to be focused on research articles. Because there was a mix of conference and journal venues, there is almost an even split of those types. For the STEM disciplines, however, the percentage is heavily skewed with journal venues which again accept and publish mostly research articles.

Table 5. Computing vs. STEM articles by report type.

Report Type	Computing [1] (n = 199)	STEM [1] (n = 143)
Research	98 (49%)	126 (88%)
Experience Report	97 (49%)	16 (11%)
Literature Review	4 (2%)	1 (1%)

[1] Data reported as number of articles and % of the category.

3.2. Study Characteristics

In this section, the characteristics of the studies described within the articles are reported upon. Information about the basic study design, research approach, research questions, duration of the study, types of comparative analyses, and evaluation are presented in the subsections.

3.2.1. What Is Being Studied

The type of educational intervention being studied is broken up into four main categories: activity, curriculum, evaluation instruments, and professional development. Professional development is any intervention designed specifically for teachers, either in-service or pre-service, generally for the purposes of training. Articles that report on the design and validation of evaluation instruments related to pre-college interventions are given the code evaluation instruments. The code curriculum is for those articles that discuss either the impact of the implementation of national curriculum or state curriculum standards; or localized curriculum efforts that span more than one activity, lesson, or unit. All other articles are coded as activity. Table 6 gives a breakdown of each type of activity for computing and STEM articles. Literature reviews were not included in this analysis. The data show that for computing, the main focus of 85% of the articles is the activities and curriculum, almost evenly split. This is not the case for STEM that is 83% focused on activities.

Table 6. Computing vs. STEM articles by type of intervention.

Focus Area	Computing [1] (n = 195)	STEM [1] (n = 142)
Activity	87 (45%)	119 (83%)
Curriculum	78 (40%)	14 (10%)
Evaluation Instrument	6 (3%)	1 (1%)
Professional Development	24 (12%)	8 (6%)

[1] Data reported as number of articles and % of the category.

3.2.2. Basic Study Design

Table 7 shows the categorized basic study design for each article. The studies described in each article were coded as cross-sectional, longitudinal, meta-study, retrospective, or not applicable. While it is not always the case that experience reports have a systematic study included in the article, many of them fall in line with the same study design characteristics as research articles. Some experience reports talk about a single intervention (cross-sectional), while others discuss an intervention over time and how it has evolved (longitudinal). Literature reviews were not included in this analysis. For some articles, it is not clear which of the two categories are being discussed and not applicable has been coded. When comparing computing to STEM, there is a similar pattern of distribution of the basic study design with cross-sectional making up a large majority of the studies. While the number of longitudinal studies found is similar between the groups, STEM has a slight lead when considered as a percentage of the whole.

Table 7. Computing vs. STEM articles by basic study design.

Study Design	Computing [1] (n = 195)	STEM [1] (n = 142)
Cross-sectional	152 (78%)	123 (87%)
Longitudinal	18 (9%)	19 (13%)
Meta-study	3 (2%)	0 (0%)
Retrospective	12 (6%)	0 (0%)
Not applicable	10 (5%)	0 (0%)

[1] Data reported as number of articles and % of the category.

3.2.3. Time Period for Longitudinal Studies

For each article that was coded as research and coded as longitudinal for its basic study design, the duration of the study as stated in the article was recorded. For the computing articles, the duration of the longitudinal study was reported in the range of one semester up to 10 years. The average duration of the longitudinal computing studies was computed to be two years. For STEM studies, the study duration was in the range of one year to 10 years and the average study duration was 3.36 years. The ranges for these two groups are arguably not different, but the average length of study is slightly higher for STEM studies.

3.2.4. Research Approach

For each article that was coded as research, the research approach was coded when described in the article. The codes used were quantitative, qualitative, mixed methods, or unspecified. The results of the coding are presented in Table 8 and show that the computing articles are actually a majority of non-quantitative approaches with 29% using qualitative research techniques and 41% using a mixed methods approach. Only 27% of the computing articles describe studies that used strictly quantitative methods. For the STEM articles, it is the opposite with 50% using quantitative techniques and only 20% using a qualitative approach, with 29% using a mixed methods approach.

Table 8. Computing vs. STEM articles by research approach.

Research Approach	Computing [1] (n = 102)	STEM [1] (n = 126)
Quantitative	28 (27%)	63 (50%)
Qualitative	30 (29%)	25 (20%)
Mixed Methods	42 (41%)	36 (29%)
Unspecified	2 (2%)	2 (1%)

[1] Data reported as number of articles and % of the category.

3.2.5. Research Questions

For each article that was coded as research, whether or not the article presented its research questions or research hypotheses was recorded. This was a binary coding and the results of the coding are presented in Table 9 and show that computing articles present their research questions and/or hypotheses more often than the STEM articles and are reporting the research questions 80% of the time, compared to only 63% of the time for STEM articles.

Table 9. Computing vs. STEM articles stating research question(s).

Research Question(s) Stated	Computing [1] (n = 102)	STEM [1] (n = 126)
Yes	82 (80%)	79 (63%)
No	20 (20%)	47 (37%)

[1] Data reported as number of articles and % of the category.

Digging deeper into this data shows that for computing, those articles that did not report a research question were 20% qualitative studies, 30% quantitative studies, and 50% mixed methods studies. For STEM, articles that did not state research questions were 19% qualitative, 62% quantitative, and 19% mixed methods studies. Based on this analysis, there does not seem to be a pattern related to the type of research design and the reporting of research questions.

3.2.6. Analysis Based on Race, Gender, or Socioeconomic Status

For each article, three independent, binary codings were produced to answer the question of whether or not the article presented analyses based on differences in race, gender, and/or socioeconomic status. All articles were included in this analysis since many experience reports present either anecdotal data or observations about differences between these demographic groups. The results of the coding are presented in Table 10 and show that the analysis of these demographics of participants is more common in the computing articles than in the STEM articles. Literature reviews were not included in this analysis.

Table 10. Computing vs. STEM articles including analysis of participants' race, gender, or socioeconomic status.

Analysis	Computing [1] (n = 195)	STEM [1] (n = 142)
Race/Ethnicity	35 (17%)	5 (3%)
Gender	59 (28%)	14 (10%)
Socioeconomic Status	19 (9%)	3 (2%)

[1] Data reported as number of articles and % of the category.

Digging a little deeper, articles that did multiple analyses were examined (i.e., independent analysis on more than one of the categories). For STEM articles, only six articles did multiple analyses, but each of those articles only looked at two of the three demographic characteristics. For computing, 24 articles did analyses on two categories, and 10 articles looked at all three. The data show that interventions affecting those of a different gender, race/ethnicity, and/or socioeconomic status are a bigger part of the discussion in computing than in STEM.

3.2.7. Evaluation

For each research article, information about the evaluation methods and instruments was recorded. Appropriate evaluation is an area that has been explored by the researchers in the context of this same set of data and discussed in greater detail than presented here [28,29]. How and what was assessed across computing and STEM articles was compared.

The freeform text for what was measured was converted into a binary code for whether or not that information was stated in the article. For "how it was measured", a *yes* was recorded if the article gave any information about measurement frequency, measurement type, or instrument used. Literature review articles were not in this part of the analysis, but all research and experience reports were included.

It was found that 182 out of 195 computing articles (93%) did specify in some way what the study intended to measure. Comparing research versus experience reports, 87 out of 97 experience reports (90%) specified what they intended to measure, and 96 out of 98 research reports (98%) made the same specification. It was found that 136 out of the 142 STEM articles (96%) specified what they intended to measure. Looking into the breakdown of research vs. experience reports shows that for experience reports, 13 out of 16 articles (81%) reported this information and 122 out of 126 research articles (97%) reported this information. Overall, the rates of reporting of this information are similar for computing and STEM.

For specifications for how it was measured, again, 182 out of 195 (93%) computing articles specified at least one of measurement frequency, measurement type, or instrument used for measurement. The breakdown for experience reports vs. research reports was the same as for the above paragraph on "what was measured". It was found that 136 out of 142 STEM (96%) articles specified at least one of measurement frequency, measurement type, or instrument used for measurement. The breakdown for experience reports vs. research reports was that 14 out of 16 experience reports (88%) gave this information and 121 out of 126 research articles (96%) gave this information. So once again, computing and STEM articles are reporting this information at similar rates.

3.3. Study Participants

In this section, the results of the coding of information about the participants in the study as reported by the articles is presented. Information about number of participants, participants' age, grade/level in school, gender, race and/or ethnicity, socioeconomic status, location, and disabilities are presented in the subsections.

3.3.1. Number of Study Participants

For each article, the number of participants as reported by the authors was recorded. Literature reviews are excluded from this analysis. For research articles, 27 computing articles (28%) and 13 STEM articles (10%) did *not* report the number of participants of the study. Therefore, the rate of non-report is almost three times as often for computing as STEM articles.

For experience reports, 39 computing articles (40%) and seven STEM articles (44%) did not report the number of participants in the educational interventions described. The rates of non-report are much higher in experience reports.

Figure 2 presents the data about the actual number of participants as a graph of the number of participants (in ranges) as a percentage of the overall. The numbers in parentheses are the actual number of articles to report the data. For this analysis, both research and experience reports were included. There is a great deal of similarity between the number of participants reported in studies in STEM articles and computing articles and the number of studies in each category reflects that. It is important to note that the ranges represented in the graph are not of equal size and reflect somewhat natural breaks and jumps in the number of participants.

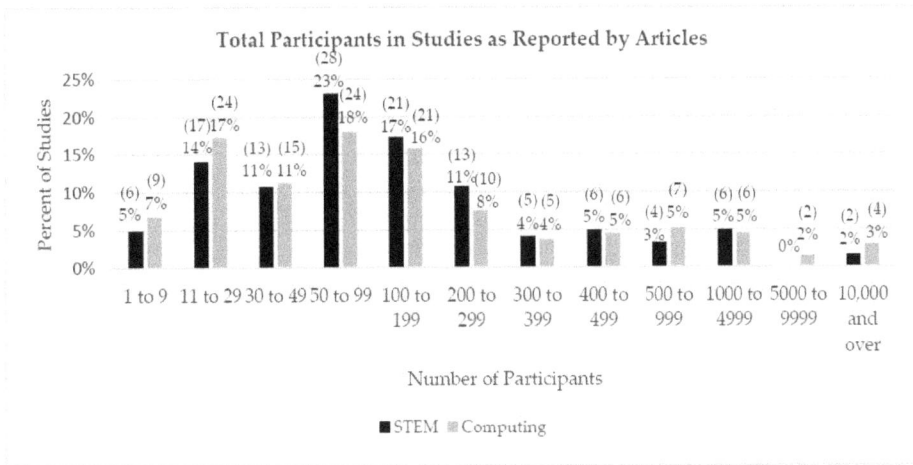

Figure 2. Computing vs. STEM number of participants reported in studies.

3.3.2. Age and Year/Grade in School

The age as well as grade level of the study participants were recorded as reported by each article. For this analysis, research and experience reports were included, but those that were categorized as professional development were excluded.

The grade/year in school was converted to the U.S. system for purposes of reporting. Non-U.S. grade levels are recorded as listed by the authors; they were then converted to the U.S. system by looking up their equivalents using internet searches.

Table 11 shows the results of this coding for computing and STEM. The demographic most frequently reported was grade level, with 43% of computing articles and 62% of STEM articles reporting. The same percentage (22%) of computing and STEM articles reported both age and grade level.

Table 11. Computing vs. STEM reporting age and grade level of participants.

Reporting	Computing [1] (n = 171)	STEM [1] (n = 134)
Age only	30 (18%)	11 (8%)
Grade Level only	73 (43%)	82 (62%)
Both age and grade level	38 (22%)	30 (22%)
Neither age or grade level	30 (18%)	10 (7%)

[1] Data reported as number of articles and % of the category.

However, the percentage of computing articles reporting neither piece of data is twice as high as the STEM articles. Of the computing articles that are reporting no information on age or grade level, only nine of the 30 are experience reports; so there are 21 research articles not reporting this information about the study participants. Only three out of 10 non-reporting STEM articles are experience reports; so even in STEM, seven research articles are not reporting this information.

Table 12 shows the number of articles reporting educational activities aimed at a specific grade level group. The data are grouped into common groupings for the U.S. system, Pre-K (before required formal schooling begins at age 5), K–4 (roughly ages 5 to 9 or 10), 5–8 (often called middle school, ages 10 or 11 to 13 or 14), and 9–12 (commonly called high school, ages 14 or 15 to 17 or 18). Articles could have been coded into more than one category if the study participants bridged the boundaries of these groups. At least one study reported participants from Pre-K to 12th grade. For computing, the largest percentage of interventions is aimed at grades 5–8, followed closely by interventions for grades 9–12. However in STEM, the largest percentage of interventions target grades 9–12, followed by grades 5–8.

Table 12. Computing vs. STEM reporting grade levels of participants.

Grade Level	Computing [1] (n = 111)	STEM [1] (n = 112)
Pre-K (before formal schooling)	3 (3%)	1 (1%)
Kindergarten–4th grade (ages 5 to 9 or 10)	31 (28%)	27 (24%)
5th grade–8th grade (ages 9 or 10 through 13 or 14)	69 (62%)	51 (46%)
9th grade–12th grade (age 13 or 14 through 17 or 18)	61 (55%)	65 (58%)

[1] Data reported as number of articles and % of the category.

3.3.3. Gender

Information about the gender of the participants as reported by the authors was recorded. Looking only at research and experience reports that did not discuss professional development, in computing, 53% reported on the gender breakdown of the participants. For STEM, 49% reported on the gender breakdown of the participants.

Looking at research studies that reported results comparing gender, 30 out of 34 computing articles (88%) and 13 out of 14 STEM articles (93%) gave a detailed gender breakdown of the participants.

3.3.4. Race and/or Ethnicity

Information about the race/ethnicity of the participants as reported by the authors was recorded. Looking only at research and experience reports that did not discuss professional development, in computing, 25% reported on the race and/or ethnicity of participants. For STEM, 34% reported on the race and/or ethnicity breakdown of the participants.

Looking at research studies that reported results comparing race/ethnicity, 14 out of 17 computing articles (82%) and four out of five STEM articles (80%) gave a detailed race and/or ethnicity breakdown of the participants.

3.3.5. Socioeconomic Status

Information about the socioeconomic of the participants as reported by the authors was recorded. Looking only at research and experience reports that did not discuss professional development, in computing, 14% reported on the socioeconomic status of the participants. For STEM, 29% reported on the socioeconomic status of the participants.

Looking at research studies that reported results comparing socioeconomic status, four out of five computing articles (80%) and two out of three STEM articles (67%) gave a detailed breakdown of the socioeconomic status of the participants.

3.3.6. Disabilities

For each article, a binary code was produced as to whether or not the article mentions students with disabilities or accommodations for students with disabilities. It should be noted that these are, in fact, vastly different concerns, but for the purposes of this literature review, the lack of discussion of disability found in either set of articles did not seem to warrant further categorization. For computing, only two articles mention anything about the disability of the participants (1% of the research/experience articles that are not professional development). For STEM, five articles mention disability status (4% of the research/experience reports that are not professional development).

3.3.7. Participant Demographic reporting

Table 13 summarizes the information presented in Section 3.3.1–Section 3.3.6 in a single table.

Table 13. Computing vs. STEM participant demographics reporting frequency.

Participant Demographic	Computing [1] (n = 111)	STEM [1] (n = 134)
Age/grade level of participants	141 (82%)	124 (93%)
Gender of participants	91 (53%)	66 (49%)
Race and/or ethnicity of participants	43 (25%)	45 (34%)
Socioeconomic status of participants	24 (14%)	39 (29%)
Disability information about participants	2 (1%)	5 (4%)

[1] Data reported as number of articles and % of the category.

3.4. Additional Study Information

In this section, the results of the coding of additional information about the study/intervention as reported by the articles is presented. As described in Table 4, many different pieces of data about the instructors of the intervention and about the activity itself were recorded. The analysis for this section will focus on much of this data in aggregate. In particular, the focus is on the location of where the intervention/study took place, reporting about instructor demographics and reporting about activity demographics.

3.4.1. Location of Intervention/Activity

For each article, the location of the study was recorded when presented as part of the description of the study. The location of the intervention/activity was not assumed based on the location/institution of the authors of the article. For this analysis, literature review articles were removed. For computing, 126 out of 195 articles (65%) specified where the study/intervention took place. For STEM, 113 out of 142 articles (80%) specified where the study/intervention took place.

For both computing and STEM, 60% of the studies took place inside the U.S. No other country had more than 5% of the studies from either computing or STEM. There were 34 different countries represented in the computing articles and 29 different countries represented in the STEM articles. Countries from all continents except Antarctica were represented in the articles. There were two STEM articles that did give location information but it was not specific enough to a country. One study talked about a "town in South America" and another discussed that the participants were from 31 countries, but did not give a listing of those countries.

3.4.2. Instructor/Teacher Demographics

For each article, information about the teacher/instructor/leader of the intervention or activity was captured for the following demographic information: who the instructor was (i.e., classroom teacher, graduate student), number of instructors, prior experience of instructor in the teaching subject matter, gender of instructor, and race/ethnicity information of instructor. For this analysis, only articles that focused on an activity or professional development were considered because those are the types of articles that would be best suited to talk about an instructor.

The number of articles that gave any of the above information is at most 27% for computing articles, but 55% for STEM articles. Table 14 shows the breakdown of how often instructor demographics were discussed.

Table 14. Computing vs. STEM reporting instructor demographics.

Instructor Demographic	Computing [1] (n = 111)	STEM [1] (n = 120)
Who instructed/led intervention	30 (27%)	66 (55%)
Instructor gender	12 (11%)	10 (8%)
Instructure race/ethnicity	3 (3%)	3 (2%)
Number of instructors	30 (27%)	48 (40%)
Prior experience of instructor	16 (14%)	23 (19%)

[1] Data reported as number of articles and % of the category.

3.4.3. Activity/Intervention Duration

In this literature review, information was recorded about the activities/interventions as described in the articles. Table 4 describes the program elements that were recorded for activity demographics. For this analysis, the focus is on the following data:

- Type of activity (e.g., informal classroom activity, formal classroom activity/curriculum)
- Curriculum used
- Tools/Language used
- Delivery method (e.g., lab, lecture, project-based, team-based)
- Learning objectives (or goals) of the intervention
- Duration of the intervention

Freeform text entries were coded into binary *yes/no* entries for this analysis. Only articles that described activities or professional development are included. Articles that describe curriculum are not included. Table 15 provides a summary of these results. For computing, a high percentage of articles identify the type of activity that is being conducted (84%) as well as the curriculum and/or tools/languages used (87%). Computing articles do not report learning objectives for the activities at a high rate, with only 18% of the articles reporting learning objectives. However, expanding the definition of learning objective to include a statement about the general goals for the activity that may or may not be learning objectives, the number of articles reporting that information is 84 and removing for duplication, 92 out of 111 articles (83%) report either or both pieces of this information.

Table 15. Computing vs. STEM reporting activity demographics.

Activity Demographic	Computing [1] (n = 111)	STEM [1] (n = 120)
Type of activity	93 (84%)	103 (86%)
Curriculum, tools, language used	97 (87%)	64 (53%)
Method of delivery/instruction	69 (62%)	100 (83%)
Learning objectives	20 (18%)	9 (8%)
Duration	67 (60%)	86 (72%)

[1] Data reported as number of articles and % of the category.

For STEM articles, a high percentage of articles identify the type of activity that is being conducted (86%), but the curriculum and/or tools/languages used are reported by only 53% of the articles. STEM articles are also less likely to contain learning objectives for the activities, with only 8% of the articles reporting learning objectives. However, if the definition is expanded to include any statement about the general goals for the activity that may or may not be learning objectives, the number of articles reporting that information is 47 and, removing for duplication, 43 out of 120 articles (36%) report either or both pieces of this information (36%). STEM articles still report less of this information than computing. STEM articles, however, report more frequently on the method of instruction for the activities at 83% compared to at 62% of computing articles reporting.

4. Discussion

The last step of the literature review framework, Step 5, defined in [22], is to interpret the findings. This section discusses and interprets the findings of this literature review and the comparison of information reported within computing and STEM articles.

In response to the research questions, R1 was concerned with describing what data were collected/reported in computing education. R2 was similar in nature, but with a focus on closely related STEM fields. The third research question, R3, was concerned with the similarities and differences in the reporting between these two groups.

4.1. Techniques for Data Collection and Reporting in Computing versus STEM

To address the first research question, a majority of the STEM fields are using research approaches and styles similar to computing. A majority of the STEM studies are cross-sectional and more heavily skewed towards quantitative methods as opposed to computing. Because of the predominance of quantitative methods, the number of participants was analyzed to see if the studies being reported in STEM articles were of much larger size than those in computing articles. Looking at the reported data (see Figure 2), there are no large differences, save for a slightly higher percentage of STEM studies that have participants in the 50–99 range. In terms of studies with greater than 100 participants, the percentages are nearly identical in all categories. Therefore, the use of quantitative methods is not directly influenced by the number of participants in the study. So, a key difference in the techniques is a stronger reliance on quantitative techniques for STEM articles, irrespective of the number of participants.

Based on previous work [13,14], it was hypothesized that in the more established STEM disciplines, a greater reliance on longitudinal studies was present. Unfortunately, that was not the case in this review with only 19 articles (13%) reporting on longitudinal studies. The article number is almost equal to the computing articles found (18), even if the percentages are not the same. Perhaps a key difference in the STEM articles is that the average length of the longitudinal studies reported upon is longer by over a full year. However, the maximum study duration is 10 years in both disciplines in these articles and this seems about correct. If a student participates in an activity around age 10 (which is where a significant proportion of activities seem to be targeted), then the study follows that student into a college/university. So, in the case of longitudinal work, there was not significant differences in duration or vastly different techniques employed found in this literature review.

One area where computing is doing something that did not appear in STEM disciplines is retrospective studies. Six percent (6%) of the studies in the computing literature were categorized as retrospective, or asking participants to look back on events that happened previously and answer questions about them at the current time. Often times these studies are used to determine how an event or activity influenced where the participant is in the present time. These types of studies differ from longitudinal studies in that the participants from an intervention are not tracked over time by the researchers, but rather participants are asked about something they may have experienced from a different group of researchers. There was no evidence of these types of studies in the STEM articles.

Another area in which computing is different to STEM is in the comparative analysis of the participants based on certain demographic characteristics (i.e., race, gender, socioeconomic status). Computing studies are twice to five times as likely to compare participants grouped by demographic characteristics as STEM studies. Broadening participation in computing has been a long-standing effort in the computing community, heavily supported and funded by government grants and programs [30], which could explain some of this difference.

In terms of age/grade level studied, both groups presented studies focused primarily on middle and high school (grades 5–12), with around a quarter of the studies (28% for computing, 24% for STEM) looking at issues in grades K–4, and very few studies (3% or less for both groups) looking at students in the pre-kindergarten years. So, from this perspective, all the disciplines are focusing their efforts on students in the upper grade levels of primary and secondary education.

4.2. Similarities and Differences in Reporting for Computing and STEM

Turning to the second research question, identifying the similarities and differences in reporting, the two groups have strengths and weaknesses in different areas—some of them mutually strong or weak. Table 16 summarizes the differences in reporting over the various categories analyzed by this literature review. What is important to remember, however, is that even when computing or STEM reports more frequently, or they are comparable, none of the categories was reporting the information 100% of the time and for many of the categories, reporting was actually very low. Since this study was borne out of a desire to improve replicability of educational research, it is important for both the computing education research community and STEM education research community and publication venues to work to improve overall reporting of the relevant information about their research studies [16,21].

Table 16. Categories of reporting and which group (computing or STEM) had more reporting.

Computing	STEM	Comparable
Research questions	Number of study participants	Evaluation
Comparison on gender, race/ethnicity, socioeconomic status	Participant age/grade level	Participant gender
	Participant socioeconomic status	Participant race/ethnicity
	Disability	Activity demographics
	Location reporting	
	Instructor demographics	

4.3. More Frequent Reporting from Computing

4.3.1. Research Questions

It is vitally important for research articles to report their research questions in a manner which is clear and easily distinguishable in the text. Computing articles contain this information in 80% of the articles, but STEM only has a report rate of 63%.

4.3.2. Comparisons Based on Demographic Characteristics

Computing has more articles reporting on the comparisons of participants based on demographic groups of gender (28% vs. 10%), race/ethnicity (17% vs. 3%), and socioeconomic status (9% vs. 2%). While this is not a necessary feature of a study, it is interesting to note that computing simply is studying the impact of the interventions

4.4. More Frequent Reporting from STEM

4.4.1. Number of Participants

STEM reported the number of participants more frequently in research studies, with only 10% of the articles categorized as research not reporting. For computing, that number is 28% of research articles not reporting number of participants. In either case, it could be argued that this number should be 0% and that all research articles should report the number of participants in the study.

Computing has a significantly larger proportion of experience reports as compared to STEM (49% to 11%), and actually reports at a slightly higher rate in this category (60% reporting for computing, 56% reporting for STEM). For experience reports, it could be argued that reporting the number of participants is not required in the reporting because the article does not present a formal research study. However, this information plays an important role in a reader's understanding of the intervention and the subsequent conclusions drawn. Having information about class size or how many students total participated in an activity helps the reader to understand how applicable the observations might be in their circumstance.

Looking at the data for research and experience reports in aggregate, STEM reports more frequently, with 91% of STEM articles containing such data (research or experience reporting), while computing has only 63% of articles reporting the number of participants.

4.4.2. Age, Grade, Level of Participants

Participant age and/or grade level in school was not reported by 7% of the STEM articles studied, and not reported by 18% of the computing articles. This information is extremely important to understand the context of the classroom the intervention takes place in. The environment of a secondary school is very different from that of early elementary/primary school. Furthermore, terminology is problematic when discussing grade and level in school due to the vast differences in educational systems and names. Even within the U.S., terms such as "middle school" and "high school" can mean different things to different school systems. When possible, it is always best to couple the reporting with ages of participants or typical age ranges of students in that level if explicit age data are not collected. Doing so will help all readers, especially those from regions in which the educational system is different to that studied by the researchers.

4.4.3. Socioeconomic Status

STEM articles were twice as likely to present information about participant socioeconomic status than computing articles (29% vs. 14%). Most often, this was done at the school/community level, which seems appropriate due to privacy concerns. Understanding the socioeconomic climate of where the intervention takes place can provide important insight to how or why an intervention does or does not work.

4.4.4. Disability Information

To say that STEM had more frequent reporting in this area hides the fact that at 4%, the reporting is still poor. The fact that computing only talks about this issue 1% of the time is the only thing that gives STEM the edge in this area. More work is needed in both areas to ensure that disability information and accommodation information becomes part of the discussion in the pre-college research space.

4.4.5. Location Where the Invention Took Place

STEM reports location of intervention at a slightly higher rate than computing (80% to 65%). However, looking at distribution of locations, the studies are still predominantly U.S. studies. The number of additional countries represented is roughly the same for computing and STEM. This predominance of U.S. studies could be the result of venue bias since only English-language venues were considered, bar the results of [14], which expanded a literature review in computing to include many non-U.S.-based venues did not show significant differences in the proportion of studies taking place outside the U.S.

4.4.6. Instructor Demographics

For the five instructor demographics studied, summarized in Table 14, STEM reported the information at a higher rate (at times double the rate) in all but two instances, instructor gender and instructor race/ethnicity, where computing reported at a 3% and 1% higher rate respectively. In this case, STEM reports this information more frequently, particularly about who actually led the intervention as part of the study. It may be the case that researchers assume that readers know that they led the intervention or that a classroom teacher would lead the intervention as created by the researcher, but this information should be stated so that readers understand the classroom environment.

4.5. Reporting Comparable Computing versus STEM

4.5.1. Evaluation

Both groups reported evaluation in terms of what they intended to measure equally well. The analysis for this study is somewhat superficial in terms of evaluation. The use of validated measures or rigor of evaluation protocol as described by the articles was not analyzed. Future work in this area would be needed to examine more closely the use of validated instruments and other best practice evaluation methods for the two groups.

4.5.2. Gender of Participants, Race/Ethnicity of Participants

Both groups reported on participant demographics in terms of gender and race/ethnicity with about the same frequency, but the percentages were barely at 50% for gender and slightly more than 25% for race/ethnicity. While the demographic breakdown of the participants may not be germane to the research questions being studied, understanding the context of the classroom environment is important to the understanding of the work. So being explicit about these demographic factors helps to situate the intervention. Even if the demographic information is reported for the school/community level, it helps create a picture of what the classroom looks like.

4.5.3. Activity Demographics

For the five activity demographics studied, summarized in Table 15, computing reports more frequently for two of them, and STEM for three, but the differences in reporting are not as large as in other categories, and thus this was classified as being done equally well on both sides. The one area where computing is reporting more often is in the area of curriculum and tools/languages used. This is possibly an artifact of the discipline. Computing is incredibly focused on the technology and/or programming language used for instruction, so it is often discussed more often than the actual way in which the technology/tool/language is being presented, which computing is reporting less often. This could also be an artifact of the age of the discipline. As an example, mathematics decided a very long time ago to use Arabic numerals as opposed to Roman numerals (or others) as their language of expression. Computing has yet to adopt a universal language of expression for programming and is likely decades away from doing so, if it will happen at all. Therefore, there is a very important need to know about the language/tool when discussing these interventions.

4.6. Guides for Improving Reporting

This systematic literature review shows that there is room for improvement in the reporting of educational research in both computing and STEM education. Resources have been created for computing education researchers that can apply equally well to STEM education researchers. The first, a guide for reporting program elements (https://csedresearch.org/guides/) [31], is based on a comprehensive examination of 297 articles in computing education and was derived from noting the gaps in reporting as described in [16].

To encourage researchers to report data more fully and consistently, a list of recommendations for reporting on these interventions was also developed [16]. These recommendations have been reprinted here as Figure 3.

The second, a guide for reviewers to consider when reviewing articles (https://csedresearch.org/check-articles/) [32], was informed through the work in the initial design and creation of the site with a focus group of potential users (computing education researchers, practitioners, and evaluators) [26]. Through the 10-week discussion period, one theme that emerged was how to assess the research quality of the items being included in the repository and the discussions resulted in the following framework [reprinted here as Table 17].

Category	As applicable, provide:	Example
Student Demographics	Student ages and specific grade levels (both)	"ages 5-8"; "grades 4-5"; "15 in grade 6 (ages 10-12), 26 in grade 7 (ages 11-13)"; avoid country-specific or non-standardized terms ("middle school")
	Number of students	"24 students participated"; "3 sections of 15 students each"
	Gender of students	"all female students"; "4 male and 16 female"; "male and female students" (if breakdown unknown)
	Specific locations of students, including city, state, and country	"activity was held at University of X in AnyTown, State/Region, Country"
	Prior CS education of students (as specific as possible)	"students had no prior computing courses"; "15% of students had taken an introduction to computing course prior to the activity";
	Prior CS experience (informal curriculum, out of school activities)	"20% of students had participated in hour of code last academic year"; "16% of students were involved in after school robotics club"
	Race/ethnicity of students	"20% of participants were Caucasian, 18% were African-American, 20% Hispanic, and 42% did not specify race/ethnicity"
	Socio-economic status of students	"5% of population (U.S.) receive free/reduced lunch"
Instructor Demographics	Number of instructors	"activity was led by 2 instructors who took turns teaching and helping students, along with 3 teaching assistants to assist during work periods"
	Who taught the activity	"activity was run by the researcher"; "activity was run by a school teacher"; "activity was run by a second year undergraduate student majoring in Computer Science"
	Prior experience of instructors (as specific as possible)	"instructor taught summer camps for 15 years and taught in the computing department of a university for 20 years"
	Gender of instructors	"the instructors were both male"; "there were two male instructors, one female instructor, and three female teaching assistants"
	Race/ethnicity of instructors	"the instructors were white"; "one instructor was African American and one was Hispanic"
Activity Components	Clearly defined learning objectives (specific skills/knowledge activity to be taught or attitudes to be changed)	"By the end of the activity, students were expected to be able to program proficiently with Prolog and demonstrate that knowledge through a series of short group demonstrations to the class"; the activity was designed to increase student interest in technology careers"
	Type of activity	"this one-on-one tutoring activity"; "the activity was a competition designed to..."
	Required or elective	"this was an elective activity"; "this activity was required of all students in the 6th grade"
	When activity was offered	"this was a summer camp"; "club met after school"; "activity was done during the school day"
	Curriculum used	"curriculum was created by instructor (URL, if posted)"; "Code.org materials were used (give URL)"; "materials from the Scratch website were used (give URL)"
	Teaching Method	"pair programming was used"; "students were given time in the lab to work in teams"; "students listened to the presenters"
	Tool/language used	"projects were completed in Scratch"; "projects were completed using Arduino boards"
	Duration of activity, including contact hours	"workshop ran 3 days for 45 minutes each day"; "club met after school twice a month for one hour each meeting for the entire school year (35 weeks)"
	Average number of students in each session (if multiple sessions/classes/workshops)	"there was an average of 20 students per session"
	Accommodations for learners with disabilities	"students with disabilities were accommodated using their current IEP"; "activities were reviewed for accessibility for students with vision or hearing disabilities"
	Date of the activity (month(s), year(s))	"activity ran from August 2015 to May 2016"; "the camp took place in July 2013"
	Materials/resources needed (including physical space and material costs of the activity)	"activity required use of a computer lab with the XYZ software installed (which can be downloaded as a free trial version from URL)"; "The camp required the use of a computer lab as well as facilities for lunch and snacks throughout the day. The cost per student in supplies was $50."
	Amount of time needed to prepare for the activity	"the instructors spent four weeks planning for the activities of the camp"
	Appropriate CSTA Categories and Levels (or equivalent) for the activity	"this activity encompasses CSTA practices P2 and P5 and is at level 2, and includes coverage of the following subconcepts from the CS-Troubleshooting concept"

Figure 3. Recommendations for reporting.

Table 17. Checklist for research articles.

Purpose, Goals, Intent, Clarity: Do the authors ...

- Make a case for why the reader should care about the problem?
- Provide their contact information for the activity/study organizer/instructor/designer?
- Clearly and explicitly state the research question(s) and hypothesis?
- Clearly state the study's objectives, including articulating any learning outcomes?
- Use correct language related to educational researcher?
- Provide any definitions used that are crucial to the study?
- Specify the research question(s) the study sought to answer?

Study Design: Do the authors ...

- Indicate the research methodology used and the rationale for that choice?
- Use an appropriate design related to its type of study?
- Describe the methodology in sufficient detail for another researcher to replicate the study?
- Describe the methodological framework (quantitative, qualitative, mixed methods) in terms of educational research? (Qualitative: case studies, ethnography, longitudinal, etc.; Quantitative: (quasi) experimental designs, survey, etc.)
- Describe any efforts to offset the novelty effect, Hawthorne effect, John Henry effect?
- Use and rigorously apply instruments appropriate to the research question?
- Describe and provide the instruments used within the study?
- Fully describe the setting for the study (location, classrooms, courses, schools)?
- Use an appropriate instrument to measure impact?
- Consider sample size and whether it is sufficient?

Activity/Intervention: Do the authors ...

- Fully describe the intervention and/or activities?
- Explain how the activity is suitable to the targeted participant group (age/range/experience/etc.)?
- Describe the skill, knowledge, or disposition that was being targeted?
- Describe the length and frequency of the intervention (hours, days, months)?
- Describe who conducted the intervention, including qualifications?

Ethics: Do the authors ...

- Disclose their International Review Board (IRB) approval process and methods to ensure participant privacy, confidentiality, and protection?
- Disclose any costs/funding sources to conduct any aspect of the research/activity in order to assess possible bias?
- Disclose whether or not participants or researchers receive monetary or gift incentives?
- Include researcher qualifications and how researcher bias has been mitigated?
- Declare any personal, organizational, or institutional biases?

Participants: Do the authors ...

- Include participant demographic information, including age, grade range, gender, race/ethnicity, socioeconomic status?
- Include number of participants in the study?
- Include recruitment process for participants (volunteer? required?)?
- Describe sampling technique used?

Data Analysis: Do the authors ...

- Indicate the analysis methods and tools used and the rationale for those choices?
- Describe how the data analysis methods were appropriate for the design?
- Fully describe the analysis methods with sufficient detail for replication?
- For quantitative frameworks, describe all statistical tests used and a rationale for non-standard measures used? Include or provide a link to the raw assessment data for others to verify/analyze? Distinguish between correlation and causality?
- For qualitative frameworks, describe how the data were analyzed, how inter-rater reliability was maintained, and provide researcher reflexivity statement?

Results: Do the authors ...

- Provide a compelling argument (sample size, quantitative or qualitative analysis, etc.) for the significance of its results?
- Describe the results of the study?
- Explore the implications of the results on research, policy, and practice?
- Describe how this research and/or results fit into the larger context of related research?
- Consider whether the results are appropriate for the scale of the intervention?
- Describe limitations of the study, including issues related to ability to generalize, sample size, confounding variables, whether or not participants were randomized or not representative, with any alternative hypothesis stated?
- Include data (sample size, statistical analysis, etc.) indicating its significance?

4.7. Threats to Validity

Section 2.4 acknowledges some of the threats to the validity of this study, particularly around bias in sampling for the literature review. However, another important threat to the validity of this work is human error, both in the information that was overlooked or missed in the extraction of data from the articles as well as information that may have been misinterpreted. While every effort was made to record the actual text from the articles as the data were being extracted, there were times when the actual sentences needed to be summarized or rephrased to conform to the categories of data being collected.

The data curated for the computing articles have undergone a data extraction as well as a data verification process. The STEM articles underwent only a data extraction process with no secondary review. However, the extraction was done by a senior researcher working on the project who developed and coached others on the protocol, once again, to mitigate potential errors for this study.

In addition, the research team has a background in computing education and general education techniques, but not a background in other STEM education research. It is possible that this lack of knowledge could introduce interpretation error when extracting data from the STEM articles.

5. Conclusions

In order to improve the credibility of educational research in K–12 as well as undergraduate STEM+C, it is imperative for educational researchers to carefully record and report participant demographics as well as program elements of the intervention. This particular study was formed to determine whether computing education is lagging behind other STEM disciplines in terms of the accurate reporting of and study of these types of educational interventions at the pre-college level.

Overall, this comparative literature review answered a key question in terms of understanding the differences in reporting in the computing and STEM literature. As such, the researchers considered the possibility that other STEM disciplines may help understand how reporting demographic and program data in computing education research compares and what can be improved. While this review uncovered deficiencies on both sides, more often on the computing side, there were times when computing had a higher level of reporting.

The results bring forward possible questions for future consideration including what mechanisms can be employed to ensure more thorough reporting of these factors in research studies. Is there a way to bring more recognition of the importance of these issues to the community? With more investment in computing education in recent years, will a literature review 5 years from now still uncover the same deficiencies in reporting?

By bringing these issues of reporting into the conversation, there may be a shift in the way articles report on their experiments and findings. With stakeholders such as the U.S. National Science Foundation starting to make a push for more replication and reproducibility, it is anticipated that any such shift will lead to more utility in the research results and greater ability for others to replicate studies, thereby adding credibility to the results. By so doing, best practices can be better formed through an aggregation of higher integrity, empirical evidence.

Author Contributions: Conceptualization, A.D. and M.M.M.; Data curation, M.M.M.; Formal analysis, A.D.; Funding acquisition, A.D. and M.M.M.; Investigation, A.D. and M.M.M.; Methodology, A.D. and M.M.M.; Project administration, A.D.; Supervision, M.M.M.; Validation, A.D.; Visualization, A.D.; Writing—Original Draft, A.D. and M.M.M.; Writing—Review and Editing, A.D. and M.M.M.

Funding: This research was funded by U.S. National Science Foundation, grant numbers 1625005, 1625335, 1757402, and 1745199.

Conflicts of Interest: The authors declare no conflict of interest.

References

1. Computer Science for All. Available online: https://obamawhitehouse.archives.gov/blog/2016/01/30/computer-science-all (accessed on 30 January 2019).
2. Guzdial, M. Bringing Computer Science to U.S. Schools, State by State. *Commun. ACM* **2016**, *59*, 24–25. Available online: https://doi.org/10.1145/2898963 (accessed on 30 January 2019). [CrossRef]
3. 2018 State of Computer Science Education: Policy and Implementation. Available online: https://code.org/files/2018_state_of_cs.pdf (accessed on 30 January 2019).
4. CSTA K–12 Computer Science Standards. Available online: https://www.csteachers.org/page/standards (accessed on 30 January 2019).
5. ISTE Standards. Available online: https://www.iste.org/standards (accessed on 30 January 2019).
6. National Curriculum in England: Computing Programmes of Study. Available online: https://www.gov.uk/government/publications/national-curriculum-in-england-computing-programmes-of-study (accessed on 30 January 2019).
7. Australian Curriculum: Digital Technologies. Available online: https://www.australiancurriculum.edu.au/f-10-curriculum/technologies/digital-technologies/ (accessed on 30 January 2019).
8. National Centre for Computing Education. Available online: https://www.computingatschool.org.uk/ (accessed on 30 January 2019).
9. Khan Academy: Computer Programming. Available online: https://www.khanacademy.org/computing/computer-programming (accessed on 30 January 2019).
10. Girls Who Code. Available online: https://girlswhocode.com (accessed on 30 January 2019).
11. Code Academy. Available online: https://www.codecademy.com/ (accessed on 30 January 2019).
12. Code.org: Teach Computer Science. Available online: https://studio.code.org/courses?view=teacher (accessed on 30 January 2019).
13. Decker, A.; McGill, M.M.; Settle, A. Towards a Common Framework for Evaluating Computing Outreach Activities. In Proceedings of the 47th ACM Technical Symposium on Computer Science Education, Memphis, TN, USA, 2–5 March 2016; ACM: New York, NY, USA, 2016; pp. 627–632. [CrossRef]
14. Decker, A.; McGill, M. Pre-College Computing Outreach Research: Towards Improving the Practice. In Proceedings of the 48th SIGCSE Technical Symposium on Computer Science Education, Seattle, WA, USA, 8–11 March 2017; ACM: New York, NY, USA, 2017; pp. 153–158. [CrossRef]
15. Schmidt, S. Shall we really do it again? The powerful concept of replication is neglected in the social sciences. *Rev. Gen. Psychol.* **2009**, *13*, 90–100. [CrossRef]
16. McGill, M.; Decker, A.; Abbott, Z. Improving Research and Experience Reports of Pre-College Computing Activities: A Gap Analysis. In Proceedings of the 49th SIGCSE Technical Symposium of Computer Science Education, Baltimore, MD, USA, 21–24 February 2018; ACM: New York, NY, USA, 2018; pp. 964–969. [CrossRef]
17. Ahadi, A.; Hellas, A.; Ihantola, P.; Korhonen, A.; Petersen, A. Replication in computing education research: Researcher attitudes and experiences. In Proceedings of the 16th Koli Calling International Conference on Computing Education Research, Koli, Finland, 24–27 November 2016; ACM: New York, NY, USA, 2016; pp. 2–11. [CrossRef]
18. Cooper, M.M. The Replication Crisis and Chemistry Education Research. *J. Chem. Educ.* **2018**, *95*, 1–2. Available online: https://pubs.acs.org/doi/10.1021/acs.jchemed.7b00907 (accessed on 13 March 2019). [CrossRef]
19. Breining, G. Addressing the Research Replication Crisis. Available online: https://news.aamc.org/medical-education/article/academic-medicine-research-replication-crisis/ (accessed on 13 March 2019).
20. Makel, M.C.; Plucker, J.A. Facts Are More Important Than Novelty: Replication in the Education Sciences. *Educ. Res.* **2014**, *43*. Available online: https://journals.sagepub.com/stoken/rbtfl/w5mrNxPVD8zSg/full (accessed on 2 February 2019). [CrossRef]
21. National Science Foundation. Companion Guidelines on Replication & Reproducibility in Education Research. Available online: https://nsf.gov/pubs/2019/nsf19022/nsf19022.pdf (accessed on 13 March 2019).
22. Khan, K.S.; Kunz, R.; Kleijnen, J.; Antes, G. Five steps to conducting a systematic review. *J. R. Soc. Med.* **2003**, *96*, 118–121. Available online: http://www.ncbi.nlm.nih.gov/pmc/articles/PMC539417/ (accessed on 30 January 2019). [CrossRef] [PubMed]

23.   Gonzalez, H.B.; Kuenzi, J.J. Science, Technology, Engineering, and Mathematics (STEM) Education: A Primer. Congressional Research Service 7-5700, Washington, DC. Available online: http://www.fas.org/sgp/crs/misc/R42642.pdf (accessed on 30 January 2019).

24.   Freeman, S.; Eddy, S.L.; McDonough, M.; Smith, M.K.; Okoroafor, N.; Jordt, H.; Wenderoth, M.P. Active Learning Increases Student Performance in Science, Engineering, and Mathematics. *Proc. Natl. Acad. Sci. USA* **2014**, *111*, 8410–8415. Available online: https://www.pnas.org/content/pnas/111/23/8410.full.pdf (accessed on 30 January 2019). [CrossRef] [PubMed]

25.   Creswell, J.W. *Educational Research: Planning, Conducting, and Evaluating Quantitative*; Prentice Hall: Upper Saddle River, NJ, USA, 2002; pp. 146–166.

26.   Computer Science Education Repository. Available online: https://csedresearch.org (accessed on 30 January 2019).

27.   McGill, M.; Decker, A. Defining Requirements for a Repository to Meet the Needs of K–12 Computer Science Educators, Researchers, and Evaluators. In Proceedings of the 2018 Frontiers in Education Conference, San Jose, CA, USA, 3–6 October 2018; IEEE: New York, NY, USA, 2018.

28.   Decker, A.; McGill, M. A Topical Review of Evaluation Instruments for Computing Education. In Proceedings of the 50th SIGCSE Technical Symposium of Computer Science Education, Minneapolis, MN, USA, 27 February–2 March 2019; ACM: New York, NY, USA, 2019; pp. 558–564. [CrossRef]

29.   McGill, M.; Decker, A.; Haynie, K.; McKlin, T. A Gap Analysis of Noncognitive Constructs in Evaluation Instruments Designed for Computing Education. In Proceedings of the 50th SIGCSE Technical Symposium of Computer Science Education, Minneapolis, MN, USA, 27 February–2 March 2019; ACM: New York, NY, USA, 2019; pp. 706–712. [CrossRef]

30.   CISE Strategic Plan for Broadening Participation. Available online: https://www.nsf.gov/cise/oad/cise_bp.jsp (accessed on 30 January 2019).

31.   Reporting Tips. Available online: https://csedresearch.org/guides/ (accessed on 30 January 2019).

32.   Checklist for Research Articles. Available online: https://csedresearch.org/check-articles/ (accessed on 30 January 2019).

education
sciences

MDPI

Article

Ants Go Marching—Integrating Computer Science into Teacher Professional Development with NetLogo

Mike Borowczak [1,*] and Andrea C. Burrows [2]

[1]   Department of Computer Science, College of Engineering and Applied Science, University of Wyoming,
      1000 E University Ave, Laramie, WY 82071, USA
[2]   School of Teacher Education, College of Education, University of Wyoming, 1000 E University Ave, Laramie,
      WY 82071, USA; Andrea.Burrows@uwyo.edu
*   Correspondence: Mike.Borowczak@uwyo.edu

Received: 1 February 2019; Accepted: 20 March 2019; Published: 26 March 2019

check for
updates

Abstract: There is a clear call for pre-collegiate students in the United States to become literate in computer science (CS) concepts and practices through integrated, authentic experiences and instruction. Yet, a majority of in-service and pre-service pre-collegiate teachers (instructing children aged five to 18) lack the fundamental skills and self-efficacy to adequately and effectively integrate CS into existing curricula. In this study, 30 pre-collegiate teachers who represent a wide band of experience, grade-levels, and prior CS familiarity participated in a 16-day professional development (PD) course to enhance their content knowledge and self-efficacy in integrating CS into existing lessons and curricula. Using both qualitative and quantitative methodology, a social constructivist approach guided the researchers in the development of the PD, as well as the data collection and analysis on teacher content knowledge and perceptions through a mixed-methods study. Ultimately, participants were introduced to CS concepts and practices through NetLogo, which is a popular multi-agent simulator. The results show that although the pre-collegiate teachers adopted CS instruction, the CS implementation within their curricula was limited to the activities and scope of the PD with few adaptations and minimal systemic change in implementation behaviors.

Keywords: computer science education; computer science; computer science integration; pre-collegiate teacher; K–12 teacher; science education; engineering education

1. Introduction

While technological devices dominate the world today, advanced artificial intelligence (AI) will dominate the day to day functions in the world of tomorrow [1]. The change requires a shift from a technology literate workforce to a highly-skilled workforce knowledgeable in both discipline domains such as science, technology, engineering, and mathematics (STEM), as well as computer science (CS). The good news is that CS is embedded within many workforce STEM careers [2,3]; however, the bad news is that based on current pre-collegiate teacher (those teaching in Kindergarten through 12th grade—K–12—in the United States) CS self-efficacy and skills, CS remains disjointed from many pre-collegiate STEM courses [4,5]. While many informal definitions exist for the exact nature of CS, it can be simply defined as the science of problem solving within a computational context [6]. The distinction between CS, computational thinking (CT), software engineering, and programming is not well defined when only exploring the practical applications rather than the theoretical constructs and underpinnings of the computing spectrum. The distinction is further confounded, as most university-level CS programs prepare software engineers, who utilize broad CT skills, to combine highly specialized CS theory and some specific domain knowledge, to develop software systems through the actionable skill of programming. While most novices might view the entirety of the computing spectrum from the visible tip of the iceberg as programming, the theory and core competencies below the surface form the true basis for a highly skilled CS workforce (Figure 1).

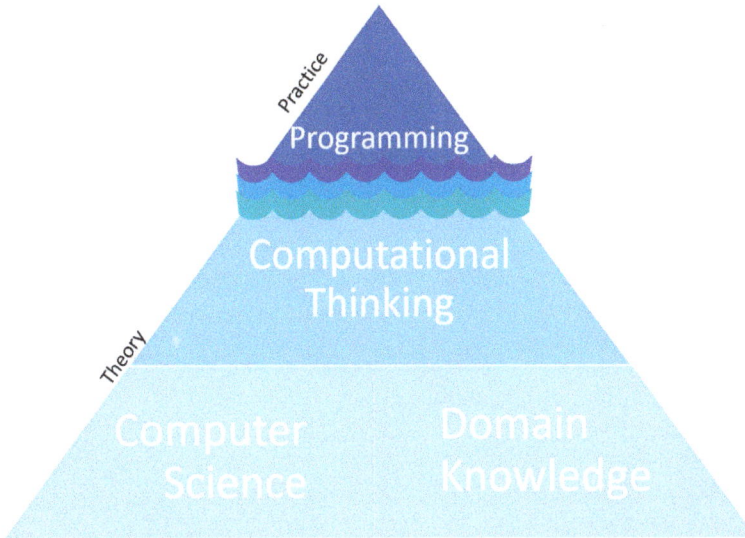

Figure 1. The computing spectrum is shown here as an iceberg model. While the actionable skill of programming is prominently visible to many, the theory and core competencies of computing lie well below the surface.

A more concrete analogy of this model of the computing spectrum surrounds the use of toy construction blocks. Given enough time, one can pick up and learn how to use blocks to create objects (programming), given a tool box of sample construction models (e.g., an arch), one can build more complex structures (computational thinking), and finally if given the foundational theories (domain knowledge) of physics (e.g., forces, material characteristics) and mathematical tools, one can design new custom structures given specific requirements (e.g., computer science and domain knowledge).

In the future, computer scientists and STEM professionals who cannot integrate specific domain knowledge and CS are unlikely to outpace the advances in modern AI and machine learning. For this study, the term 'integration' is key, and integration refers to the blending of CS concepts into already established STEM and other disciplines. Thus, this research study continues to explore the impact of integrating new CS content knowledge into pre-collegiate teachers' prior STEM domain knowledge to produce practical applications through existing pre-collegiate STEM teaching [7]. The incorporation of CS-based problem solving in pre-collegiate classrooms and experiences is substantiated and reinforced through the engineering skills and practices specifically identified in the Next Generation Science Standards (NGSS) [8]. Therefore, pre-collegiate students benefit from the incorporation of CS into their STEM coursework because of the additional exposure to 21st century skills and critical thinking skills, such as those emphasized in the NGSS science and engineering practices (SEP), crosscutting concepts (CCC), and disciplinary core ideas (DCI). Computer science enables these skills such as problem solving, designing solutions, evaluating and analyzing data, peer collaboration, and the oral, written, and electronic dissemination of results.

Currently, CS is taught as a standalone subject in both pre-collegiate and collegiate classrooms. This approach is in sharp contrast to the current use or integration of CS within a variety of STEM fields—from biology, to chemistry, to astronomy, to statistics. The authors argue that pre-collegiate teachers can assist in building a 21st century workforce by incorporating basic CS skills into their established curricula, engaging in effective pedagogy, and experimenting with traditional and cutting-edge resources. The challenge is increasing pre-collegiate teacher self-efficacy within a CS construct without the benefit of a degree in a CS field. The purpose of this study was to investigate a readily accessible online resource, NetLogo, to determine if pre-collegiate teachers' use of NetLogo during professional development (PD) impacts their fundamental CS knowledge, skills, and subject integration.

In this paper, modeling refers to the creation of abstract representations in code. NetLogo is a multi-agent simulator that uses the Logo programming language and was designed for pre-collegiate classroom modeling [9]. The quintessential "Hello World" model for NetLogo consists of modeling ant behavior and pheromone release with food sources [10]. The "Ants" NetLogo model consists of modeling one type of agent, an ant, to move randomly until it detects a chemical 'scent' and then move toward higher concentrations of the scent. Furthermore, an ant releases this chemical scent when it has found food; thus, as more ants locate the scent trail, and thus food, the scent trail itself is reinforced. The inclusion of a free modeling and simulation programming language and environment (web or computer-based), NetLogo [11], offered the pre-collegiate teachers in the PD the opportunity to prepare and develop the skills to incorporate CS concepts into STEM activities. The authors of this study strived to teach the pre-collegiate teachers and pre-collegiate students to think like computer scientists, engineers, and engineering educators to promote modeling.

2. Purpose, Problem, and Research Question

Computer science is in the spotlight of current United States' (U.S.) education policy [12] and the media. While it is recognized that more working CS professionals are needed in the U.S., the path on how to motivate pre-collegiate students into CS majors and careers remains unclear [13]. Currently, most pre-collegiate CS teachers have a collegiate background involving varying degrees of CS, and this process is not scalable to reach all pre-collegiate students. In order to reach as many pre-collegiate teachers as possible, accessible opportunities such as teacher PD need to be offered [14]. The authors of this study address a challenge that today's pre-collegiate teachers face in implementing CS concepts into existing curricula by creating a PD that included: (1) integrating CS into current instruction; (2) explicitly defining real-world CS examples; and (3) showcasing core CS concepts for content knowledge gains. If pre-collegiate teachers possess ample CS content knowledge and high self-efficacy, from PDs or other resources, then they are more likely to incorporate CS into their curricula [6]. This study showcases how pre-collegiate teachers engaged with CS and NetLogo over a 16-day PD called RAMPED, which stands of Robotics, Applied Mathematics, Physics, and Engineering Design. Following the recommendations of other researchers [15], the authors of this study examined: How can pre-collegiate STEM teachers, who have limited CS or programming knowledge, incorporate CS concepts for their STEM classrooms? Due to the research team's interest in the use of the PD material, the central research question of interest evolved to become: *"How do pre-collegiate STEM teachers view their CS skill set before and after the PD, and do their perceptions align with what they know and how they plan to use CS in their classrooms?"*

3. Theoretical Framework and Literature Review

The authors embraced a social constructivism theoretical framework, where interactions between people (in this case the pre-collegiate teachers) allowed for the creation of connections, and content understanding of the CS material presented and assisted in developing CS self-efficacy and perceptions [16]. NetLogo, as presented here, was based on the group construction of NetLogo ideas, code meanings and changes, and simulated modeling experiences. Teachers created pre-collegiate classroom ideas for CS and NetLogo; their collaborations were collected as evidence. Additionally, the authors utilized Pea and Collins' concept of the fourth wave of science education reform [17] which:

> ... involves the emergence of a systemic approach to designing learning environments for advancing coherent understanding of science subject matter by learners. Science educators and researchers have recognized the need for [mindful] coordination of curriculum

design, activities, and tools to support different teaching methods that can foster students' expertise in linking and connecting disparate ideas concerning science, embedded learning assessments that can guide instructional practices, and teacher professional development supports that can foster continued learning about how to improve teaching practice.

Using technology (e.g., NetLogo programming language) with pre-collegiate teachers, so that they explored and created using CS concepts in K–12 classrooms, was an extension of prior research. Computer science is explored in the following literature review sections related to four main areas including: (1) NetLogo and CS background; (2) pre-collegiate students using and learning CS; (3) pre-collegiate teachers using and learning CS; and (4) higher education students and faculty using and learning CS. These four themes are highlighted in Section 3.2 and add context to the authors' work.

3.1. Background of the Study

For context to the PD, in the following paragraphs, the authors outline what the pre-collegiate teachers investigated for the NetLogo session, and how the material relates to other subjects. The two-day NetLogo PD session was held during the intensive two-week summer PD that was followed by PD support days during the academic year (for a total of 16 days of PD with three dedicated to NetLogo). Pre-collegiate teachers investigated the relationship between common science and manufacturing processes and the design of algorithms to solve optimization and design problems that have no apparent brute-force solution. Of specific focus were investigations of: (1) the biomimicry in genetic algorithms (biological concepts within genetics of population diversity, selection, mutations, and termination) and (2) the relationship between the physical properties of systems (such as the heating and cooling of metals and the balancing of interconnected spring networks) to the creation of megalithic and nanoscopic structures.

The foundations of genetics rely on the intersection of biology, math, and chemistry. During the first part of the teacher-centric investigations on how genetics influences the design of mathematical algorithms, the session built up the baseline knowledge for the pre-collegiate teachers, relying first on the existing knowledge of the pre-collegiate teachers, and then scaffolding and extending the explanation of new concepts by domain content experts. Pre-collegiate teachers then engaged in hands-on, minds-on active learning sessions, with a genetic algorithm that created valid mathematical and chemical equations. After the hands-on/minds-on approach, teachers developed their skill set in either the Python or Sketch programming languages (based on their students' age/skill sets and personal self-selection). Finally, pre-collegiate teachers modified a genetic algorithm template (in Python or Sketch) to solve a simple "game of life" that required setting parameters of birth rate, death rate, and food densities for multiple populations to achieve the maximal survival of a targeted species.

After exposure to the use of genetic-based algorithms, the pre-collegiate teachers investigated algorithms rooted in physics and chemistry. A similar pattern of using the groups' prior knowledge enabled a more realistic starting point for the domain experts to scaffold and improve teachers' understanding. One primary focus of discussion was Hooke's Law (springs) and annealing (forming/breaking crystal lattice structures). Again, the group of teachers chose/investigated two separate algorithms that solved the same problem of where to optimally place human settlements within a geographic area. The session continued by supplementing the prior day's experiences in Python or Sketch, and culminated in the teacher's modification of the "settlement code" to include more realistic constraints, and then compared the results to actual geological settlements.

During the follow-up day session during the academic year, the pre-collegiate teachers were exposed to applications and models of systems that were derived from naturally existing phenomenon, which is an area of research generally encapsulated by "biomorphic systems," "bio-inspired systems," or "biologically derived systems." This one-day session focused more on the physical structures of elements (wings, nests, animal skin coloration) as well on how organisms form collectives based on their fundamental characteristics and interactions with their environment (e.g., flocking birds, schooling fish, ant-food gathering). The ideas of population genetics, survival, and cost, were explored in conjunction with these observable phenomena.

Overall, previous research [18] has indicated "involvement with modeling scientific phenomena and complex systems can play a powerful role in science learning" (p. 151). There have been successes in advancing engineering education and CS through modeling, science standards, and more; however, there is room for improvement in terms of motivating pre-collegiate teachers to use engineering and CS in pre-collegiate classrooms. The study's PD aimed to improve CS content knowledge and motivate pre-collegiate teachers to integrate CS into their STEM disciplines.

3.2. Modeling through NetLogo

In this section, the four literature review themes relate to teaching teachers to think like engineers, and are important for CS and engineering educators at all levels to consider. The first theme of significance to CS and engineering educators focuses on background information about the descriptions of NetLogo as a multi-agent programming language and modeling environment [11,19–22]. NetLogo is a multi-agent simulator that leverages the popular Logo programming language, which was originally developed as a 'learning language.' Multi-agent simulators define the characteristics and/or behaviors of a specific agent (e.g., ant, worker ant, queen ant). Then, the simulator allows an end user to create many replicas of that agent in a predefined world (e.g., ant colony, a flock of birds, atoms, photons). Lastly, the simulator controls and records the interactions of the agents within the world according to the predefined (programmed) rules (e.g., ants following pheromone trails, birds flocking, atoms binding, the behavior of light) [23,24]. Note that an educational use of modeling (e.g., I do, we do, you do) is different than the scientific use of modeling (creation of abstract representation) utilized in this study.

3.2.1. Pre-Collegiate Student Interactions with CS

Secondly, another major literature theme explores pre-collegiate student technology use with CS interactions [15,25–28]. Ultimately, there are a plethora of CS projects for researchers to explore with pre-collegiate teachers and students by using NetLogo or other technologies such as Arduinos and Raspberry Pis, (which the pre-collegiate teachers explored in other RAMPED PD sessions). Although there are several experiential opportunities showcased in the literature, pre-collegiate teachers still struggle to incorporate authentic science, engineering, and CS into their established classroom subjects for their students [29,30].

3.2.2. Pre-Collegiate Teacher Interactions with CS

In the third theme, educational researchers show extensive examples of pre-collegiate teachers using CS in curriculum and instruction, but it is usually in a focused and narrow manner of CS content delivery [9,15,25,31–39]. Thus, based on these works, researchers know that pre-collegiate teachers are attempting and are sometimes successful at incorporating CS into their classrooms. The pre-collegiate teachers' attempted use of CS speaks to the Task Force on Cyberlearning [40] as they call for "research to establish successful ways of using … technologies to enhance educational opportunities and strengthen proven methods of learning" (p. 7). This is where a PD [or similar program] fits into assisting pre-collegiate teachers with CS in classrooms. Additionally, educational researchers have made arguments that "the cognitive and sociocultural factors related to learning complex systems knowledge are relevant and challenging areas for learning sciences research" [41] (p. 11). Thus, teaching pre-collegiate teachers to utilize CS exploration is complicated, and should be systemic and studied rigorously.

3.2.3. Higher Education Interactions with CS

Finally, although an extension of pre-collegiate teaching, CS is still relevant and needed in higher education, and is encouraged by researchers as well [9,18,31,34,35,38,42–47]. However, as Blikstein and Wilensky [38] point out:

A common element in those [higher education] programs is to introduce courses in which students design products and solutions for real-world problems, engaging in actual engineering projects. These initiatives have [been] met with some success and are proliferating into many engineering schools. Despite their success, they have not addressed one key issue in transforming engineering education: extending the pedagogical and motivational advantages of design-based courses to theory-based engineering courses, which constitute the majority of the coursework in a typical engineering degree, and in which traditional pedagogical approaches are still predominant (p. 17).

Hence, higher education instructor content and pedagogy and the translation of those elements to pre-collegiate teachers is an area in need of examination and additional study. Computer science can bridge the design to theory issue [4,6,12].

Overall based on the current literature detailed in Section 3.2 there is a clear need for CS instruction, and work in this area is ongoing. Additionally, researchers are now looking beyond the use of CS, and call for an integrated STEM approach [48]. Thus, the need for CS in society, CS in pre-collegiate classrooms, and the call for an integrated STEM approach are the basis for this study.

4. Materials and Methods

With this PD context, experts conducted six independent sessions in two-day blocks during RAMPED, which was a 16-day, year-long engineering education PD focused on CS applications. Nearly two dozen pre-collegiate teachers (n = 22) from a subset of the 30 total STEM teachers participated in the NetLogo PD sessions. In this group of pre-collegiate teachers, several teachers represented a program, SWARMS (Sustaining Wyoming's Advancing Reach in Mathematics and Science), that supports STEM teaching certification with collegiate funding. Although not the focus of the study, the SWARMS teachers were beginning teachers who needed the additional support of this type of CS PD, although they were technologically savvy. The NetLogo session differed from the other five sessions in that it was taught through learner-centric, inquiry-based activities rather than traditional lectures. Remembering that the research question was how pre-collegiate STEM teachers perceive their CS skill set *before and after the PD, and if the perceptions align with what they know and how they plan to use CS in their classrooms*, the research team collected pre and post-CS content knowledge and self-efficacy data via surveys (including open-ended questions), informal interviews, and artifacts. The research team included faculty from education, CS, physics/astronomy, and engineering. Additionally, an independent evaluator collected qualitative data on PD satisfaction and classroom implementation planning along with quantitative pre and post-content competency data to complement the perception data.

4.1. The Study and Participants

The data for this study were collected intensively during the course of the 2016 16-day engineering education PD for pre-collegiate STEM teachers, and were aimed at enhancing their CS content knowledge and self-efficacy. Of the 22 pre-collegiate NetLogo teacher participants (from a total of 30 STEM pre-collegiate teachers), complete data sets exist for only 20 teachers. The participants equally represented elementary, middle school, and high school teachers in the study. Seven of the pre-collegiate teachers were male, and the other 15 were female. The authors refer to the pre-collegiate teachers as STEM teachers as all taught science or mathematics, and additionally, five of the teachers also taught art, engineering, or technology. The PD focused on CS real-world applications, and the research team implemented six individual PD sessions. Each PD session consisted of two days, which were focused on core CS concepts embedded within authentic uses of CS. The two-day PD sessions included: (1) NetLogo Naturally Inspired (NNI), (2) Astronomy and Space, (3) Robotics, (4) Virtual Reality, (5) Arduinos, and (6) Raspberry Pi. For context, the pre-collegiate teachers chose four of the six sessions to attend during the initial 10-day PD. The pre-collegiate teachers then attended all six extension sessions during the academic year, for a total of 16 participation days. Each session was led by a content expert, with additional guidance and material resources provided by education experts.

The NetLogo session, in comparison to the five other sessions (baseline), was taught through a guided inquiry approach rather than traditional lecture. For example, at the beginning of the first day of the session, participants were presented with a challenge using one of the "Hello World" programs for NetLogo, "Ants" [10], which was described earlier. What follows is a condensed version of those challenges: (1) change the color of the ants, (2) increase the number of food piles that the ants can choose from, (3) introduce the concepts of energy (and death) into the system, (4) introduce reproduction into the system, and (5) introduce some population mutation into the system. These five challenges quickly allowed participants to become acquainted with the language syntax, forced them to utilize fundamental CS techniques to reason and solve the problems, and finally think about the challenges and problems that CS solves that programming alone cannot. This preceded the connections described in Section 3.1.

This study focused on 22 pre-collegiate teachers' CS content knowledge changes, CS self-efficacy, and planned classroom implementation of CS. Pre-collegiate teachers that completed the data set (n = 20) had the following general characteristics: 65% were elementary school teachers (teaching children between five and 14 years old), 63% were science-focused teachers, they had an average of 12.9 years teaching experience, and taught 125.5 students per year, with about 12% of those students on individualized education plans (IEPs).

In order to improve pre-collegiate teacher self-efficacy and CS content knowledge, the RAMPED PD introduced pre-collegiate STEM teachers to real-world applications to CS. Thus, a formal assessment instrument consisted of questions spanning CS applications and fundamental CS theory. The research team created the content questions and administered the pre-assessment and post-assessment instrument to assess pre-collegiate STEM teacher CS knowledge and self-efficacy. This particular study only utilizes a subset of the assessment questions (see Table 1 for the subset of questions) to form a targeted assessment to compare and contrast the NetLogo sessions to other PD sessions. Table 1 highlights seven questions along with the CS concept(s) that they address. Six of the seven questions were related to actual code statements in one of three programming languages: C++, Python, or LOGO, while question seven (Q7), regarding the illustration of sequential operation, only contained graphical illustrations.

Table 1. Subset of assessment questions and corresponding computer science (CS) concept(s) from the full professional development (PD) survey. NNI: NetLogo Naturally Inspired.

Question	Session	Assessment Question (Summary)	CS Concept(s)
Q5	Baseline	Which command queries a robot's joint state?	Syntax
Q7	Baseline	Which of these illustrates sequential operation?	Control Structures
Q14	Baseline	Print out the numbers 1–10	Variables
Q17a	NNI	Show 1000 rolls of a fair 21-sided die	Control Structures
Q17b	NNI	Create a process to swap to two numbers	Syntax
Q17c	NNI	Take a number and add one to it	Variables
Q17d	NNI	Report if a number is even or odd	Boolean Logic

Overall, data were collected several times throughout the study. The participants in the PD answered these previously stated seven survey questions prior to the start of the summer PD session weeks (pre-pre), prior to the specific two-day PD session (pre), immediately after the two-day PD session (post), and immediately after the summer PD session (post-post). These four data sets form the basis for the short-term and long-term impact of the CS content knowledge gains among the pre-collegiate STEM teachers. Thus, each teacher answered the survey questions four times, and the research team collected these data along with other data sets. Interview and artifact data (e.g., lesson plans) were also collected. It is important to note that the authors of this study are not promoting a certain PD or curricula, but instead are promoting a certain mindset in the creation of any PD where there is an emphasis on integration, modeling, and CS concepts.

4.2. Limitations

There are several limitations of the study. Frist, the participant pool is limited to a self-selected group of 20 participants who were admitted on a first-come, first-served basis for a paid PD opportunity, and they chose to complete all of the pre-test and post-test data. Second, the group of participants came largely from the same region and state. Third, the PD was short in terms of teaching a new technical content area to novice pre-collegiate teachers, although the total time spent (120 h) was well above the traditional PD threshold. Fourth, the results in this paper are not generalized due to a limited participant sample, plus an exclusive focus on CS in real-world specific applications. Fifth, the implementation survey was administered three months after the PD concluded; however, the results are not finalized, as the pre-collegiate teachers continue to slowly adopt CS classroom strategies. Sixth, the assessment instrument was custom tailored for the RAMPED PD, and as such had limited reliability and validity. Finally, all of the research team, including the STEM faculty, had significant prior experience in outreach and PD for non-technical audiences; this may be atypical in other technically focused PDs, and may influence the approach of the team, and thus may have skewed the reported results in this study.

5. Analysis and Results

5.1. Qualitative Results

The pre-collegiate teachers answered two types of qualitative data collection, including informal interview questions regarding the individual PD sessions (during working lunches), as well as open-ended questions on the full PD survey. The PD team looked for evidence of content knowledge and perceptions of CS integration. A synthesis of responses shows that the pre-collegiate STEM teachers planned to implement NetLogo into their classrooms at higher rates than the baseline of the other five PD sessions. The research team's summary of the teacher responses from the open-ended questions is summarized in Table 2. Two themes that were identified from their responses included: the cost of the activity implementation and the planned activity type (e.g., inquiry-based, after school club). Also shown in Table 2 are the results of the three-month post-summer PD survey where pre-collegiate teachers reported on both their planned (potential) and already executed (current) CS classroom implementation. The pre-collegiate teachers shared the CS activities that they had planned to use or had already piloted originating from the RAMPED PD experiences (see Table 2).

Table 2. Synthesized aggregation of teaching implementation plan, the current and potential implementation rate, cost, the planned activity, and the PD session type (Inquiry, Explanation, Lecture).

	Topic.	Current (Potential) Implementation	Cost (USD)	Planned Activity	PD Session
	NetLogo	10% (45%)	Free	Inquiry, Family Science Night	Inq. & Exp.
Baseline	Arduino	5% (20%)	<$50	Electricity Unit	Lec. & Inq.
	Raspberry Pi	5% (30%)	<$50	Integrated Project; Afterschool Club	Lec. & Inq.
	Space	0% (10%)	Free	*Unknown*	Lec. & Inq.
	Virtual Reality	5% (25%)	$25–100+	Lecture and Lab	Lec. & Inq.

Along with these implementation data, the following are examples of comments from the pre-collegiate STEM teacher informal interviews and open-ended questions regarding their perceptions of CS integration into STEM:

- [I need] a little more on why a swap is so important in NetLogo or any programming language
- I love the idea of using Net Logo for modeling scenarios with students
- Love the program [NetLogo], my familiarity improved substantially through the workshop, but also with the practice and working with [colleagues]
- [I will use the] applicable web-based opportunities
- My coding background is weak, so I had a hard time figuring out how to modify the code, including for the simulations. However, exposure to the simulations was excellent, so hopefully I can [identify] some of them and use them in class.
- [Doing this workshop has] re-establish[ed] the possibility of using one or more of the simulations models. A benefit would be initial student exposure to coding and using the library of simulations and manipulating the variables already coded.
- [I enjoyed] reviewing the web model and trying to change it.
- The hands-on pieces and the sequence cards were helpful in reading code in a clearer manner.

The research team identified positive terminology regarding participant engagement (e.g., love; excellent; use them; re-established; enjoyed) as well as terms expressing challenges (e.g., a little more; hard time figuring out how; weak) in their responses to NetLogo classroom use. Before PD, the majority of the pre-collegiate teachers (90%) did not know about NetLogo and the potential CS applications. During and after the NetLogo session, the pre-collegiate teachers entertained the idea of integrating CS concepts into their STEM courses.

In actual classroom implementation, one of the elementary teachers used the NetLogo's model's library simulation entitled 'Ants' [10] with her fourth-grade class. The teacher reported that the students changed the size of the ants, the color of the ants, and added a patch of food for the ants by adjusting the NetLogo code. This 'Ant' NetLogo lesson complemented the teacher's life science unit through focusing on biological evolution's unity and diversity. From the NGSS disciplinary core idea on biological evolution 3-LS4-3 [8], the students constructed an argument with evidence that in a particular habitat, some organisms can survive well, some survive less well, and some cannot survive at all. In early 2019, almost three years after the RAMPED PD, this same teacher explained:

"I have been working with NetLogo in my fourth-grade classroom going on three years now. I began using the online platform in my class after learning about it during a summer PD. In the summer program I rewrote pieces of code in an existing program on erosion to tailor it for fourth-grade science standards. I also created a pre and post-assessment to go with the model to gain data on student learning. The model went well the first year, and students were able to use the model that I had created to see how the flow rate impacted erosion over time. I also used the idea of if/then statements to have my students write a flow chart for the standard subtraction algorithm. It was the first time that I saw students really understand what an algorithm was and why it worked.

When I went to use my model in the second year, NetLogo had changed the program to where my model was no longer operable in the new program, and I had not saved it to the online commons. I unfortunately did not have the time to recode the program, and so I looked for other ways to use NetLogo. My district had also switched to Chrome books, and so the only platform available was online instead of the desktop application. I decided to use NetLogo as a space to teach some simple coding, since our school at that time did not have a coding program. NetLogo was a great way to get students into coding since it is color-coded and is more simple than other coding languages. Students were able to dive in and change the color, size, and shape of the 'turtles' without much experience. I also had the students simply explore the online library to see what other models were out there. I had students pick a model and talk about what the model showed and how it could be manipulated.

[With the] Hour of Code curriculum, and I no longer felt the need to do coding with NetLogo in my classroom. Students were instead using Scratch and other coding programs to create animations and explore. I am starting to look at NetLogo again with an eye toward physics and modeling collisions of objects to help my students better grasp what is happening, since we do not have the instrumentation to measure the energy change in a collision, and the change is not always discernable to the naked fourth-grade eye. I have found that NetLogo gives me a place to allow my students to model with numerous repetitions, and is highly effective as a supplement to my science instruction."

Also in early 2019, again almost three years after the RAMPED PD, another teacher provided the following vignette:

"When I was the [high school] psychology teacher, a [science teacher] and I (behavioral science) used NetLogo to integrate CS into two problems that had overlap: how a virus spreads and how a social meme spreads across a social network. Students were broken into two groups to look at corresponding NetLogo models and given some basic introduction to coding through these models. In pairs, they made predictions, changed variables, and then tried to make suggestions for how both models could improve. The context of my segment about how a social meme spreads across a network were related to cultural change and cognitive bias (in particular, confirmation bias/motivated reasoning), and the attempts to address the culture problem endemic in [the state] of toxic peer victimization (bullying, peer cruelty, social/relational aggression, cyberbullying) and a local project. It helped students to visualize content [they had] just become familiar with when we jig-sawed Gladwell's Tipping Point in understanding the role of surveillance in identifying mavens, connectors, and salespeople/persuaders that could be enlisted in the effort, and the design of 'sticky' memes to help cause a cultural change or shift. Unfortunately, due to budget cuts, I was reassigned to teach financial literacy, and was not able to continue addressing the cultural problems in [the state]. The applicability of NetLogo also assisted [the science teacher] and [nursing teacher] in the common project that we began the first year [while] helping students understand virology and epidemiology to introduce discussions of vaccination and infection control for CNAs [or certified nursing assistants]."

5.2. Quantitative Results

5.2.1. CS Content Scores

In addition to the CS integration perception data, 20 PD participants responded to all of the content knowledge survey questions on four separate occasions. As discussed in the previous section, the four data collection points of interest in this study focus on the time immediately surrounding the PD, with a pre-summer PD assessment (pre-pre), a pre-PD session assessment (pre), a post-PD session assessment (post), and a post-summer PD assessment (post-post). The average correct score results from a seven-question subset across all 22 participants is shown in Table 3. The trend between the first three assessments is strictly increasing, and the most fluctuation occurs between the post-session assessment (Post) and the post-summer PD assessment (post-post).

Table 3. Percentage of correct CS content answers for PD participants.

Question.	Pre-Pre	Pre	Post	Post-Post
5	6%	18%	44%	26%
7	39%	45%	90%	82%
14	32%	39%	55%	86%
17a	60%	60%	68%	100%
17b	29%	55%	59%	80%
17c	30%	35%	36%	50%
17d	48%	53%	70%	62%

5.2.2. CS—NetLogo Pre-Collegiate Self-Efficacy Scores

The self-efficacy of the pre-collegiate teachers was measured quantitatively on a five-point Likert-scale, with 1 representing "not skillful at all," and 5 representing "extremely skillful." The number of responses to the anonymous self-efficacy survey varied between pre and post, with 22 in pre-PD responses, and 21 post-PD responses. Table 4 shows the overall NetLogo session participant self-efficacy results. When comparing the pre to post results, perhaps most interesting is the overall shift in self-efficacy. Prior to the PD, only 18% (4/22) of pre-collegiate teachers rated themselves at higher NetLogo skill levels (4 or 5); after the PD session 67% (14/21), the same sample rated themselves at higher NetLogo skill levels (4 or 5). This change from four to 14 represents an over 200% increase in the number of pre-collegiate teachers with high self-efficacy after the PD session. When looking at participants rating themselves as average or better (3, 4, or 5), the self-efficacy rate changed from 50% (11/22) to 95% (20/21).

Table 4. Self-efficacy assessment by PD participants pre and post-NetLogo PD session.

Pre (n = 22)	3	8	7	2	2
Post (n = 21)	-	1	6	9	5
Skill Level	1	2	3	4	5
	Not Skillful		*Average*	*Extremely Skillful*	

5.2.3. PD Session Usefulness and Satisfaction

In addition to implementation surveys, content knowledge assessment, and self-efficacy assessments, the PD participants were asked to reflect and provide feedback on the PD itself. Table 5 shows a summary of this anonymous feedback. Immediately after the PD session, during an exit interview, pre-collegiate teachers were asked, "on a three-point scale Likert scale, how useful is NetLogo to you?" Of the 20 respondents, 95% of the pre-collegiate teachers stated that NetLogo was useful to them (moderate extent, 6; larger extent, 13), with only one respondent saying that the session was useful to a negligible extent. The research team asked about the pre-collegiate teacher overall satisfaction, and of the 22 pre-collegiate teachers interviewed after the NetLogo session, over 75% reported being satisfied with the session [1/22 completely dissatisfied (5%), 3/22 mostly dissatisfied (14%), 2/22 moderately satisfied (9%), 5/22 mostly satisfied (23%), and 11/22 completely satisfied (50%)]. Finally, when asked if the NetLogo workshop "stretched teacher thinking into their classrooms", over 85% of teachers believed that it did to a moderate or large extent [8/22 moderate extent (36%), and 12/22 large extent (55%)]. Overall, teachers enjoyed and planned to use integrated CS and NetLogo concepts in their pre-collegiate classrooms after the PD, and expressed that this was in part because their perceived level of CS and NetLogo expertise had increased.

Table 5. Participant assessment of session usefulness and impact.

	Low		Moderate		High
Session Usefulness (n = 20)	1	0	6	0	13
Session Satisfaction (n = 22)	1	3	2	5	11
Stretched Thinking (n = 22)	2	0	8	0	12

6. Conclusions and Implications

While CS is becoming a "must teach" subject for pre-collegiate teachers, as seen in the literature review, rarely is it incorporated within all STEM disciplines and grade levels. Teachers' lack of CS integration is due in part to a lack of specific CS content knowledge, self-efficacy, and resources to effectively incorporate CS within existing curricula. This limited study shows that using a specific tool or programming language, such as NetLogo, in a PD can create pre-collegiate teacher comfort with the tool along with pre-collegiate teacher classroom use. As seen in Table 3, the pre-collegiate teacher content knowledge scores exhibit a positive increase for all of the questions pre-pre to post, pre-pre to post-post, pre to post, and pre to post-post; this provides support that the NetLogo PD session had a positive impact on short-term (two-week) and long-term (one-year) CS content knowledge. Additionally, most of the pre-collegiate teachers required sustainability and authentic CS integration support, given the 16-day PD with a total of three days with NetLogo immersion. A three-day intensive session can offer beginning CS content knowledge and bolster self-efficacy, but it cannot offer pre-collegiate teachers the in-depth CS knowledge that is need for spontaneous examples during classroom implementation. The participants' CS engagement is encouraging in light of the need for engineering and integrated CS in pre-collegiate classrooms. It is reassuring that overall, the pre-collegiate teachers enjoyed and participated in the NetLogo sessions and planned to use the resource in their classrooms.

The pre-collegiate teacher challenges emphasize the need for pre-collegiate teacher sustained engineering and CS expert support. The teachers identified CS and NetLogo implementation challenges that were traditional in nature (e.g., understanding the programming language) as well as non-traditional (e.g., changing class assignments). In pre-collegiate teacher feedback and artifacts, the authors noticed that there were few real-world examples incorporated with the use of NetLogo in the classroom. This raises concern, as the PD emphasized real-world connections to modeling. The authors speculate that the pre-collegiate teachers need more time to fully understand and internalize the real-world applications of the modeling software as well as more chances for expert collaboration. If the desire to use CS is present, but there are hurdles for pre-collegiate teachers to overcome, then CS instructors from institutes of higher education can assist in filling this gap. As stated earlier, the authors do know about Trautman's blog showcasing the graphic 'Coding Confidence versus Competence,' and admit that this same path might have allowed the pre-collegiate teachers to cling to the 'hand-holding honeymoon' phase of the integration sessions, including the NetLogo experience. However, three years after the PD, two of the NetLogo pre-collegiate teacher participants were utilizing NetLogo in the classroom when possible. This showcases a long-lasting impact from the NetLogo PD, even if it is a small participant pool sample.

The authors argue that pre-collegiate teachers can learn basic CS fundamentals through exploration in a constructivist environment with a free, easily accessible programming language (such as NetLogo) and without structured, lecture-oriented sessions. Potential implications, given a larger focused study, are widespread, as pre-collegiate teachers can potentially increase their own CS content knowledge and self-efficacy. For example, if a teacher participated in free, online modules at their own pace, could that lead to as much of an increase in CS self-efficacy and content knowledge? This could influence integrated CS implementation, which can lead to the incorporation of more CS into pre-collegiate daily activities and standards-based instruction. Finally, the authors believe that STEM teachers, in conjunction with CS content experts, can use NetLogo or a similar technology, as a tool within CS PD. Additionally, the authors propose that pre-collegiate STEM teachers could self-engage or create a NetLogo professional learning community (PLC) to augment these exploratory CS opportunities. Experience with CS and NetLogo appears to increase teacher content knowledge and self-efficacy, and the evidence revealed that pre-collegiate teachers were able to create STEM lessons that incorporated engineering, CS, and NetLogo. Future work could validate studies such as this one and expand STEM teachers' knowledge on what works to incorporate CS into pre-collegiate classrooms. Teaching pre-collegiate teachers to think like engineers and computer scientists is important, timely, and needed. This study shows how integrating CS into existing standards-based curricula can have short and long-term impacts in pre-collegiate classrooms.

Interestingly, although not the focus of this study, five of the six sessions were taught by faculty that used a traditional lecture followed by inquiry experiences, but the NetLogo session was taught by a faculty member who used a brief introduction, and then allowed the pre-collegiate teachers to explore the possibilities of NetLogo modeling in their own exploratory modes (and offered explanations along the way). Could the session approach make the difference in pre-collegiate teacher use of NetLogo? Just as the ants march toward survival in the NetLogo simulation, pre-collegiate teachers are faced with moving forward and integrating CS into STEM disciplines to prepare future generations for the demands and needs of a computing-centric career. Similar to ants finding food, pre-collegiate teachers who adopt and develop integrated CS materials become beacons to other pre-collegiate teachers, enabling them to address the collective need for CS integration throughout the pre-collegiate education system. The need for CS and the standards that call for CS and CS-like skills are present and currently appearing; thus, pre-collegiate teachers need an institute of higher education or other programs' support in varied dimensions and on copious occasions to allow as many pre-collegiate teachers as possible to embrace and utilize integrated CS in classrooms. Based on the data and analysis presented, the authors offer that NetLogo (or any other similar) technology, when used in an exploratory, inquiry-based fashion, is capable of enabling teachers to incorporate CS into their pre-collegiate classrooms especially when pre-collegiate teachers embrace content learning and show increasing perception of their abilities within the CS context.

Author Contributions: Conceptualization, M.B., A.C.B.; methodology, M.B.; validation, M.B., A.C.B.; formal analysis, M.B.; investigation, M.B., A.C.B.; resources, M.B., A.C.B.; data curation, M.B., A.C.B.; writing—original draft, M.B., A.C.B.; writing—revision and editing, A.C.B., M.B.; visualization, M.B., A.C.B.; supervision, M.B., A.C.B.; project administration, A.C.B.; funding acquisition, A.C.B.

Funding: This work was supported by 1) US federal grant, RAMPED, under No Child Left Behind (NCLB) (P.L.107F110, Title II, Part B) administered by the Wyoming Department of Education (MSP Grant #1601506MSPA2); and 2) National Science Foundation (NSF) Noyce—called SWARMS—(NSF Grant# 1339853). Any opinions, findings, conclusions or recommendations expressed in this material are those of the authors and do not necessarily reflect the views of the National Science Foundation.

Acknowledgments: This work is a revised and extended analysis and discussion of data presented in short-paper published by the authors: Burrows, A.C. and Borowczak, M. "Teaching Teachers to Think Like Engineers Using NetLogo," which, appeared in the proceedings of the 2017 ASEE Annual Conference & Exposition, Columbus, OH, USA, 2017. The authors would like to acknowledge all the pre-collegiate teacher participants from the RAMPED PD, and especially Crystal and Joshua for their specific insights and feedback to this work.

Conflicts of Interest: The authors declare no conflict of interest.

References

1. Pew Research Center. AI, Robotics, and the Future of Jobs. Available online: http://www.pewinternet.org/2014/08/06/future-of-jobs/ (accessed on 10 December 2018).
2. U.S. Bureau of Labor Statistics. Available online: https://www.bls.gov/ooh/computer-and-information-technology/home.htm (accessed on 10 December 2018).
3. U.S. Bureau of Labor Statistics. Available online: https://www.bls.gov/spotlight/2017/science-technology-engineering-and-mathematics-stem-occupations-past-present-and-future/pdf/science-technology-engineering-and-mathematics-stem-occupations-past-present-and-future.pdf (accessed on 10 December 2018).

4. Hubwieser, P.; Giannakos, M.; Berges, M.; Brinda, T.; Diethelm, I.; Magenheim, J.; Pal, Y.; Jackova, J.; Jasute, E. A Global Snapshot of Computer Science Education in K-12 Schools. In Proceedings of the 2015 ITiCSE on Working Group Reports, Vilnius, Lithuania, 4–8 July 2015; pp. 65–83.

5. Celik, V.; Yesilyurt, E. Attitudes to technology, perceived computer self-efficacy and computer anxiety as predictors of computer supported education. *Comput. Educ.* **2013**, *60*, 148–158. [CrossRef]

6. Burrows, A.C.; Borowczak, M.; Slater, T.F.; Haynes, J.C. Teaching computer science and engineering through robotics: Science and art form. *Probl. Educ. 21st Century* **2012**, *47*, 6–15.

7. Leonard, J.; Buss, A.; Gamboa, R.; Mitchell, M.; Fashola, O.S.; Hubert, T.; Almughyirah, S. Using robotics and game design to enhance Children's self-efficacy, STEM attitudes, and computational thinking skills. *J. Sci. Educ. Technol.* **2016**, *25*, 860–876. [CrossRef]

8. NGSS Lead States. *Next Generation Science Standards: For States by States*; National Academies Press: Washington, DC, USA, 2013.

9. Wilensky, U.; Papert, S. Restructurations: Reformulations of knowledge disciplines through new representational forms. In Proceedings of the Constructionism 2010: Constructionist approaches to Creative Learning, Thinking, and Education: Lessons for the 21st Century, Paris, France, 16–20 August 2010.

10. Wilensky, U. NetLogo Ants Model. Center for Connected Learning and Computer-Based Modeling. Northwestern University: Evanston, IL, USA. Available online: http://ccl.northwestern.edu/netlogo/models/Ants (accessed on 10 December 2018).

11. Wilensky, U.; NetLogo. Center for Connected Learning and Computer-Based Modeling. Northwestern University: Evanston, IL, USA. Available online: http://ccl.northwestern.edu/netlogo (accessed on 10 December 2018).

12. Obama, B. The President's Radio Address: Giving Every Student an Opportunity to Learn Through Computer Science for All. Office of the Press Secretary, The White House. Available online: https://www.whitehouse.gov/the-press-office/2016/01/30/weekly-address-giving-every-student-opportunity-learn-through-computer (accessed on 10 December 2018).

13. Cannady, M.A.; Greenwald, E.; Harris, K.N. Problematizing the STEM Pipeline Metaphor: Is the STEM Pipeline Metaphor Serving Our Students and the STEM Workforce? *Sci. Educ.* **2014**, *98*, 443–460. [CrossRef]

14. Borowczak, M.; Burrows, A.C. Interactive Web Notebooks Using the Cloud to Enable CS in K–16+ Classrooms and PDs. In Proceedings of the 2017 ASEE Annual Conference & Exposition, Columbus, OH, USA, 24–28 June 2017.

15. Sengupta, P.; Dickes, A.; Farris, A.V.; Karan, A.; Martin, D.; Wright, M. Programming in pre-collegiate science classrooms. *Commun. ACM* **2015**, *58*, 33–35.

16. Vygotsky, L. Interaction between learning and development. In *Readings on the Development of Children*; Gauvain, M., Cole, M., Eds.; Scientific American Books: New York, NY, USA, 1978; pp. 34–40.

17. Pea, R.D.; Collins, A. Learning how to do science education: Four waves of reform. In *Designing coherent science education*; Kali, Y., Linn, M.C., Roseman, J.E., Eds.; Teachers College Press: New York, NY, USA, 2008.

18. Hashem, K.; Mioduser, D. The Contribution of Learning by Modeling (LbM) to Students' Understanding of Complexity Concepts. *Int. J. e-Educ. e-Business, e-Manag. e-Learn.* **2011**, *1*, 151.

19. Blikstein, P.; Abrahamson, D.; Wilensky, U. Netlogo: Where we are, where we're going. In Proceedings of the annual meeting of Interaction Design and Children, Boulder, Colorado, 8–10 June 2005.

20. Tisue, S.; Wilensky, U. Netlogo: A simple environment for modeling complexity. In Proceedings of the International Conference on Complex Systems, Boston, MA, USA, 16–21 May 2004; Volume 21, pp. 16–21.

21. Tisue, S.; Wilensky, U. NetLogo: Design and implementation of a multi-agent modeling environment. In Proceedings of the Agent 2004 Conference on Social Dynamics: Interaction, Reflexivity and Emergence, Chicago, IL, USA, 7–9 October 2004; pp. 7–9.

22. Wilensky, U. Modeling nature's emergent patterns with multi-agent languages. In Proceedings of the 8th Conference of EuroLogo, Linz, Austria, 21–25 August 2001; pp. 1–6.

23. Goel, A.K.; Rugaber, S.; Vattam, S. Structure, behavior, and function of complex systems: The structure, behavior, and function modeling language. *Artif. Intell. Eng. Des. Anal. Manuf.* **2009**, *23*, 23–35. [CrossRef]

24. Malan, D.J.; Leitner, H.H. Scratch for budding computer scientists. *ACM SIGCSE Bull.* **2007**, *39*, 223–227. [CrossRef]

25. Basu, S.; Dickes, A.; Kinnebrew, J.S.; Sengupta, P.; Biswas, G. CTSiM: A Computational Thinking Environment for Learning Science through Simulation and Modeling. In Proceedings of the 5th International Conference on Computer Supported Education, Aachen, Germany, 6–8 May 2013; pp. 369–378.
26. Berland, L.K.; Reiser, B.J. Classroom communities' adaptations of the practice of scientific argumentation. *Sci. Educ.* **2011**, *95*, 191–216. [CrossRef]
27. Svihla, V.; Linn, M.C. A design-based approach to fostering understanding of global climate change. *Int. J. Sci. Educ.* **2012**, *34*, 651–676. [CrossRef]
28. Vattam, S.; Goel, A.K.; Rugaber, S.; Hmelo-Silver, C.E.; Jordan, R.; Gray, S.; Sinha, S. Understanding Complex Natural Systems by Articulating Structure-Behavior-Function Models. *Educ. Technol. Soc.* **2011**, *14*, 66–81.
29. Burrows, A.C. Partnerships: A systemic study of two professional developments with university faculty and K–12 teachers of science, technology, engineering, and mathematics. *Probl. Educ. 21st Century* **2015**, *65*, 28–38.
30. Burrows, A.C.; DiPompeo, M.A.; Myers, A.D.; Hickox, R.C.; Borowczak, M.; French, D.A.; Schwortz, A.C. Authentic science experiences: Pre-collegiate science educators' successes and challenges during professional development. *Probl. Educ. 21st Century* **2016**, *70*, 59–73.
31. Blikstein, P. Digital fabrication and 'making' in education: The democratization of invention. *FabLabs Mach. Mak. Invent.* **2013**, *4*, 1–21.
32. Donnelly, D.F.; Linn, M.C.; Ludvigsen, S. Impacts and characteristics of computer-based science inquiry learning environments for precollege students. *Rev. Educ. Res.* **2014**, *84*, 572–608. [CrossRef]
33. Grover, S.; Pea, R. Computational Thinking in K–12 A Review of the State of the Field. *Educ. Res.* **2013**, *42*, 38–43. [CrossRef]
34. Klašnja-Milićević, A.; Vesin, B.; Ivanović, M.; Budimac, Z. E-Learning personalization based on hybrid recommendation strategy and learning style identification. *Comput. Educ.* **2011**, *56*, 885–899. [CrossRef]
35. Maroulis, S.; Guimera, R.; Petry, H.; Stringer, M.J.; Gomez, L.M.; Amaral, L.A.N.; Wilensky, U. Complex systems view of educational policy research. *Science* **2010**, *330*, 38–39. [CrossRef] [PubMed]
36. Pathak, S.A.; Kim, B.; Jacobson, M.J.; Zhang, B. Learning the physics of electricity: A qualitative analysis of collaborative processes involved in productive failure. *Int. J. Comput.-Support. Collab. Learn.* **2011**, *6*, 57–73. [CrossRef]
37. Sengupta, P.; Kinnebrew, J.S.; Basu, S.; Biswas, G.; Clark, D. Integrating computational thinking with pre-collegiate science education using agent-based computation: A theoretical framework. *Educ. Inf. Technol.* **2013**, *18*, 351–380. [CrossRef]
38. Shen, J.; Lei, J.; Chang, H.Y.; Namdar, B. Technology-enhanced, modeling-based instruction (TMBI) in science education. In *Handbook of Research on Educational Communications and Technology*; Springer: New York, NY, USA, 2014; pp. 529–540.
39. Wilensky, U.; Brady, C.E.; Horn, M.S. Fostering computational literacy in science classrooms. *Commun. ACM* **2014**, *57*, 24–28. [CrossRef]
40. Borgman, C.L.; Abelson, H.; Dirks, L.; Johnson, R.; Koedinger, K.R.; Linn, M.C.; Lynch, C.A.; Oblinger, D.G.P.; Roy, D.S.; Katie Smith, M.S.; et al. *Fostering Learning in the Networked World: The Cyberlearning Opportunity and Challenge. A 21st Century Agenda for the National Science Foundation*; Report of the NSF Task Force on Cyberlearning; DIANE Publishing Company: Collingdale, PA, USA, 2008.
41. Jacobson, M.J.; Wilensky, U. Complex systems in education: Scientific and educational importance and implications for the learning sciences. *J. Learn. Sci.* **2006**, *15*, 11–34. [CrossRef]
42. Blikstein, P. Using learning analytics to assess students' behavior in open-ended programming tasks. In Proceedings of the 1st International Conference on Learning Analytics and Knowledge, Banff, AB, Canada, 27 February–1 March 2011.
43. Blikstein, P.; Wilensky, U. Less is more: Agent-based simulation as a powerful learning tool in materials science. In Proceedings of the IV International Joint Conference on Autonomous Agents and Multiagent Systems (AAMAS 2005), Utrecht, Holland, The Netherlands, 25–29 July 2005.
44. Blikstein, P.; Wilensky, U. *MaterialSim: A constructionist agent-based modeling approach to engineering education. Designs for Learning Environments of the Future*; Springer: Boston, MA, USA, 2010; pp. 17–60.
45. Chiu, M.H.; Wu, H.K. The roles of multimedia in the teaching and learning of the triplet relationship in chemistry. In *Multiple Representations in Chemical Education*; Springer: Netherlands, The Netherlands, 2009; pp. 251–283.

46. Levy, S.T.; Wilensky, U. Crossing levels and representations: The Connected Chemistry (CC1) curriculum. *J. Sci. Educ. Technol.* **2009**, *18*, 224–242.
47. Sengupta, P.; Wilensky, U. Learning electricity with NIELS: Thinking with electrons and thinking in levels. *Int. J. Comput. Math. Learn.* **2009**, *14*, 21–50. [CrossRef]
48. Burrows, A.C.; Garofalo, J.; Barbato, S.; Christensen, R.; Grant, M.; Parrish, J.; Thomas, C.; Tyler-Wood, T. Integrated STEM and Current Directions in the STEM Community. *Contemp. Issues Technol. Teach. Educ.* **2017**, *17*, 478–482.

education sciences

MDPI

Article

An Entrepreneurship Venture for Training K–12 Teachers to Use Engineering as a Context for Learning

Anant R. Kukreti [1,*] and Jack Broering [2]

[1] Department of Biomedical, Chemical, and Environmental Engineering, University of Cincinnati, 2600 Clifton Ave, Cincinnati, OH 45221, USA

[2] University of Cincinnati, 2600 Clifton Ave, Cincinnati, OH 45221, USA; jack.broering@gmail.com

* Correspondence: anant.kukreti@uc.edu; Tel.: +1-513-919-5217

Received: 6 November 2018; Accepted: 6 March 2019; Published: 11 March 2019

check for updates

Abstract: In this paper, the authors present their experiences from participating in a National Science Foundation (NSF) I-Corps L training program established for business startups, using Blank's Lean LaunchPad, Osterwalder's Business Model Canvas, and associated tools. They used the entrepreneurial skills acquired through this training to scale-up their emerging innovation, the Cincinnati Engineering Enhanced Math and Science Program (CEEMS), which had been developed, implemented, and evaluated with successful results over a period of seven years in a targeted 14 school-district partnership in Greater Cincinnati. The overriding goal was to improve student learning and success rates in K–12 math and science courses by helping to accelerate the process of bringing effective educational innovation, CEEMS, to scale. In CEEMS, teachers were trained in using challenge-based learning (CBL) and the engineering design process (EDP), teaching pedagogies to transform their classrooms into student-centered, hands-on learning environments, while also assisting students to improve their evaluation scores related to science, math, and engineering instruction. CEEMS teachers acquired the necessary skills through coursework, professional development (PD) workshops, and longitudinal professional guidance provided by assigned coaches over a period of two years to become proficient in developing CBL–EDP curriculum, teaching it, and assessing student learning and reflecting after teaching. The authors have documented how they used customer market research conducted during the I-Corps L training to define their minimum viable product (MVP) to duplicate the successful CEEMS methodology through a condensed ($\leq$16 week) self-paced, completely online training program with virtual coaching support. The authors also describe the process they used to move forward very quickly from an MVP to a more complete product offering, its branding, the process of trademarking it, and finally licensing it to an established non-profit organization (NPO) for future marketing. Details of the whole experience are presented with the hope that it will serve as a useful guide for other venture creators.

Keywords: challenge-based learning; engineering design process; student engagement; online professional development training; coaching

---

1. Introduction

1.1. The Need

The American Association for the Advancement of Science (AAAS), the National Research Council (NRC), and the National Science Foundation (NSF) all promote student-centered pedagogies, such as inquiry, constructivism, and project-based learning, as ways to increase student engagement and achievement in science [1]. K–12 teachers are required to teach state mandated academic standards for specific courses and grade levels. Additionally, they also face high-stakes testing accountability, classroom management, and interruptions to instructional time due to testing, assemblies, special programs, etc. With the advent of the Next Generation Science Standards (NGSS) [2], many states (even those who have not adopted NGSS) have placed more of an emphasis on incorporating engineering design into science standards. While Common Core State Standards (CCSS) for Mathematical Practice [3] do not directly mention engineering, they promote teaching students "habits of mind". Engineering design is one vehicle to develop these critical habits. In a math classroom, engineering design challenges engage students through problem solving, critical thinking, sense making, reasoning, collaboration, communication, precise measurement, collection and analysis, graphing of data, and so on. In order to encourage the use of engineering design, *Understanding the Status and Improving the Prospects* [4] advocates for a more systematic linkage between engineering design and scientific and mathematical inquiry to improve learning. As such, engineering design has a key role in both NGSS and CCSS.

Despite this new engineering focus, K–12 science and mathematics teachers are often intimidated and unsure how to incorporate engineering practices in their classrooms. As a result, professional development (PD) has emerged to address this very issue. The most powerful instrument for change lies at the core of education—teaching itself [5–7]. Successful learning is a shared experience between a knowledgeable, enthusiastic teacher and curious, self-assured students [8–13]. The efficacy of combining PD that improves teaching effectiveness with standards-based (K–12) curriculum is becoming evident [14–17], as are better ways of retaining effective teachers [18]. Teacher education needs to be iterative; it depends on sustained, coherent, collaborative, and reflective high-quality PD [19–22], high-level science content [23], and an understanding of the social, contextual, and distributed nature of learning [24].

The components of an integrated framework in science, technology, engineering, and math (STEM) education often include a trans-disciplinary curriculum and an inquiry-based approach [25–29]. Embedded in it is authentic learning, engineering education and the engineering design process (EDP), project-based and problem-based learning (PBL), career exploration, and a collaborative learning environment. Currently, K–12 schools often give students an incomplete and inaccurate depiction of what engineering entails because methods differ between the sciences and engineering. Thus, there is a pressing need for in-service training that will prepare instructors to instruct in engineering as well as math and science.

In science education, engineering design is increasingly being viewed as a gateway to authentic learning that can support increased student understanding of scientific concepts (e.g., [30–32]). Mehalik et al. [33] suggest that a systems design approach for teaching science concepts is superior in terms of knowledge gain, engagement, and retention when compared to a scripted inquiry approach. Parallel to design approaches are those that show how science becomes the vehicle for prompting design, as is the case with PBL pedagogy (e.g., [34]). For example, an inquiry project designed by Snetsinger et al. [35] began with the question "How can one harness the energy of the wind to create electricity?" and students worked in teams to address the design challenge. Whether the approach to science is through design or design through science, the convergence between science and engineering design are explored in ways that represent the real world [36]. Design has the potential to stimulate interest and make science accessible to all.

In order to capture the attention and aspirations of students, innovative, real-world applicable units prove particularly valuable; however, they require teachers who are not only confident in their abilities to design and implement them, but are also given the opportunity to do so. In order to develop units that highlight real world problem solving, teachers often benefit from having a structure to scaffold their lesson. Challenge-based learning (CBL) provides that structure or scaffolding. In CBL, scaffolding structures guide student progress through the challenge [37]. CBL environments can mimic design or provide motivating reasons for students to solve problems to address a societal issue and in the process learn STEM content. The success of these approaches for learning engineering has been demonstrated [38,39]. The advantage over traditional design activity is that when this is situated as science and math activity instead, students are more likely to fully explore variables, rather than stop when design criteria are met [38–42]. A CBL STEM classroom creates learning environments designed to engage students in "doing" and facilitating students' active engagement in their own learning [43].

1.2. Our Response to the Needs: A Teacher PD Program for Select School Districts in Cincinnati

The Cincinnati Engineering Enhanced Mathematics and Science Program (CEEMS) [44] was a $9.2 million targeted Math and Science Partnership (MSP) grant (#DGE-1102990) funded by NSF from 2011 to 2018, for which the primary author of this paper was the Principal Investigator and the co-author was a Resource Team Member (coach) on the project team. The CEEMS vision was to establish a cadre of in-service teachers, who would implement the authentic articulation of engineering with science and mathematics in 6–12th grade classrooms. It afforded a much-needed opportunity to study how students learn mathematics and science when engineering is used as the context. CEEMS was led by the University of Cincinnati as the higher education Core Partner in partnership with 14 Core Partner school districts. CEEMS worked to meet the growing need for engineering-educated teachers who were equipped to provide learners with opportunities to meet the NGSS, CCSS for Mathematical Practice, and Ohio's Learning Standards [45] for K–12 science and mathematics while acquiring universal skills (21st-Century Learning Skills). CEEMS was unique in that teachers were trained under coaches to develop and teach curricular units in which CBL and the EDP were integrated and individually suited to their own classroom.

The CEEMS CBL approach [46–51] has its roots in the seminal work freely disseminated by Apple, Inc. [52]. In this version of CBL, students begin with a big idea, such as public health. They collaborate in teams to generate an *essential question*, offer insight on how that big idea relates to it, and the class as a whole then state it as a *challenge* that they would like to solve. After the challenge is defined, the entire class generates *guiding questions* that need to be answered. Student teams seek to find answers to the guiding questions by participating in a variety of learning activities, conducting research, learning new material (independently, in groups or as part of a teacher-led lesson), performing experiments, interviewing, and exploring various avenues to assist in crafting the best solution to the challenge. CEEMS adds a twist by requiring that the challenge be solved using the EDP. By synthesizing CBL and the EDP, teachers use the challenge to get students engaged and interested in the problem and then guide them to use the EDP to seek out multiple solutions. Put simply, the EDP is a series of steps that engineers follow to devise solutions for problems. More details about the EDP are presented later in this paper. However, the nature of the EDP is inherently flexible because there are constraints, trade-offs, and performance objectives for any challenge or problem that make a variety of potential solutions available. As such, the EDP is an iterative process that requires constant revision and optimization. Using prior knowledge and experiences, students identify the best alternative and implement the most efficient solution. Finally, student teams share their solution to the challenge using one of many possible formats such as oral presentations, written reports, marketing flyers, videos, and other creative means.

It should be noted that CBL is similar to, yet distinct from, both project-based learning and problem-based learning. All three pedagogies are student-centered, interdisciplinary, collaborative, reflective, and oriented around a real-world problem. In contrast, in CEEMS, CBL provides students with the opportunity to use the EDP to define the question they want to answer, and to provide input on the challenge to be solved. While problem, project, and CBL by themselves all work well for teaching engineering, the CEEMS approach has shown that learners are often more invested in solving a problem if they define it and set the parameters themselves. Giving learners more control can prove frightening for educators. What if they choose to solve a problem that bears little relation to the state standards they are expected to learn? As a result, it requires much practice and support for teachers to become adept practitioners of a CBL–EDP integrated approach, while still ensuring that students learn the required content.

Using the CBL and EDP pedagogies in CEEMS, as described above, eight new courses (three credit hours each) focusing on engineering, science, and math content, and a seminar-based capstone course (one credit hour) were used to train in-service, 6–12th grade math or science teachers with current licensure in math or science, during the Summer Institute for Teachers (SIT). SIT participants took a total of six courses (three courses per summer) and two education seminar courses (one course per summer) over the course of two 7-week summer programs, for a total of 20 semester credit hours. The seminar-based capstone course was structured to provide PD to help the teachers design engineering challenges which incorporate the EDP that could be applied in their own classrooms using their own teaching standards. As part of this seminar course, two Resource Team Members (coaches), consisting of a retired or semi-retired educator and engineer, were assigned to each teacher. They provided critical support during the summer development of units by brainstorming ideas, reviewing units in progress, and approving those units once they reached completion. After the successful completion of this program, the University of Cincinnati provided the SIT teachers with a Certificate of Engineering Education. Teachers earned 10 credit hours per summer for a total of 20 credit hours.

CEEMS teachers develop units using established templates, which help them to organize their specific information and content in a consistent way that requires them to document how they plan to adhere to the program pedagogies throughout unit implementation. Prior to drafting their first curricular unit, teachers attend a PD workshop where they are introduced to the unit and an activity template that were developed for the CEEMS project. At least four activity templates are utilized for each curricular unit, as well as a pre-test and a post-test that are directly linked to the activities' educational outcomes. The activities are designed to answer the guiding questions identified by the students, and as such have well-defined and measurable educational outcomes. There are some key teaching strategies the teachers are required to plan and document prior to teaching, and to later revise if they are changed during teaching. In each unit template, teachers pre-identify the kinds of misconceptions students would likely have regarding the content and how these issues would be addressed. Additionally, the teachers outline how they plan to differentiate parts of the lesson activities to support the needs of different kinds of learners. The goal for the construction of templates is to maximize organization and preparation before implementation, but in such a way that successful teaching methods and areas for improvement can be easily identified. In the CBL section of the template, teachers have to describe how they plan to relate the math and science content to real world applications, STEM careers, and societal issues (ACS).

During the academic year, two resource team coaches observe a teacher's unit in action during key points (e.g., when CBL and the EDP are implemented) and then have a de-briefing session with the teacher to discuss successes and improvements. In the second year, their role remains the same. After the de-briefing, the teacher records his or her reflections on the implementation process of the unit template, makes any needed edits to the templates based on what occurred during unit implementation (for example, actual student misconceptions and any differentiations addressed), and documents assessment and evaluation results related to growth in student learning.

In summary, in CEEMS there are three important elements that prepare teachers to successfully incorporate the EDP into the teaching of core science and math content, which can be adopted and/or adapted by others. First, teachers experience engineering challenges themselves when taking the SIT courses: by engaging in teamwork and collaboration, learning from failure, and experiencing the iterative nature of the EDP. Second, the CEEMS seminar-based capstone course is structured as a PD program in which teachers are accountable to create implementable content and engineering design activities for their classrooms, which are reviewed, critiqued, and approved by resource team coaches. Finally, teachers are supported and guided as they create and implement engineering design modules. This is accomplished using resource team coaches, who guide the teachers through the process of creating and implementing lessons incorporating engineering design activities: they provide invaluable feedback as teachers reflect on their own practice.

With this tiered approach, the CEEMS project has trained 88 secondary teachers on teaching math and science content and standards using CBL and EDP pedagogies. Those 88 teachers developed, taught, and documented 327 units that utilize CBL and the EDP and align to content standards. The CEEMS secondary math and science units can be found at http://www.ceas3.uc.edu/ceems/. These teachers impacted over 18,000 6–12th grade students. Of the 88 CEEMS teachers, 32 enrolled in, and 21 have completed, the Masters in Curriculum & Instruction with Engineering Education specialization (MCIEE) degree program as of August 2018.

The CEEMS evaluation and research studies use a mixed-methods design to respond to the following questions:

(1) How do students in a design and CBL environment engage in decision making, strategic planning, evaluating a revision of plans, creative thinking, and task persistence?
(2) How do students in design and CBL environments perceive their involvement in STEM careers?
(3) What measures and instruments are most effective at capturing and documenting these leaning tasks?
(4) How are the teachers' gains in knowledge of engineering transferred into instructional plans?
(5) What supports and barriers do teachers encounter as they implement their plans with students?
(6) How do the knowledge gains and implementation factors impact the teachers' pedagogical content knowledge?

The intent of this paper is not to describe and present in detail the results of the CEEMS evaluation [53,54] and research [55] studies conducted, but the key findings from them are summarized below:

1. Student knowledge gains were higher: 8.5% higher on the post-test versus comparison teachers' students, which is statistically significant at a 95% confidence interval.
2. Engineering design practice requires that students use high-level cognitive demand, which involves making connections while solving problems: 89% of students (more than 18,000 participated) reported successfully understanding and implementing the EDP to seek and defend an optimum solution to a real-world problem with constraints.
3. Integration of CBL and EDP instructional practices ensured usage of a wider variety of active learning strategies: Classroom Observation and Analytic Protocol [56] data showed that CEEMS teachers used probative, open-ended questioning that encouraged critical thinking, as well as the EDP and CBL strategies, collaborative grouping, and use of external resources (e.g., videos) as a means to focus the lesson on real-world issues.
4. Student engagement and buy-in was ensured: In post-teaching surveys, teachers reported (100% strongly agreed or agreed) that they saw increased classroom engagement compared to when non-CEEMS units were taught.
5. Teachers saw the benefit of continued use of CEEMS teaching pedagogies (CBL and the EDP) with time: Teachers' current instructional practices (CIP) surveys indicated a significant increase of their usage of these teaching pedagogies during the project (from pre-project to one year, and pre- to post-project/two years) and one year after programming ended.
6. Over time teachers learned to negotiate successfully through barriers and lack of supports reported for student-centered reforms, and to minimize their impact.

1.3. Taking CEEMS beyond Its Partnership

The goals of the CEEMS project were admittedly ambitious—to profoundly change the STEM culture in the Greater Cincinnati area as it pertains to K–12 educational agendas over the grant period (seven years, starting in the fall of 2011). Moreover, we hoped that our project would not only serve the state of Ohio by advancing student proficiency in science, mathematics, and engineering (and, as a result, support the state's pursuit of economic success in the STEM driven milieu of the 21st century), but also provide a template for large-scale, engineering-enhanced initiatives for STEM education reform elsewhere in the country. The CEEMS research and evaluation syntheses reports [53–55] clearly documented that evidence-based approaches (CBL integrated with the EDP) to teaching that actively engage students in their own learning are more effective than traditional lecturing. Our next overriding goal was bringing these effective educational practices to scale.

For Americans to remain competitive, several governmental, corporate, and non-profit organizations and writers have been calling for transformational change in STEM education in the US for many years [57–66], particularly focusing on post-secondary STEM education. However, previous investments have not resulted in the desired level of change, even though STEM educators, researchers, and communities agree on the required change, the vision of what needs to be changed, and the evidence-based best practices that can be used. The inability to propagate and scale STEM educational innovations is the primary reason for this situation. In this paper, the authors have attempted to fill this gap by presenting how they used their participation in the NSF's Innovation Corps for Learning (I-Corps L) pilot initiative to propagate and scale CEEMS educational innovations beyond its 14 school-district partnership in Greater Cincinnati. Hopefully this documentation will help others to plan scaling up their own STEM educational innovations.

CEEMS shows that the following skills are key to successful teacher training and experience: (1) a foundational understanding of the EDP and how to use it to teach in line with current science and mathematics standards; (2) first-hand experience with the process in active and collaborative settings, just as the students will have when methods are used in the classroom; (3) experience with tools, such as the CEEMS unit database (http://www.ceas3.uc.edu/ceems/), that facilitate the development of new units to meet individual curriculum and student needs; (4) guidance by professional coaches as they create and implement engineering design modules; and (5) to document their final unit implementations with improved student knowledge results and personal reflections for other teachers.

The challenge was to use key elements from CEEMS that prepared teachers to use engineering as a context for learning, and to package them into a much shorter PD experience that individual teachers and school districts would find worthwhile and be willing and (more importantly) able to fund. Working with the I-Corps L instructional team, we identified the best methods for packaging the CEEMS PD experiences for teachers to ensure that they get enough immersion in the pedagogies of CBL and the EDP, and enough coaching support to implement with competence. The goal was to bring to scale a tested teacher PD program (CEEMS project) so that it could be sustained and even expanded before its NSF funding ended. If successful, this would significantly change the way math and science are taught in K–12 classrooms, resulting in greater student engagement and achievement. While the overall goal is to train teachers, we have also implicitly considered the educational goals for their students. By synthesizing the CEEMS and I-Corps L approaches, we expect greater numbers of students to pursue STEM disciplines and to produce a larger, more highly qualified technical workforce that more closely reflects the demographics of the US (as identified by the numerous governmental, corporate, and non-profit organizations cited earlier).

2. Research Methods

2.1. Initial Training

During the fall of 2014, NSF awarded a supplement award, I-Corps: Training Teachers to Use Engineering as a Context for Learning (NSF grant #1518619), to a select group from the CEEMS project team. As part of this award, the team participated in a seven-week course of study, along with about 20 other exemplar projects, in order to learn how the business-model design and customer development process can be used to evaluate the sustainable scalability potential of their educational innovation. The participating exemplar projects were selected by the NSF program officers from three directorates: Education and Human Resources (EHR), Computer and Information Science and Engineering (CISE), and Engineering (ENG). The facilitators and coaches for the course included a team of an NSF program officer, business entrepreneurs, university faculty, and industry experts. The training course utilized a Lean Startup [67] methodology which assumes that all you have is a series of untested hypotheses—basically, presumptions about the validity of one's educational innovation idea. The three parts to this methodology include the following: (1) a process of hypothesis testing using a business-modeling tool; (2) "getting out of the building" to test these hypotheses with prospective clients; and (3) the use of agile development [68] to rapidly iterate the product being developed.

The goals of the training course were to work with the participating teams to accomplish the following:

(1) Determine the readiness of their educational innovation for sustainable scalability as a self-supported entity that is able to systematically promote its adoption and enable and facilitate its use;
(2) Enable the team to develop a clear go/no-go decision regarding sustainable scalability of the educational innovation;
(3) Help develop a transition plan and actionable tasks to move the educational innovation forward to sustainable scalability, if the team decides to do so.

The seven-week course ran from January to February 2015 and was started in San Francisco, California with an on-site introductory three-day workshop, in which:

(1) teams were introduced to the Lean Launchpad approach;
(2) teams learned the business model development and customer development process;
(3) teams met with customers (a minimum of 25) and presented what they learned to the class.

The introductory workshop was followed by five weekly online class sessions, and each included reading assignments from the *Startup Owner's Manual* [67], watching online lecturettes, and reporting results via PowerPoint of their "getting out of the building" and "testing our business model assumption" experiences. Each of the five online classes had two parts: an hour and a half for team presentations, and an hour class discussion of the weekly online lecturettes. At the end of February, all teams met for the final lessons-learned workshop where each team presented the lessons learned from their exploration of sustainable scalability and presented a two-minute video showcasing those lessons and their plans to move forward. Each team had the opportunity to meet with the teaching team and receive critical feedback to refine and finalize their final deliverables.

Throughout the program we engaged in customer discovery interviews to understand the potential adopters, collaborators, and users. We used Blank's Lean LaunchPad [69] approach, which is an entrepreneurial method created by Steve Blank to develop a business model by talking to potential customers. As such, we were instructed to conduct at least 100 interviews to test hypotheses related to the nine elements of Osterwalder's Business Model Canvas (see Figure 1): value propositions, customer segments, channels, relationships, revenue streams, key partners, activities, resources, and cost structure. To aid in our collection of research data (our interviews), we utilized Launchpad Central (https://www.launchpadcentral.com/), which permitted the storage of interview summaries as well as a feature that allowed us to continually refine our business model. This feature, the Business Model Canvas, provided a template that we updated throughout our training and customer interviews, and that we shared with our assigned coaches, who reviewed our work and critiqued it, enabling us to continually improve our product. This tool was very useful to help us better define our product offering, as well as to consider the trade-offs that we needed to make.

The customer interviews were analyzed to identify customer types and their needs, and the results obtained were represented in the Value Proposition Canvas (VPC) shown in Figure 2. During the training, the VPC was completed twice: once after the interviews were completed to represent what a typical customer desires, and a second time after the minimum viable product (MVP) had been envisioned, with plans to present it on the final day of the training.

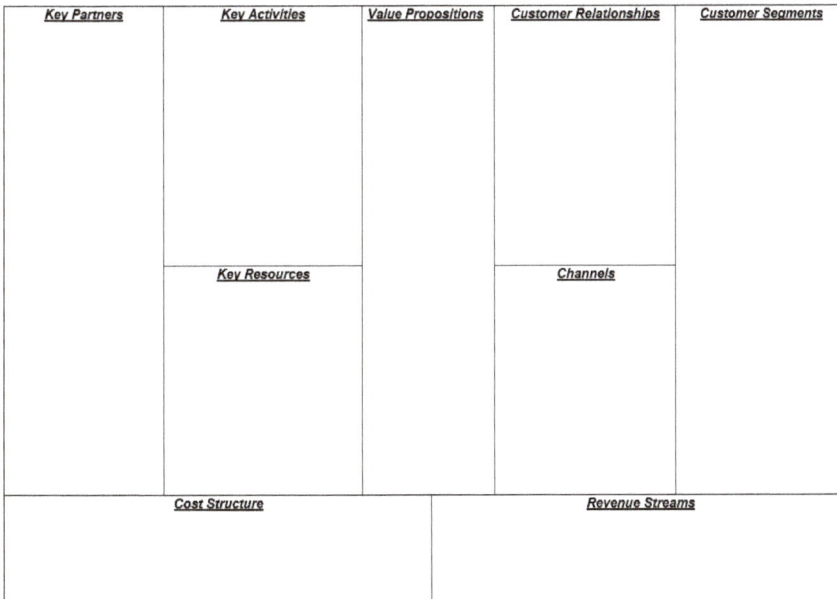

Figure 1. Business Model Canvas (BMC) (adapted from [69]).

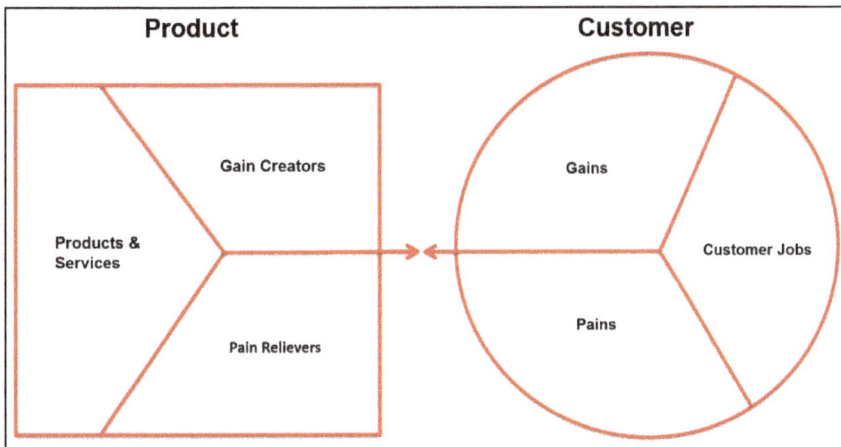

Figure 2. Value Proposition Canvas (VPC) (adapted from [69]).

2.2. Our Development Process

Figure 3 illustrates the flow of the development process we used to create our final product offering. The product in this case is a professional development program (referred to also as a workshop in this paper) for K–12 school teachers and administrators called STEMucation Academy (the official trademark for its name was obtained by the University of Cincinnati Research Institute (UCRI), an Ohio non-profit corporation, on 24 March 2016, from the United States Patent and Trademark Office). Though the flowchart may seem quite complex, it will in fact become quite understandable with more in-depth descriptions to follow.

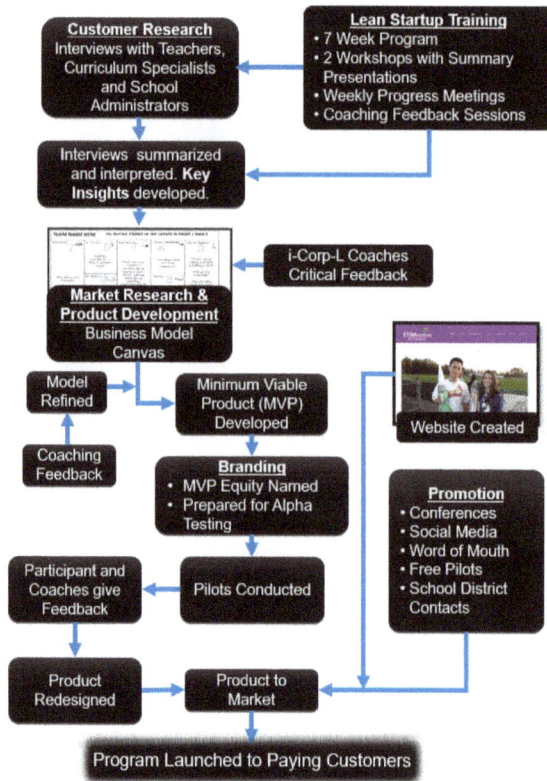

Figure 3. Program development flowchart.

2.3. Customer Research

In the Lean Startup terminology, interviewing customers is all about "getting out of the building" with the purpose of testing the hypotheses that we had formed about our proposed product. Our initial hypotheses were:

(1)   science and math K–12 teachers will value the CEEMS [44] model;
(2)   there are relatively few alternatives;
(3)   we can develop a scalable CEEMS model that retains value.

Our customer research was broad in scope. We reached out to responders from 17 different states for a total of 117 interviews. We targeted 10 to 15 interviews per week. The interviews were tailored to the individual being interviewed based on their ability to focus on pre-selected questions relative to our program development. A typical interviewee was a school administrator, math or science K–12 teacher, curriculum director, the owner or user of a competitive product, etc. These interviews were about 20 min in length and were usually attended by two team members, one to ask the questions and keep the interview on track, and a second to take notes. The interviews were done both face-to-face where practical, and at other times over the phone, to avoid high travel costs. Upon completion of the interview, notes were summarized and input into Launchpad Central. A sample of a summarized interview is shown below:

Interviewee: STEM Facilitator, school in Oklahoma

"Oklahoma has its own science standards which are similar to NGSS minus evolution and climate change. Interviewee used to be science curriculum coordinator before he took on current position. Involved in [a state of Oklahoma funded] MSP (Math & Science Partnership) program where teachers invest two weeks in PD-half of PD involves pedagogy and half of time they are working with OU researcher on actual research. Believes meaningful PD cannot be shorter than two weeks. Waiting list for MSP PD as it is very popular. His MSP does struggle with Saturday follow up only 1/3 show up; teachers have family priorities on Saturdays. Measurement tools for own MSP mostly focuses on teacher change; has some data related to student performance but that is hard to quantify. Some teachers going through MSP then were motivated to seek advanced degrees. In their district most science teachers have less than five years of experience; many have science minors rather than science majors and therefore are lacking in content. As soon as teachers achieve a paradigm shift and get it, they leave district or become consultants. Teacher PD needs to focus on how science works, what science is, and how to integrate science practices. There is no $ in Oklahoma district budgets for outside PD in science and social studies. All PD funds are directed to English/LA and math. All science PD must occur at district level; best is informal in nature when conversations occur about curriculum. Teachers are required to do 15 h of PD per year and can easily get that by coming to district sponsored PD; some PD offered at district is not science specific."

Furthermore, key insights were developed as they related to our hypotheses. These concise summaries were an excellent way for us manage the large amount of information we collected from our 100+ interviews. As an example, the key insight we developed for the above interview was:

"No money in Oklahoma districts for outside PD in science or social studies; all science PD must be homegrown due to lack of funds or rely on grant funding. Does not think PD experience will be meaningful if it is less than two weeks; measuring teacher change may be enough to prove effectiveness."

Referring to the flowchart shown in Figure 3, the top three boxes have been addressed and we are ready to discuss the Market Research and Product Development step. In this step we began completing the Business Model Canvas. As shown in Figure 1, the Business Model Canvas represents a visual overview of the nine building blocks for building a business model [69]. These nine steps are further described in Table 1.

Our training objective then was to gather the information necessary to build a successful business model through customer interviews, getting constant and critical feedback from the I-Corps L coaches, and by evolving our model as we documented our learnings using the very visual Business Model Canvas.

Table 1. The nine building blocks for building a business model.

Building Block	Description
Customer Segments	An organization serves one or several customer segments
Value Propositions	The business model seeks to solve customer problems and satisfy customer needs with value propositions
Channels	Value propositions are delivered through communication, distribution, and sales channels
Customer Relationships	Customer relationships are established and maintained with each customer segment
Revenue Streams	Revenue streams result from value propositions successfully offered to customers
Key Resources	Key resources are the assets required to offer and deliver the previously described elements
Key Activities	Key resources achieve their goals by performing a number of key activities
Key Partnerships	Some activities are outsourced and some resources are acquired outside the enterprise
Cost Structure	The business model elements result in the cost structure

2.4. Our Value Proposition

Early on in our training we were asked to define what we hoped to accomplish. This seemed like it should be a relatively simple task, but the process took quite some time to reach an agreement within our team. The first step in this process was to name our team, so as to better identify ourselves with other I-Corps L teams, as well as with the training staff. Our initial team name was Best Engineered STEM Teachers (BEST), which we used throughout our training and in the early stages of our product development. We later found out that the BEST acronym had been used to represent another organization. Later on, after completion of our training, we adopted the name STEMucation Academy, which is trademarked and in use today.

The second order of business was to succinctly articulate our value proposition. That is, what we offered to our potential customers that was truly unique and would help to meet some of their unmet needs. This was an evolutionary process, as we continuously collected input from potential customers. By "getting out of the building" and talking to potential end-users, we were able to fine-tune our initial proposition. Our value proposition migrated from one of simply helping teachers and administrators, to one of "transforming the classroom into a student-centered, hands-on, real-world learning environment". After the initial pilot of our proposed product, we established that in addition to science teachers, math teachers were an important customer as well. In retrospect, the value proposition is a dynamic statement that continues to evolve even today.

2.5. Establishing Customer Types and Needs

Understanding who the customer is and what their needs are was the most important part of the process. Initially we believed that our customers were middle and high-school science teachers, much like those science teachers that attended the CEEMS program at the University of Cincinnati. Although these are important customers, they were not the only customers. Through our customer research we found four different customer types, also referred to as a "customer archetype". The four archetypes identified were: (1) STEM-focused Teachers and Admin "Evangelists", (2) Novice Science Teachers, (3) Seasoned Science Teachers, and (4) School and District Administrators. It is worth mentioning again that during the I-Corps L training we limited our customer base to secondary-school science teachers and the decision makers who have an impact on their professional development (e.g., administrators, curriculum directors, etc.). Later this was extended to include K–12 in-service math and science teachers across elementary school to high-school grade bands. Each of these customer archetypes have their own unique set of motivations, pain points, and professional development needs that influence their purchasing decisions with respect to professional development. Through our customer research and coaching feedback, we identified those unique needs, which are summarized in Figure 4.

The STEM-Focused Teacher and Admin "Evangelists" are grouped together because of their similar needs. In this case, both are working to integrate STEM lessons into their school district. The "Evangelist" is one who sees the need and is working hard to change the school culture through the introduction of new teaching methods.

The Novice Science Teacher and the Seasoned Science Teacher are differentiated here as they typically have different requirements set by their school district that they must meet. A novice or relatively new teacher might be required to gain a master's degree, and so is seeking courses that offer college credit toward their degree. They are also more likely to need more time at home, due to family or community activities. The Seasoned Science Teacher may have already achieved their master's degree and is simply looking to attain continuing education credits, trying to keep updated on advancing teaching pedagogies, or trying to "stay fresh" as a veteran teacher.

The School and District Administrators are seeking to meet requirements mandated by the state, or they may want to improve their school's education rating, which is usually measured by their state. They typically work to motivate their employees and (more specifically) teaching staff. Introducing new initiatives such as a new STEM program might be a positive or a negative motivational circumstance, depending on how the end-user perceives it. Positioned appropriately, STEM education can have a very positive influence on the life of an administrator as measured by student outcomes. Higher standardized test scores, more student engagement, and motivated teachers are all needs that might be addressed through an appropriate professional development program.

Using the feedback received from the customer interviews, the Value Proposition Canvas was completed, which is shown in Figure 5.

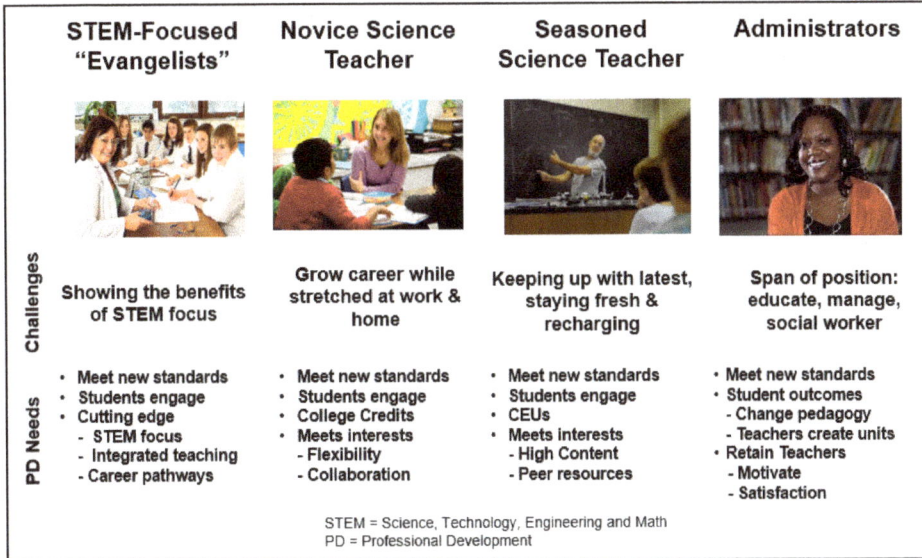

Figure 4. Customer archetypes.

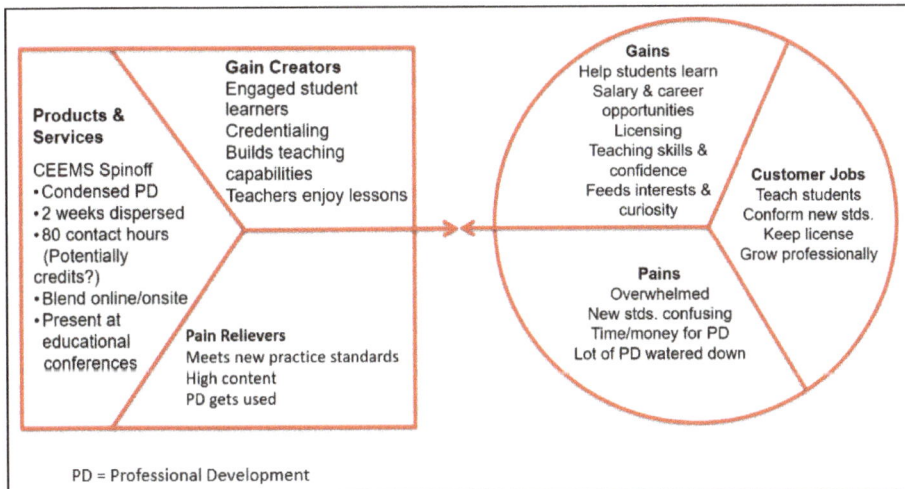

Figure 5. Completed Value Proposition Canvas after customer interviews.

2.6. Marketing Channels

When one purchases an item at a place of business such as a grocery store, you typically don't think about how it got onto the store shelf. Fortunately, we don't have to think about the person that produced the item, nor do we have to think about the warehouse employee or the truck driver who delivered the item to the store. It is important therefore to think about this supply stream or channel and consider how we might make it transparent to the end-user similar to the grocery store analogy.

Initially, the product offering for our professional development program focused on an on-site workshop at the customer's facility or at a site of their choosing. This model closely mirrored the CEEMS program that brought teachers together for a variety of workshops at a university facility. This on-site workshop model had an advantage if the customer was in close proximity to the instructors. One of our goals, however, was to develop a national program, and as such the on-site workshop model proved to be a potential showstopper due to the higher travel costs associated with it. From our interviews, we found that 40% of those interviewed supported the online approach and another 30% "somewhat supported" it. For those that did not support the online training, there were a variety of reasons, as reflected in the comments below:

"I am more motivated to work hard if I have to physically go somewhere."

"If the PD or course was online, I would likely procrastinate."

"I have three kids and feel I would need to physically get out of the house in order to get work done."

"I enjoy the interpersonal interaction that accompanies face to face PD."

"Online programs are often 'flat' and not inspiring."

A second factor that we needed to consider was that the customer (i.e., math or science teacher) needed a flexible way of obtaining the training to fit their busy schedule. As such, we began evaluating online training delivery. This seemed to meet the needs of most customer archetypes discussed earlier and afforded us the opportunity to take advantage of a growing trend in education, online training.

Our channel to market then became a two pronged approach to address those that supported the online approach, as well as hosting on-site workshops to address the needs of those that preferred the face-to-face approach.

2.7. Customer Relationships

Two key features of the CEEMS program were (1) the assignment of a personal coach to each of the program participants to assist them as they developed their units of instruction, and (2) the ability to collaborate with other teachers on their units of instruction. These features were validated in our customer interviews, as a number of interviewees expressed an interest in a personal coach and collaborating with other teachers:

"Having access to coaches and other teachers is important as it helps gain confidence in using CBL and EDP."

"Collaboration with other life science teachers is very important."

"I am open to the online channel but believe that meeting fact to face with other teachers in her district would be beneficial. I do not think that this model will work well if a teacher signs up by themselves."

As noted by these comments, interviewees felt that a relationship with their coach and other teachers would be beneficial to them in developing their lessons. In this day and age, collaboration tools such as Skype, Facetime, WebEx, and Google Hangouts solve the technical challenges of collaboration both with other teachers as well as with a coach. The biggest challenge in establishing these collaborative groups, then, is to be able to get them together at the same scheduled time—something that can only be overcome if it is scheduled at the start of the training program.

2.8. Revenue Streams

The revenue stream represents the cash a company generates from each customer segment. Costs must be subtracted from revenues to create earnings [69]. For our professional development program, the bulk of the cash generated will come from customers signing up for the professional development workshops. Costs associated with implementing the workshops include website domain purchase, annual website maintenance costs, cost of printing advertising materials, workshop and conference handouts, and conference registration fees. As a startup, the upfront costs were covered by grants and donations. A portion of the labor costs were donated to get the startup up and running. During the pilot stage of the startup, all participants attending the workshops were given free access to course materials in exchange for completing the course and providing feedback.

2.9. Key Resources

Key resources can be categorized as physical (facilities, machines, etc.), intellectual (brands, patents, copyrights, etc.), human (people working on PD) and financial (cash, lines of credit, etc.). The resources needed are often underestimated and, as a result, the product development suffers. As an example, our team identified the resources listed in Table 2 that needed to be procured to allow us to go forward with our professional development program. The second column represents how these were addressed, and the third column shows a relative cost (high > $1000/month, medium = $250–1000/month, low < $250/month).

Table 2. Identified key resources.

Key Resource	How Key Resource was Addressed	Relative Cost
Entrepreneur Training	I-Corp L seven-week training program	None (Funded by grant)
A conference room for team meetings	Used conference room at University of Cincinnati where 2 of our team members were employed	None
A Learning Management System (LMS) for workshop course administration	Used BlackBoard and CourseSites for initial pilots. Google Drive tools also used as an alternative.	None
Instructional designer to develop the course outline and manage the LMS	Designer hired and expenses shared with another department	High
Course Developer	Course materials created by Team Members	Medium
Workshop Coaches	Identified a list of CEEMS teachers and Resource Team Members as potential coaches for workshop participants	Low to Medium
Web Site Developer	Outsourced to Northern Kentucky University	Medium
Branding and Brochures	STEMucation Academy branding and brochures created images.	Low
Intellectual Property Protection	Materials copyrighted	None
Workshop Materials	Conference workshops required materials for Engineering Design Process activities	Low
Conference Registration Fees	Paid through existing grants	Low
Startup Funding for aforementioned items	Available from existing grants	High

2.10. Key Activities

"These are the most important actions a company must take to operate successfully" [69]. For our endeavor, initially the five key activities we identified included those noted in Figure 6. Each of these items were identified either through the successful implementation in the CEEMS program, or as a need identified from our customer interviews. Of the five key activities identified, three have either been implemented or refined going forward. The two items that still need attention are numbers 3 and 5, which are mechanisms to connect teachers and build professional learning communities. As we grow the number of teachers that enter the program going forward, these activities will gain more focus.

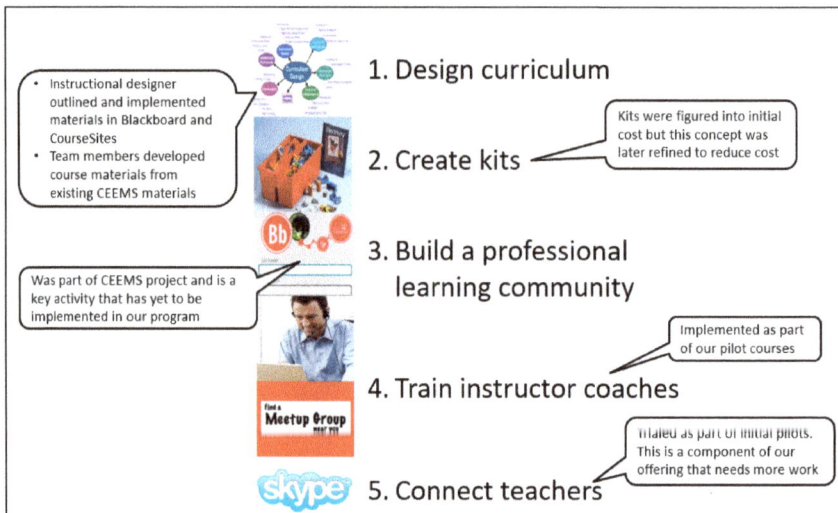

Figure 6. Key activities.

2.11. Key Partnerships

Osterwalder and Pigneur [69] state: "Key partnerships include the network of suppliers and partners that make the business model work." A number of key partnerships have helped to build our program and are listed here:

University of Cincinnati (UC): One of our initial partnerships was with the University of Cincinnati, which provided a number of resources that helped with the initial development of STEMucation Academy. Some of these resources included the incorporation of our program materials into following for-credit course:

ENGR 7050: Engineering Education Certificate Capstone (3 credits) (University of Cincinnati, 2018): This capstone course provides a structured and supported process for certificate participants to implement what they have learned through certificate courses. Participants will be required to develop and implement one full curricular unit of instruction that utilizes engineering design-based challenges within a course that they teach. Participants will have a mentor to guide them through this process. Completed activities and units are to be written using a common framework and published to an open education resource so other teachers can use them. The course is configured to be taken by a teacher after completing the required course, Engineering Foundations, during a semester when the teacher could teach the unit in a class while simultaneously taking the course.

Other resources that UC provided included the copyrighting of STEMucation Academy, use of a conference room and facilities, use of development software (including BlackBoard, Kaltura, and Articulate), and access to an instructional designer. This partnership has continued through the University of Cincinnati Research Institute (UCRI), an NPO affiliated with UC, and which obtained the trademark for STEMucation Academy.

Northern Kentucky University (NKU): NKU's Center for Applied Informatics supplied the manpower to develop and maintain our website, stemucationacademy.com, which will be highlighted later in this article.

2.12. Cost Structure

The cost structure refers to all of the costs incurred to operate the business model, including startup and ongoing costs. We estimated our startup costs to be around $75K for curriculum development, website development, marketing, and other contingencies. Our fixed costs included website maintenance, domain name fees, and conference fees. Our variable costs were related to the workshop size and frequency.

An initial breakdown of the revenue and costs associated with our program is shown in Figure 7. Based on feedback received during our customer interviews, we targeted $250 as an entry level cost for a one-day workshop. As can be seen in Figure 7, over 50% of the cost was compensation for coaches supporting a participant in the program. As coaching was identified as a key component of the program, this high-value feature was required to support the development of high-quality units of instruction for the classroom. Note that there was no profit built into this model which we later altered to cover future development costs.

Revenue	$250/Teacher
Cost	$250/Teacher
Director	$9
Coaches	$140
Units	$45
Recruiting	$6
Infrastructure	$30
Contingency	$20

Figure 7. Initial breakdown of cash flow per workshop attendee.

2.13. Insights from Our Customer Research

Key Identified Needs: In general, customers expressed a variety of needs that they felt should be addressed by a STEM-based professional development program. Some of the expressed needs are as follows:

- Teachers often found that professional development programs were of no value to them if they could not take what they'd learned back to the classroom and implement it. It is important therefore that new knowledge be easily implementable when teachers finish with the professional development program.
- The ability to collaborate with fellow teachers is necessary to enable them to discuss new lesson ideas, reinforce their knowledge of the new pedagogy, and permit them to discuss best classroom practices.
- Coaching was a very popular concept that most believed would enable them to become more adept at using the CBL pedagogy.
- Creating their own lessons was not only an important concept to the teachers, but to administrators as well, as it provided more flexibility to create lesson plans that are tailored to student needs.
- Classroom practices that stimulate student engagement were identified as necessary.
- A reasonable cost (~$250 for PD) was identified as necessary.

Competitive Comparison: Given the key identified needs, understanding how our proposed program compared to competitive offerings involved an exercise in identifying who we were competing with, what they offered, and their cost structure. A summary of our findings is shown in Table 3. We did attempt to get cost numbers, but have not mentioned these since it was difficult to get reliable numbers for some competitive programs already available (the range varied from free to $23,000). The key differentiators that we compared included the use of engineering practices (both in science and math), the focus on student-centered lessons (i.e., student engagement), the offering of ongoing coaching during the development of a unit of instruction, and the inclusion of a new teaching practice (CBL with the EDP integrated into it). These differentiators were believed to be those that would set our program apart from other programs of a similar nature and, as can be seen from Table 3, most PD offerings are deficient in one or more areas. This comparison gave us more confidence that we can continue to move forward with our proposed model.

Table 3. Competitive comparison.

Type	Examples	Description	BEST Differentiators			
			Engineering Practices	Student Centered	Ongoing Coaching	Δ Teacher Practice
Online Content	Khan Academy MOOCs [1]	Online STEM [5] resources & classroom ideas				
National Science Organizations	AAAS [2] Project 2061	Science curriculum & instruction				
	NSTA [3]	Workshops/Online Science Matters	✔			
	ASEE [4]	STEM Conference associated	✔			
National STEM Program	Engineering Is Elementary	Content & application lessons	✔			
	Project Lead the Way	Blended STEM professional development that links activities to engineering	✔	✔ Problem-based learning only	✔ Not longitudinal	✔
BEST	Online & Face-to-face Workshops	Science & Engineering Practices and Student Driven	✔	✔	✔	✔

1 A MOOC is *a course of study made available over the Internet without charge to a very large number of people*
2 *American Association for the Advancement of Science*
3 *National Science Teachers Association*
4 *American Society of Engineering Education*
5 *Science, Technology, Engineering and Math*

Note: PD is a highly fragmented market; each School District has their own/local PD offerings that will vary in cost, quality and are additional competitors; Lot of "garbage" PD out there which makes teachers skeptical.

2.14. Final Business Model Canvas and Customer and Revenue Flow

Our I-Corps L team, BEST, completed 100 or more interviews and in week three we did a channel pivot from blended online and on-site (via a national/regional teacher aggregator) to online with meet-ups supplementing online classes. This required a significant revision in our value proposition and customer segments. Our development is reflected in the changes to our Business Model Canvas (early stage in Figure 8, and final in Figure 9). The final customer and revenue flow for our final Business Model Canvas is represented in Figure 10.

Key Partners	Key Activities	Value Propositions	Customer Relationships	Customer Segments
• Learning management system (course/chat/discussion board) (e.g., Blackboard) • Endorsement (e.g., Change the equation designation as ready to scale) • Large Foundation/business interested in promoting STEM[1] for scholarships • Skype and Meetup	• Create content for online instruction • Create kit including components & instructions • Create online community of practice & lesson archive • Identify & train instructors and coaches to support online PD[2] • Identify infrastructure for teacher to teacher connections	• Helps meet the new standards that require engineering & technology in teaching science and math • Students are engaged because they understand why learning is relevant to them and the lessons are fun and interactive	• BEST[3] with teachers: personalized training & coaching and co-creation of lessons. • BEST with administrators: Expert resource on STEM education • Teacher with teacher: Peer coach and lesson sharing, community of practice facilitated by BEST	• Segment 1: School administrators & agencies that set budgets and approve teacher professional development • Segment 2a: Secondary science teachers seeking a master's degree and/or college credit to maintain their license and advance their teaching skills • Segment 2b: Secondary science teachers who want to earn continuing education units to maintain their license and build their STEM teaching skills
	Key Resources Physical • Facilities office & kit storage (University of Cincinnati) • Virtual • Learning management system • Online infrastructure • Website with controlled access • Infrastructure to facilitate teacher to teacher connections Human • Curriculum designer • Course administrator, instructors and coaches • Web site developer & Manager • Contract packers Intellectual Property • Branding (name, logo) • Copyright • Financial • Start-up Funding		**Channels** Marketing • Online • Direct mail • Education conferences Instruction Online/Onsite Initial Sites • Educational conferences that attract large numbers of teachers • Large school districts with 30+ teachers Follow-on Sites • Schools districts for a group of teachers	

Cost Structure	Revenue Streams

1. STEM—Science, Technology, Engineering and Math; 2. PD—Professional Development; 3. BEST—Best Engineered STEM Teachers

Figure 8. Business Model Canvas—early stage.

Key Partners	Key Activities	Value Propositions	Customer Relationships	Customer Segments
• National science and math associations (AAAS[1]) • National & regional teacher associations NCTM[2], NSTA[3], ASEE[4], SECO[5], etc.) • Administrator Associations (AASA[6]) • STEM[7] Organizations • Educational service organizations • Teacher unions • Longer term—Organizations that set national & state curriculum and teacher PD[8] requirements (e.g., Department of Education)	• Create content for online course • Create website with online community for practice and lesson archive • Identify and train instructors & coaches to support online PD • Create kit including components & instructions	• BEST[9] is a teacher recommended, online professional development program that helps secondary teachers meet new science and engineering practices • Teachers transform their classrooms into a student centered, hands-on, real-world, learning environments where students become critical thinkers & problem solvers	• BEST with Teachers: personalized training & coaching and co-creation of lessons • BEST with Administrators: Expert resource on STEM education • Teacher with Teacher: Peer coach and lesson sharing, community of practice facilitated by BEST	1. Science & math Teachers for grades 6–12 a. <5 yrs. experience seeking a master's degree and/or college credit to maintain their license and advance their teaching skills b. Experienced teachers >5 years and < 20 years who want to earn continuing education units to maintain their license and build their STEM teaching skills 2. School administrators & agencies that set budgets and approve teacher professional development
	Key Resources • Trained & available workshop instructors • Contract coaches to support & mentor • Program management and development • Business growth and marketing • Web design & development • Local facilities for workshops		**Channels** • Direct sales via schools, education associations & conferences • Administrator & teacher referrals based on positive outcomes • Combined online & onsite ○ University of Cincinnati for master's credits ○ Local school for groups of teachers	

Cost Structure	Revenue Streams
• Instructor salaries • Program development and administration • Website & instruction materials	• Revenue will come from tuition and PD workshop fees. Group discounts. ○ The intent is that we become a sustainable entity (nonprofit). ○ Once a recognized brand: potential for expanded services & revenue

1 AAAS—American Association for the Advancement of Science
2 NCTM—National Council of Teachers of Mathematics
3 NSTA—National Science Teachers of America
4 ASEE—American Society of Engineering Education
5 SECO—Science Education Council of Ohio
6 AASA—American Association of School Administrators
7 STEM—Science, Technology, Engineering and Math
8 PD—Professional Development
9 BEST— Best Engineered STEM Teachers

Figure 9. Business Model Canvas—final.

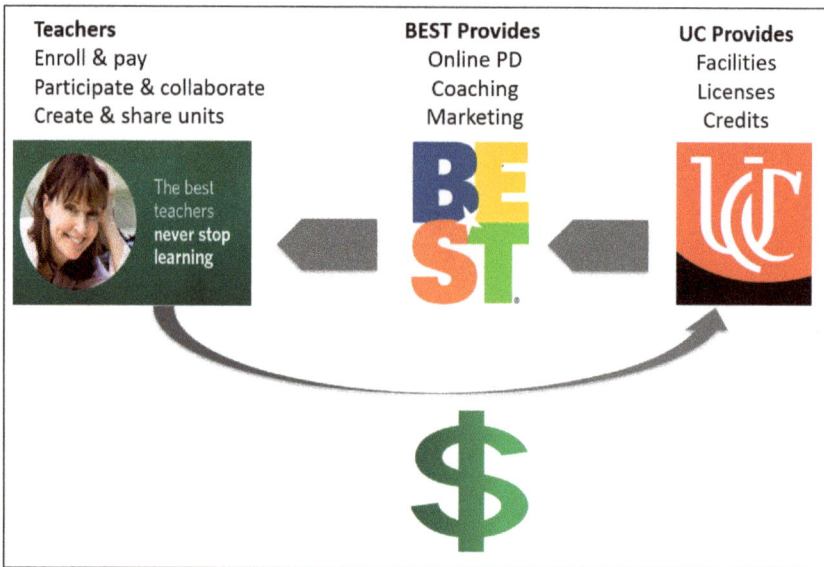

Figure 10. Customer and revenue flow.

3. Results

3.1. The Creation of an Online Professional Development Program with Virtual Coaching: The MVP

As we moved forward, we believe we had a grasp of what potential customers needed and what they were willing to spend for a professional development (PD) program focused on a CBL pedagogy that also uses the EDP to solve the challenge. Referring back to Figure 3, we are now moving into the space of creating a minimum viable product (MVP). An MVP is "a concise summary of the smallest possible group of features that will work as a stand-alone product while still solving at least the 'core' problem and demonstrating the product's value" [70].

In our case, the initial years of the CEEMS program (2012/2013) served as the basis for the MVP; it was easily developed into a customer product. Customer feedback was positive as was our 2015 American Society of Engineering Education conference experience, so it allowed us to move forward very quickly from the MVP to a more complete product offering.

In this section, we will describe the attributes of one of the workshops that was developed: the Advanced Online Workshop. In particular, this workshop encompasses all the basic components of the CEEMS PD training program (i.e., the Engineering Education Certificate Capstone course). Other workshop options and a full online PD program that can be taken for course credit are described later.

Keeping our customer interview data in mind, we set out to further develop our MVP into a professional development program that would enable teachers to transform their classrooms into student-centered, hands-on, real-world learning environments where their students could become multifaceted critical thinkers and problem solvers. This program purposefully habituates the EDP into a teacher's mindset, who creates engineering challenges for their students to solve. For those not familiar with the EDP, Figure 11 illustrates this process. Engineers typically start by clearly defining the problem to be solved ("identify and define") and then background research is done to clarify what is known about the problem ("gather information"). As is typically the case, multiple solutions to the problem are identified ("identify alternatives") before an initial solution is selected to go forward with ("select solutions"). This initial solution is trialed ("implement solution") and appraised for its effectiveness in solving the problem ("evaluate solution"). The initial solution might then be modified ('refine') and the process is repeated until an acceptable solution is found. Throughout this process, there is continual communication ("communicate") with team members and stakeholders and the final solution is then communicated to the key project stakeholders ("communicate solution").

Furthermore, by breaking our training program into modules that correlate with the critical steps of the EDP, we sought to raise awareness of the EDP and to provide teachers with an opportunity to use it as they developed their unit of instruction. As such, the first module introduces engineering design while the remaining modules (2–8) follow the steps of the EDP as noted in Figure 11. Module 8 covers both the refinement of unit documents (based on coaching feedback) as well as the communication of the unit documents to the Program Coordinator for archiving (STEMucation Academy website). The "communicate" box in the center of the diagram is not a step in the process but instead represents the communication process that occurs between the coach and the participant as the unit documents are developed.

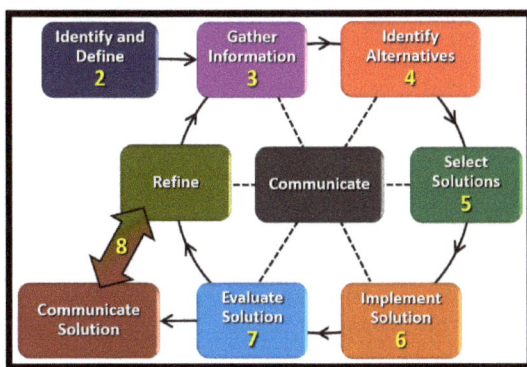

Figure 11. The engineering design process.

Structure of the Program Learning Modules: Each learning module is broken down into learning objectives, an introduction to the module, and homework assignments. Hyperlinks are used to access a variety of documents such as templates, questionnaires, and supplemental reading materials. The six coaching meetings that are required are also incorporated into the modules with fixed agendas to permit both the coach and participant to cover any pertinent issues.

All of the modules are targeted to be completed in 12–16 weeks, depending on when the participant implements the unit of instruction in their classroom, completes the follow-up reflection, and meets a final time with their Coach for a sign-off on the workshop deliverables. It is entirely possible for a teacher to complete the modules much earlier than 12 weeks.

The End Result: Each participant will end up completing a unit of instruction which includes a unit plan and multiple activity plans. The unit plan is an overview of the unit and is used to describe the CBL elements: the big idea, the hook, possible essential and guiding questions, the challenge, career connections, and societal relevance. Typically, there are a minimum of four activity plans that describe exactly what must be done to complete the activity. The activity plans include such things as activity objectives, activity guiding questions, advance preparation requirements, assessments, a materials list, procedures, projected misconceptions, and any differentiation notes. Normally, the last activity is a description of the challenge to be solved using the EDP. These plans are written in a manner so that another teacher may easily and efficiently implement them in their own classrooms.

Examples of some of the units that were developed in the CEEMS program are given in Table 4. Each of the units developed through CEEMS or STEMucation Academy are public resources and are therefore available for free to teachers.

Table 4. Unit examples from the CEEMS program.

Unit Name	Grade and Subject	Hyperlink
Aiken's Angry Birds	High School Physical Science	http://stemucationacademy.com/aiken-angry-birds/
Designer Dogs	Grade 8 Science	http://stemucationacademy.com/designing-dogs/
Feel The Noise	High School Pre-Calculus/Calculus	http://stemucationacademy.com/feel-the-noise/
Trains Always Win	Grade 8 Algebra	http://stemucationacademy.com/trains-always-win/

The Process to Monitor, Guide, and Evaluate Progress: As noted, a Coach is assigned to each workshop participant. The coach's role is to mentor the participant and to monitor and evaluate their progress. To aid the coach in assessing a participant's pre-workshop knowledge, a pre-assessment is given. This assessment appraises the participant's knowledge of such things as CBL, the EDP, 21st-century skills, and collaborative learning. The results of the assessment are used by the coach to determine where participants need to focus their energy. If the participant demonstrates adequate knowledge, this may lead to reducing or eliminating sections of the course.

In the virtual environment, it is necessary to continuously monitor the progress of the participant using a variety of feedback mechanisms. We utilize homework assignments, a rubric, and an oral evaluation guide that stimulates discussions between the participant and the coach. Prior to the implementation of a unit of instruction in the classroom, a pre-implementation checklist is completed by the participant. After the unit is taught, a post-implementation checklist is completed and is used to guide the participant in putting the finishing touches on their unit materials. Part of this post-implementation checklist is to complete a reflection that involves writing notes to themselves or other teachers who might implement the unit in their own classrooms. These notes typically point out areas of the unit that went well or areas that did not go as planned. These notes are essentially a way of reducing problems when the unit is presented again in the future, or that another teacher may have in implementing the unit.

Course participants are asked to provide photos, videos, and samples of student work from the implementation of their unit in the classroom. This supplemental material further documents the unit to aid other teachers in the future. This record is also a way for the coach to assess the participant's work and ultimately to assess the completeness of the unit. Each of these feedback instruments provides valuable insights into the participant's progress and permits mid-course corrections to be made if appropriate. Typically, the participant will complete a module and only then gain access to the next one upon the coach's approval.

Program Completion Requirements: As noted, the workshop has numerous checkpoints that provide continuous feedback to the coach in order to monitor a participant's progress. By the time participants implement their units of instruction, there is a good sense of how well they performed, how good their documentation is, and a decision to assign course credit can then easily be made, if that option is to be used.

It is important to note that if deemed appropriate for other teachers to use, materials that are created by the participant will be archived on an open-source website. An archive of unit materials currently exists on the University of Cincinnati CEEMS website [44] as well as on the STEMucation Academy website [71].

3.2. Branding the MVP

This section details the process used for branding the MVP and the decisions made regarding its visual representation, with the hope that these will serve as useful guides for other venture creators.

Brand Name and Trademark: After the close of the I-Corps L training, the first task at hand for the group was to change its name from Best Engineered STEM Teachers (BEST), as other programs were already using that acronym. The criteria the group used for branding (name and visual identity) included the following items:

(1)   It must be consistent with mission and vision, which were fixed as follows:

   ○   Mission: Our program is a teacher-recommended, online professional development program that helps teachers meet new science/mathematics and engineering practice standards.

   ○   Vision: Created to help teachers transform their classrooms into student-centered, hands-on learning environments.

(2)   It must clearly communicate the provided services (what it is). We selected the brand name as STEMucation Academy, which combined the words "STEM" (science, technology, engineering, and mathematics) and "education" to convey the message the program offers professional development training in "STEM education". The official trademark for the name was obtained by the University of Cincinnati Research Institute (UCRI), an Ohio non-profit corporation affiliated with UC. The domain name stemucationacademy.org and stemucationacademy.com were also purchased for web development and email usage, respectively.

(3)   It must demonstrate the benefits of our service—assisting teachers to improve their evaluation scores related to science, mathematics, and engineering instruction.

(4)   It has meaning to target audiences. The STEMucation Academy brand is one that generates feelings of confidence, approachability, collaboration, and individualization.

(5)   It must be distinguishable from other PD organizations in that it facilitates the development of new units as needed to meet individual curriculum and student needs, and be guided and vetted by professional coaches.

   Logo Look and Usage: Under the guidance of the I-Corps L team, a graphic designer developed a logo based on the initiative's equity, and its inspiration is a star along with the name STEMucation Academy (Figure 12).

Figure 12. STEMucation logo.

3.3. Testing Our Model

   From our customer feedback and an analysis of our competition, our initial professional development model was designed to target science teachers teaching grades 6 to 12. To test some of the aspects of our model, we piloted a face-to-face training workshop, "Integrating Engineering into Your Science Classroom," at the American Society for Engineering Education (ASEE) Annual Conference and Exposition on 13 June 2015 as part of the K–12 workshop series organized by the ASEE's K–12 division. Also, this was the first time the branding of STEMucation Academy, described in the previous section, was used in the PowerPoint presentation, handouts, and promotional materials prepared for the event. The overall goal of this experiential learning workshop was to develop and execute a student-centered engineering design challenge based on academic standards. The team envisioned the possibility of converting this entire experience into an online teacher PD program including individualized coaching to aid teachers in the development of a design challenge-based unit for his/her classroom. This workshop consisted of a 75-minute session that was free to those attending the ASEE Conference. Ten participants attended the workshop. Two veteran exemplar CEEMS high-school teachers (math and science) were recruited to direct the workshop, and the contents and delivery modalities were designed by the I-Corps L team in collaboration with them. Overall the workshop was well received. Some positive outcomes:

- We were able to implement an engineering design activity to simulate a classroom challenge
- Participants were able to work on their own unit of instruction and presented their plans
- We received first-hand feedback from the ultimate users on what our planned online PD program or workshops should make clear:

  ○ What does it look like to teach STEM by integrating engineering into one's classroom?
  ○ How can and does science and math education benefit from including the EDP?

3.4. Creating the Marketing Website

Providing information to current program graduates and potential future customers is provided through an online website at stemucationacademy.com. As most individuals are familiar with website navigation, we will point out just a few tips for navigating the website.

The website contains seven major segments: Home, About, Training Options, Units, Resources, Register, and Contact. The Home page features comments from the Program Director and Program Coordinator as well as scrolling photos taken during CBL classroom activities and various training programs. The About page provides background information on the benefits of CBL, key program attributes such as higher student achievement, and the highly valued personal coaching assistance the program provides. Training Options illustrates the features and costs of the four training programs, including two online and two on-site workshops. For the One-Day Introductory On-Site Workshop and the Introductory Online Workshop, a single engineering design challenge activity is developed and implemented in the classroom. For the Three-Day and the Advanced Online Workshops, a full CBL–EDP unit of instruction is developed which includes at least four activities, one of which is solving a challenge using the EDP. A fifth option includes customized workshops to fit customer needs. To aid teachers in the development of materials for their classes, the Units option provides access to classroom-ready units of instruction that utilize the CBL methodology with integration of the EDP to solve the challenge. The Resources page includes materials that were presented at a conference as well as journal articles published by the CEEMS project team that provide more background information on the CBL and EDP teaching methodologies. The Register page can be used by those who would like to sign up for one of the workshops and Contact can be used to get more information. The Register section includes a step-by-step process for registration, submission of documents to make the enrollment payment, instructions when they will be informed of the assigned coach and the go-ahead to start the training program and obligations thereafter. The contact form will send an email message to teacherpd@stemucationacademy.com, which is monitored continuously by the STEMucation Academy Program Coordinator.

3.5. Alpha Testing: Piloting the Online PD Program

The STEMucation Academy's online PD program was fully developed and available for internal testing by the end of the 2015 Fall Semester. It was piloted with six individual in-service teachers for free during the 2016 Summer and Fall semesters. Teachers were recruited from a nationwide search, and a group of six teachers completed the program together in the 2017 Spring Semester. The group of six in-service teachers who completed the program together were enrolled in a course they were taking at the University of Cincinnati College of Education, Criminal Justice, and Human Services, though not all students enrolled in the course took the online PD program. This enabled us to test the modalities of the "teacher collaboration" aspect modeled in the online PD program (teachers disparately located and teachers taking a course together). Since STEMucation Academy is self-paced, it required 3–6 weeks for teachers to complete the program, depending when the unit was scheduled for teaching. This verified that our projected completion period of 12–16 weeks, as mentioned in Section 3.1, was more than realistic. Past veteran CEEMS teachers and Resource Team Members (CEEMS coaches) were employed as coaches for both these pilot programs. In both online pilot implementations, the teachers who completed the program reported that they felt much more comfortable and competent in their ability to create and teach a unit incorporating an engineering design challenge in an end-of-the-program survey. They also praised the flexible nature of the online format. A few of the quotes provided by the participants of the online PD program are mentioned below:

- "I liked that I could go at my own pace, look ahead to all of the modules so I could get the whole picture before actually doing each module, and I liked that there was someone I could contact to bounce ideas off."
- "The self-pace was great!"
- "I liked how I could go back and re-watch something to help me understand."
- "The resources were great."
- "My coach was great! She was very helpful and supportive."
- "I had an awesome coach who I enjoyed working with. She was always giving me ideas and helped me in any way."
- "I liked the timeline of the workshop. Having due dates for parts of the STEM unit was helpful. Working with a mentor was also helpful."

In the end-of-the-program survey for the pilot implementations, the teachers who completed the program reported that overall:

(1) they felt much more comfortable and competent in their ability to create and teach a unit incorporating an engineering design challenge;
(2) the coach was great and was the key support to their success in completing the online PD course;
(3) the breakdown of modules into engineering process steps was helpful in learning about the EDP.

Besides the above strengths, some challenges were also reported, which resulted in making following changes in the online PD program:

A. Fluency in Using Blackboard: CourseSites by Blackboard was used to offer the STEMucation Academy's online PD program for both pilots. A debrief with the coaches was held after each pilot. Generally, the feedback received from the coaches was positive. All coaches felt that even though CourseSites was an appropriate platform for the online PD program, they reported that a few student teachers initially had challenges navigating CourseSites. Overall coaches felt the student teachers were capable of mastering all subject areas, were communicative, and put forth an above-average amount of effort to master the techniques being taught in the online PD program. Due to the issues arising from the use of CourseSites, an alternative learning management system was sought. As most coaches and participants are familiar with cloud-based products such as Google Drive, YouTube, and Microsoft Office products such as Word and PowerPoint, a decision was made to convert the online program materials to a format that allowed the participants and coaches to get "up and running" more quickly. This also permitted modifications to the online program to be made by personnel not experienced in the use of CourseSites. A study guide was created for each of the eight STEMucation Academy modules. These study guides are in PDF format, which is universally readable on all types of digital devices including tablets, smartphones, and computers. The study guides include a module overview, module objectives, assignments, and other instructions to help the participant navigate the course. Hyperlinks to videos and other course supplements are imbedded in the modules. At the time of writing this paper, the new format has been evaluated and is being used by teachers currently enrolled in the STEMucation Academy's online PD course.

B. Need for Better Management of the Discussion Board: Some participants expressed a need for better management of the discussion board to ensure timely interactions with the coaches and on-time completion of the modules. Based on this feedback and the fact that the course participants did not always participate in one-on-one discussions with their coach, the discussion board was dropped and the one-on-one meetings between participant and coach became mandatory. This alternate form of communication allows the coach to better assess the participants' progress and, if needed, offer mid-course corrections.

C.   Issues with Purpose and Submission of Rubrics.   We found participants wanted more explanation of the course requirements and the rubric elements used to assign a grade. Having a clear definition of expected performance would help the participant understand what their work product should focus on. Each of the eight modules contain a number of assignments and each assignment has one or more rubric elements associated with it. Overall there are more than 20 rubric elements distributed over the eight modules. A sample rubric element is illustrated in Table 5.

Table 5. Sample rubric.

Rubric Element	Excellent (100–90%)	Acceptable (89–60%)	Unacceptable (59–0%)
Possible Essential Questions	At least 3 possible Essential Questions have been clearly written and are well related to the Big Idea for each if the identified challenges	1 or 2 possible Essential Questions have been documented for each of the identified challenges	No possible Essential Questions have been documented
(15)	(15–13.5)	(13.5–9)	(8.85–0)

The rubric in this case was used to define the desired performance requirements and is broken up into 3 levels: (1) excellent performance, (2) acceptable performance, or (3) unacceptable performance. Point levels are assigned to each rubric element based on the complexity of the assignment and its relative importance to the overall course learning objectives. When the coach assigns a score, it provides an opportunity for discussion with the participant regarding their work. In some cases, the coach may recommend reworking the participant's unit and activity plans, or the coach may simply reinforce the fact that the participant's work is commensurate with an excellent or acceptable performance. By clearly defining the expected performance and articulating this to the participants prior to and during the course, it is believed that participants will develop higher-quality work.

Another aspect of the rubric was to improve consistency between the coaches who are evaluating a student teacher's performance. In a typical classroom setting, a single instructor assesses student performance and assigns a grade. This is a model of consistency, as one "evaluator" is appraising the work of each participant in the course. In the STEMucation Academy approach, multiple coaches may be involved and a potential problem with inconsistent evaluation of performance may arise due to the different expectations of the coaches. Again, the rubric provides a uniform approach to evaluating performance and helps to ensure fair assessments are made among course participants.

3.6. Moving Forward: Licensing Out the Program for Marketing

Once STEMucation Academy's online PD program was fully developed and vetted, we began looking for opportunities to license the program to an established non-profit organization (NPO) to promote and market it to paying customers. In September 2018, UCRI and UC's Innovation Office signed a licensure contract with the Science Education Council of Ohio (SECO) for the online PD program. SECO is a well-established NPO in Ohio that has been organizing professional development workshops, programs, and conferences in the region for 14 years (https://scienceeducationofohio1.wildapricot.org/). Also, SECO is the Ohio chapter of the National Science Teachers Association (NSTA). The SECO Board of Directors have agreed to license STEMucation Academy's online PD program since it provides them an opportunity to have a national footprint and bring visibility to its mission: "The Science Education Council of Ohio (SECO) is a collaborative community that believes everyone deserves the benefit of a strong science education in order to engage with an ever-changing world." SECO is developing an informational webpage related to STEMucation Academy and a registration page for enrollees on its webpage. SECO will enroll and assign coaches to the enrollees from a list of qualified, certified coaches supplied by STEMucation Academy. STEMucation Academy will maintain the course modules and provide access to the enrollees, and its Program Coordinator will be the liaison between the enrollees and the coaches to monitor progress. The Program Coordinator will also maintain a required online training program for the coaches.

Upon completion of the program, participants will receive 45 contact hours and have the option of purchasing three graduate credit hours from a partner University that SECO uses for offering graduate credits for its other PD offerings.

3.7. Ongoing Efforts for Broader Impacts

As mentioned in Section 2.1 in the CEEMS project, eight in-class graduate courses and one seminar course served as the cornerstone for all teachers during the Summer Institute for Teachers (SIT). These courses were packaged to offer the SIT participants a Graduate Secondary Engineering Education Certificate (GSEEC) from UC. Once the GSEEC program was fully established at UC, STEMucation Academy converted four key CEEMS courses to complete online courses and added a new online course that duplicated the CEEMS PD seminar course in a complete virtual environment. In this newest course, teachers work under the guidance of a coach to develop, teach, and document student learning results, and to put their units into a format for web dissemination to other teachers. The five online courses are packaged to offer a 12-credit GSEEC distance education program to reach a wider geographic audience:

The required courses (three graduate credits each) are:

- Engineering Foundations
- Engineering Education Certificate Capstone

Elective courses (option to select two, at three graduate credits each):

- Models and Applications of Physical Sciences
- Engineering Applications in Math—this contains two sections, one for high-school teachers and the other for middle-school teachers (it could also be taken by elementary school teachers)
- Engineering Models

The course descriptions for these courses and details of the GSEEC program can be found on the STEMucation Academy website [71]. STEMucation Academy is currently working out the logistics of offering this complete online 12-credit GSEEC program to paying customers and will soon be announcing its availability.

4. Concluding Remarks

The published literature clearly recognizes that the best way to improve undergraduate STEM education is by investing in math, science, engineering, and technology (STEM) K–12 teachers. A number of Federal agencies and corporate foundations have invested significant resources in an effort to improve teaching and learning across STEM disciplines. However, this has not produced the increasingly necessary transformational changes in STEM education the US desperately requires. Addressing the persistent challenges that limit evidence-based instructional practices in STEM education is still an urgent need, yet the rate and extent of large-scale adoption is very low because STEM educators, researchers, and communities do not have the basic training to systematically accelerate the process of bringing effective educational innovations to scale. Even when successful, their impact has mostly remained local to where the practices were developed.

In this paper, the authors have presented their experiences from participating in an NSF I-Corps L training program established for business startups using Blank's Lean LaunchPad, Osterwalder's Business Model Canvas, and associated tools. They used the entrepreneurial skills acquired through this training to scale-up their professional program, the Cincinnati Engineering Enhanced Math and Science Program (CEEMS). CEEMS had been developed, implemented, and evaluated with successful results over a period of seven years in a targeted 14 school-district partnership in Greater Cincinnati.

CEEMS worked intensively with secondary school (grades 6–12) math and science teachers, who participated for a two-year period in the project to develop and implement new units of instruction to meet teachers' individual curriculum and student needs. The programs specifically addressed the needed academic standards through engineering design challenges.

The main aim of CEEMS was to train teachers to encounter new emerging science/mathematics and engineering practice standards (NGSS, CCSS for Mathematical Practice, and the recently revised Ohio Learning Standards for K–12 science and mathematics juxtaposed with Universal Skills/21st-Century Learning Skills), with demonstrated and documented higher student performance. To achieve this aim, the CEEMS teachers were trained in using CBL and the EDP teaching pedagogies to transform their classrooms into student-centered, hands-on learning environments, while also assisting them to improve their evaluation scores related to science, math, and engineering instruction.

The CEEMS teachers acquired the skills to successfully implement the above through a two-year commitment to complete 20 credits of graduate coursework. Their tuition fees covered course credits and additional funds covered longitudinal face-to-face guidance, critical reviews of their work, and continuous feedback and approval by professional coaches during both the development and implementation stages. In CEEMS this was possible because NSF funds covered all these costs. Recognizing limitations in the I-Corps L project, a goal was established to bring to scale a tested teacher PD program, CEEMS, so that the practice of its primary pedagogies (CBL and the EDP) could be sustained and even expanded on when funding from the NSF ran dry. The parameters for the scale-up were set to be:

- include online and face-to-face channels of service (make both options available);
- make it self-paced and flexible to fit the teacher's curricular needs and teaching schedule;
- condense it for successful completion within a semester ($\leq$16 weeks);
- include virtual coaching to assist teachers in producing the curriculum, teaching it, assessing student learning gains, reflecting after teaching, and documenting for web dissemination to other teachers for quality assurance, guidance, and approval;
- ensure costs are fixed at a level that can be paid either by a teacher or by the school district.

The engineering design process is a simple concept to understand, but it is challenging to implement well. Like many skills, it takes practice. That is what a majority of this online PD program created, with attributes dedicated to designing and implementing units of instruction using CBL and EDP to enhance any unit of study, not just math and science. It is envisioned that this collaborative experience between the teacher and the expert coach will showcase "tricks of the trade" for implementing CBL and the EDP in a classroom setting, and increase the confidence and comfort level of the participating teacher to do more on their own later.

In this paper, the authors have documented how they used customer market research conducted during the I-Corps L training to define a minimum viable product (MVP) that incorporated the above attributes. The authors also described the process they used to move forward very quickly from an MVP to a more complete product offering, its branding, the process of trademarking it, piloting and testing the MVP, and finally licensing one of the online professional development programs for teacher training to an established non-profit organization (NPO), the Science Education Council of Ohio (SECO), for future marketing.

The MVP was branded and trademarked as STEMucation Academy by the University of Cincinnati Research Institute (UCRI), an Ohio non-profit corporation affiliated with University of Cincinnati. A dedicated website, http://stemucationacademy.com/, was developed for STEMucation Academy and maintained by the Northern Kentucky University's (NKU's) Center for Applied Informatics. This website presents details of all the PD program offerings by STEMucation Academy and the registration process for any one of those offerings.

Educ. Sci. **2019**, *9*, 54

Details of the author's I-Corps L training experience and its outcomes are presented in this paper with the hope that they will serve as a useful guide for other venture creators. In summary, the key lessons learned from our I-Corp L experience are:

pick a diverse, committed team; decide how the startup will pay for some of the early expenses, as startups cost money—look for viable partnerships that help move the project forward; most importantly, "get out of the building" to fully understand the customer needs, pains, and revenue flow to develop the MVP; and finally, identify what differentiates the MVP created from the competition.

Author Contributions: A.R.K. and J.B. contributed equally to the conceptualization, writing and revision of this article.

Funding: The authors would like to acknowledge the financial support provided by the US National Science Foundation Awards, 1102990 for the CEEMS-targeted MSP project and the supplement 1518619 for the I-Corps L project.

Acknowledgments: Any opinions, findings, conclusions, and/or recommendations are those of the investigators and do not necessarily reflect the views of the National Science Foundation. The authors also extend their deepest appreciation to Julie Steimle and Melisse May, who participated with them in the I-Corps L training program and thoughtfully and generously provided essential feedback for deciding on the next steps during and after the training. Lastly but not the least, we would like to acknowledge the generous support of the non-profit corporation the University of Cincinnati Research Institute (UCRI) for partnering and obtaining the trademark STEMucation Academy and copywriting its products.

Conflicts of Interest: The authors declare no conflict of interest.

References

1. Anderson, K.J.B. Science Education and Test-Based Accountability: Reviewing their Relationship and Exploring Implications for Future Policy. *Sci. Educ.* **2012**, *96*, 104–129. [CrossRef]
2. NGSS Lead States. *Next Generation Science Standards: For States, by States*; The National Academies Press: Washington, DC, USA, 2013; ISBN 978-0-309-27227-8.
3. Common Core State Standards Initiative (CCSSI). *Common Core State Standards for Mathematics*; National Governors Association Center for Best Practices and the Council of Chief State School Officers: Washington, DC, USA, 2010. Available online: http://www.corestandards.org/Math/Practice/ (accessed on 9 March 2019).
4. National Academy of Science, National Academy of Engineering and National Research Council. *Engineering in K–12 Education: Understanding the Status and Improving the Prospects 2009*; The National Academies Press: Washington, DC, USA, 2009. [CrossRef]
5. Griffard, P.B.; Wandersee, J.H. Challenges to Meaningful Learning Among African-American Females at an Urban Science High School. *Int. J. Sci. Educ.* **1999**, *21*, 611–632. [CrossRef]
6. Loucks-Horsley, S.; Hewson, P.W.; Love, N.; Stiles, K.E. *Designing Professional Development for Teachers of Science and Mathematics*; Corwin Press: Thousand Oaks, CA, USA, 1998; ISBN 978-1-4129-6360-2.
7. Teel, K.M.; Debruin-Parecki, A.; Covington, M.V. Teaching Strategies That Honor and Motivate Inner-city African–American Students: A School/University Collaboration. *Teach. Teach. Educ.* **1998**, *14*, 479–495. [CrossRef]
8. Mayer, R.E. Invited Reaction: Cultivating Problem-Solving Skills Through Problem-Based Approaches to Professional Development. *Hum. Resour. Dev. Q.* **2002**, *13*, 263–269. [CrossRef]
9. Hashweh, M.Z. Effects of Subject Matter Knowledge in the Teaching of Biology and Physics. *Teach. Teach. Educ.* **1987**, *3*, 109–120. [CrossRef]
10. Furguson, R. Paying for Public Education: New Evidence on How and Why Money Matters. *Harv. J. Legis.* **1991**, *28*, 465–498.
11. Kennedy, M.M. Education Reform and Subject Matter Knowledge. *Res. Sci. Teach.* **1998**, *35*, 249–263. [CrossRef]
12. Cohen, D.; Hill, H. Instructional Policy and Classroom Performance: The Mathematics Reform in California. *Teach. Coll. Rec.* **2000**, *102*, 294–343. Available online: http://www-personal.umich.edu/~{}dkcohen/cohen_hill_2000_TCR.pdf (accessed on 9 March 2019). [CrossRef]

13. Muijs, D.; Reynolds, D. School Effectiveness and Teacher Effectiveness in Mathematics: Some Preliminary Findings from the Evaluation of the Mathematics Enhancement Program (Primary). *Sch. Eff. Sch. Improv.* **2000**, *11*, 273–303. [CrossRef]

14. Cohen, D.K.; Hill, H.C. *State Policy and Classroom Performance: Mathematics Reform in California (CPRE Policy Brief)*; Consortium for Policy Research in Education: Philadelphia, PA, USA, 1998.

15. Kahle, J.B.; Meece, J.; Scantlebury, K. Urban African-American Middle School Science Students: Does Standards-Based Teaching Make a Difference? *Res. Sci. Teach.* **2000**, *37*, 1019–1041. [CrossRef]

16. Klein, S.P.; Hamilton, L.S.; McCaffrey, D.F.; Stecher, B.M.; Robyn, A.; Burroughs, D. *Teaching Practices and Student Achievement: Report of First-Year Findings from the 'Mosaic' Study of Systemic Initiatives in Mathematics and Science*; RAND Corporation: Santa Monica, CA, USA, 2000. Available online: https://www.rand.org/pubs/monograph_reports/MR1233.html (accessed on 31 October 2018).

17. Weiss, I.R.; Montgomery, D.L.; Ridgway, C.J.; Bond, S.L. *Local Systemic Change through Teacher Enhancement: Year Three Cross-Site Report*; Horizon Research Inc.: Chapel Hill, NC, USA, 1998. Available online: http://www.horizon-research.com/local-systemic-change-through-teacher-enhancement-year-three-cross-site-report (accessed on 31 October 2018).

18. National Commission on Math and Science Education for the 21st Century; Glenn. *Before It's Too Late: A Report to the Nation from the National Commission on Mathematics and Science Teaching for the 21st Century*; Department of Education: Washington, DC, USA, 2000.

19. Lieberman, A.; Grolnick, M. Networks and Reform in American Education. *Teach. Coll. Rec.* **1996**, *98*, 36–40.

20. Sparks, D. Focusing Staff Development on Improving Student Learning. In *Handbook of Research on Improving Student Achievement*; Cawelti, G., Ed.; Educational Research Service: Arlington, VA, USA, 1995; pp. 163–169, ISBN 10 1931762295.

21. Little, J.W. Teachers' Professional Development in a Climate of Educational Reform. *Educ. Eval. Policy Anal.* **1993**, *15*, 129–151.

22. Gamoran, A.; Secada, W.G.; Marrett, C.B. The Organizational Context of Teaching and Learning. In *Handbook of the Sociology of Education*; Hallinan, M.T., Ed.; Springer: New York City, NY, USA, 2000; ISBN 978-0-387-36424-7.

23. American Association for the Advancement of Science. *Atlas of Science Literacy: Project 2061*; AAAS: Washington, DC, USA, 2007; Chapter 3, ISBN 978-0871686688.

24. Putnam, R.; Borko, H. What Do New Views of Knowledge and Thinking Have to Say About Research on Teacher Learning? *Educ. Res.* **2000**, *29*, 4–15. [CrossRef]

25. Rutherford, F.J.; Ahlgren, A. *Science for All Americans*; Oxford University Press: New York City, NY, USA, 1990; ISBN 0-19-506770-3.

26. Morrison, J.S. *TIES STEM Education Monograph Series: Attributes of STEM Education*; Teaching Institute for Essential Science: Cleveland, OH, USA, 2006.

27. Meeth, L. Interdisciplinary Studies: A Matter of Definition. *Chang. Mag. High. Learn. Routl.* **1978**, *10*, 10. [CrossRef]

28. Committee on Science Learning K-8. *Taking Science to School*; The National Academies Press: Washington, DC, USA, 2007; ISBN 0-309-10205-7.

29. National Research Council. *Inquiry and the National Science Education Standards: A Guide for Teaching and Learning*; The National Academies Press: Washington, DC, USA, 2000; ISBN 0-309-06476-7.

30. Benenson, G. The Unrealized Potential of Everyday Technology as a Context for Learning. *Res. Sci. Teach.* **2001**, *38*, 730–745. [CrossRef]

31. Crismond, D. Learning and Using Science Ideas When Doing Investigate-and-Redesign Tasks: A Study of Naive, Novice, and Expert Designers Doing Constrained and Scaffolded Design Work. *Res. Sci. Teach.* **2001**, *38*, 791–820. [CrossRef]

32. Kolodner, J.L. Facilitating the Learning of Design Practices: Lessons Learned from Inquiry into Science Education. *J. Ind. Teach. Educ.* **2002**, *39*, 9–40.

33. Mehalik, M.M.; Doppelt, Y.; Schunn, C.D. Middle-School Science Through Design-Based Learning Versus Scripted Inquiry: Better Overall Science Concept Learning and Equity Gap Reduction. *J. Eng. Educ.* **2008**, *97*, 71–85. [CrossRef]

34. Greenwald, N.L. Learning from Problems. *Sci. Teach.* **2000**, *67*, 28–32.

35. Snetsinger, C.; Brewer, C.; Brown, F. Capture the Wind. *Sci. Teach.* **1999**, *66*, 38–42.

36. Lewis, T. Design and Inquiry: Bases for an Accommodation between Science and Technology Education in the Curriculum? *Res. Sci. Teach.* **2006**, *43*, 255–281. [CrossRef]

37. Schwartz, D.L.; Lin, X.; Brophy, S.; Bransford, J.D. Toward the Development of Flexibly Adaptive Designs. In *Instructional-Design Theories and Models: A New Paradigm of Instructional Theory*; Reigeluth, C.M., Ed.; Lawrence Erlbaum Associates: Mahwah, NJ, USA, 1999; Volume II, pp. 183–213.

38. Klein, S.S.; Sherwood, R. *Exemplary Science in Grades 9-12—Standards Based Success Stories*; NSTA Press: Arlington, VA, USA, 2005; pp. 43–50, ISBN 0-87355-257-1.

39. Klein, S.S.; Sherwood, R. Biomedical Engineering and Cognitive Science as the Basis for Secondary Science Curriculum Development: A Three-Year Study. *Sch. Sci. Math* **2005**, *105*, 384–401. [CrossRef]

40. Klein, S.S.; Harris, A.H. A User's Guide for the Legacy Cycle. *Educ. Hum. Dev.* **2007**, *1*, 1–16.

41. Brophy, S.B.; Klein, S.S.; Portsmore, M.; Rogers, C. Advancing Engineering Education in P-12 Classrooms. *J. Eng. Educ.* **2008**, *97*, 369–387. [CrossRef]

42. Corday, D.S.; Harris, T.R.; Klein, S.S. A Research Synthesis of the Effectiveness, Replicability, and Generality of the VaNTH Challenge-based Instructional Modules in Bioengineering. *J. Eng. Educ.* **2009**, *98*, 335–348. [CrossRef]

43. Walker, A.E.; Leary, H.; Hmelo-Silver, C.E.; Ertmer, P.A. (Eds.) *Essential Readings in Problem Based Learning: Exploring and Extending the Legacy of Howard S. Barrows*; Purdue University Press: West Lafayette, IN, USA, 2015; ISBN 9781612493688.

44. The Cincinnati Engineering Enhanced Math and Science Program (CEEMS). Available online: https://ceas.uc.edu/special_programs/ceems/CEEMS_Home.html (accessed on 31 October 2018).

45. Ohio Department of Education. *Ohio Learning Standards*. Available online: http://education.ohio.gov/Topics/Learning-in-Ohio/OLS-Graphic-Sections/Learning-Standards (accessed on 31 October 2018).

46. Steimle, J.; Kukreti, A.R.; Maltbie, C.V. Best Practice for Incorporating STEM into Rural Schools: Train and Invest in Teacher Leaders. In Proceedings of the ASEE Annual Conference and Exposition, New Orleans, LA, USA, 26–29 June 2016.

47. Kukreti, A.R.; Steimle, J. Coaching: Key to Success of Middle School/High School STEM Program. In Proceedings of the Mentoring Conference, Albuquerque, NM, USA, 25–28 October 2016.

48. Steimle, J.; Kukreti, A.R.; Meyer, H. Evaluating the Risk: In an Age of High Stakes Testing, Should Teachers Integrate Engineering Design into Traditional Science and Math Courses? In Proceedings of the ASEE Annual Conference & Exposition, Columbus, OH, USA, 25–28 June 2017.

49. Meyer, H. Integrating Engineering into an Urban Science Classroom. *Urban Learn. Teach. Res.* **2017**, *13*, 112–123.

50. Meyer, H. Teachers' Thoughts on Student Decision Making during Engineering Design Lessons. *Educ. Sci.* **2018**, *8*, 9. [CrossRef]

51. Kukreti, A.R.; Meyer, H.; Steimle, J.; Liberi, D. *Energize Your Classroom with Engineering Design Challenges: Science and Math Teachers Share Their Experiences*; NSTA Press: Arlington, VA, USA, in press; ISBN 978-1-68140-698-5.

52. Apple Inc. Challenge Based Learning. 2010. Available online: http://apple.co/2iAn4Wk (accessed on 31 October 2018).

53. Morrison, A.B.; Maltbie, C.V.; Short, A.D.; Wiechman, S.; Tellmann, J.; Swonger, G.; Dariotis, J.K. *Key Evaluation Results of the CEEMS Project, Year 7*; Evaluation Services Center, University of Cincinnati: Cincinnati, OH, USA, 2018. Available online: http://bit.ly/2017-2018-CEEMS-ESC-Final-Report (accessed on 31 October 2018).

54. Dixon, M.L.; Li, Y.; Woodruff, S.B. *Evaluation of CEEMS: The Cincinnati Engineering Enhanced Mathematics and Science Partnership Project: Annual report, 2017–2018*; Miami University, Discovery Center for Evaluation, Research, and Professional Learning: Oxford, OH, USA, 2018. Available online: http://bit.ly/2017-2018-CEEMS-Final-Eval-Report-Miami-University (accessed on 31 October 2018).

55. Meyer, H. *2017–2018 CEEMS Research Report*; University of Cincinnati, College of Education, Criminal Justice and Human Services School of Education, FUSION Center: Cincinnati, OH, USA. Available online: http://bit.ly/2017-2018-CEEMS-Final-Research-Study-Report (accessed on 31 October 2018).

56. Horizon Research Inc. Inside the Classroom Observation and Analytic Protocol. 2000. Available online: http://www.horizon-research.com/inside-the-classroom-observation-and-analytic-protocol (accessed on 20 October 2018).

57. Boyer, E.L. *Scholarship Reconsidered: Priorities of the Professoriate*; Jossey-Bass: San Francisco, CA, USA, 2014.
58. National Science Foundation. *Shaping the Future: New Expectations for Undergraduate Education in Science, Mathematics, Engineering, and Technology*; Report: NSF96139; NSF, Directorate for Education and Human Resource: Arlington, VA, USA, 1996.
59. National Research Council. *Transforming Undergraduate Education in Science, Mathematics, Engineering and Technology*; National Academy Press: Washington, DC, USA, 1999; ISBN 0-309-06294-2.
60. National Research Council. *Evaluating and Improving Undergraduate Teaching in Science, Technology, Engineering and Mathematics*; The National Academies Press: Washington, DC, USA, 2003. [CrossRef]
61. National Research Council. *Improving Undergraduate Instruction in Science, Technology, Engineering, and Mathematics: Report of a Workshop*; The National Academies Press: Washington, DC, USA, 2003. [CrossRef]
62. Committee on Science, Engineering, and Public Policy. *Rising Above the Gathering Storm: Energizing and Employing America for a Brighter Economic Future*; The National Academies Press: Washington, DC, USA, 2005. Available online: http://www.nap.edu/books/0309100399/html (accessed on 9 March 2019).
63. National Academy of Engineering. *Engineer of the 2020: Visions of Engineering in the New Century*; The National Academies Press: Washington, DC, USA, 2005. Available online: http://www.nap.edu/books/0309091624/html (accessed on 9 March 2019).
64. National Academy of Engineering. *Educating the Engineer of 2020: Adapting Engineering Education to the New Century*; The National Academies Press: Washington, DC, USA, 2005. [CrossRef]
65. Jamieson, L.H.; Lohmann, J.R. *Creating a Culture for Scholarly and Systematic Innovation in Engineering Education: Ensuring US Engineering Has the Right People with the Right Talent for a Global Society*; American Society of Engineering Educators: Washington, DC, USA, 2009.
66. National Academy of Sciences, National Academy of Engineering, and Institute of Medicine. *Rising Above the Gathering Storm, Revisited: Rapidly Approaching Category 5*; The National Academies Press: Washington, DC, USA, 2010; ISBN 978-0-309-16097-1. [CrossRef]
67. Blank, S.; Dorf, B. *The Startup Owner's Manual: The Step-by-Step Guide for Building a Great Company*; K&S Ranch, Inc.: Pescadero, CA, USA, 2012.
68. MacNeal, R. Agile Teams and Projects. In *Teamwork and Project Management (Basic Engineering Series and Tools)*, 4th ed.; Smith, K.A., Ed.; McGraw-Hill: New York City, NY, USA, 2014; pp. 143–153.
69. Osterwalder, A.; Pigneur, Y. *Business Model Generation*; John Wiley and Sons Inc.: Hoboken, NJ, USA, 2010.
70. Value Proposition Canvas Template. Available online: https://www.peterjthomson.com/2013/11/value-proposition-canvas/ (accessed on 31 October 2018).
71. STEMucation Academy. *Training Workshops and Unit of Instruction Resources for Teachers*. 2018. Available online: http://stemucationacademy.com (accessed on 9 March 2019).

education
sciences

MDPI

Article

Exploring Secondary Students' Alternative Conceptions about Engineering Design Technology

Anila Asghar [1,*], Ying-Syuan Huang [1], Kenneth Elliott [2] and Yannick Skelling [3]

[1]   Department of Integrated Studies in Education, McGill University, Montreal, QC H3A 2M1, Canada;
     ying.huang6@mail.mcgill.ca
[2]   Independent Researcher, McGill University, Montreal, QC H3A 2M1, Canada; kelliott@videotron.ca
[3]   Département de didactique, Université du Québec à Montréal (UQAM), Montreal, QC H2X 3R9, Canada;
     skelling.yannick@gmail.com
*   Correspondence: anila.asghar@mcgill.ca; Tel.: +1514-398-4527 (ext. 094194)

Received: 11 January 2019; Accepted: 18 February 2019; Published: 24 February 2019

check for
updates

Abstract: This paper presents the assessment items that were developed by science and technology teachers in Québec to explore their students' alternative ideas about engineering design technology and technological systems. These assessment items were administered to Secondary Cycle One students in Francophone and Anglophone schools in Québec to elicit their ideas about the foundational technology concepts included in the science and technology curriculum. Students' responses are presented to share their alternative and scientific explanations. In addition, various approaches to facilitate a deeper understanding of scientific models and mechanistic reasoning in students are also discussed.

Keywords: science; technology; engineering; mathematics (STEM) education; engineering design technology; students' alternative conceptions; conceptual change; conceptual assessment items; inquiry-based science and technology; learner-centered pedagogy; assessment tool

1. Introduction

This paper aims to share the resources that we have developed in collaboration with secondary science and technology teachers in Québec to support the teaching of engineering design technology. To this end, we present the assessment tools that were developed by the teachers to elicit their students' alternative ideas about technology and technological systems. These assessment items were administered to Secondary Cycle One students (grades seven and eight) in Francophone and Anglophone schools in Québec to elicit their alternative ideas about the foundational technology concepts included in the science and technology curriculum in Québec. We hope that science educators will benefit from the tools that their fellow colleagues developed to facilitate the integration of science and technology while teaching the Québec Education Program. This paper is organized into five sections. First, we provide an overview of the Science and Technology program in Quebec. Then, we review the literature on students' intuitive or alternative conceptions in science. In the subsequent sections, we describe the study methods, present an analysis of the key findings focusing in secondary students' intuitive conceptions of technological systems, and discuss the pedagogical implications of this work, relative to the literature on conceptual change approaches to science and technology education.

The Québec Education Program (QEP) is a competency-based curriculum divided into six Subject Domains, with Mathematics, Science, and Technology being one of them [1]. Each subject has competencies that must be developed by the students through Elementary and Secondary school. The discipline-specific and cross-curricular competencies aim to develop students' intellectual capacities and appropriate social skills that will enable them to respond to complex changes in their environment [1]. According to the QEP,

> One aim of a competency-based program is to ensure that students' learnings serve as tools for both action and thought, which is a form of action. Unlike a skill, which may be applied in isolation, a competency makes use of several resources and is itself used in fairly complex contexts. [2] (p. 4)

The content for each subject area for each cycle is defined by the QEP and is used to develop the competencies. One of the major changes introduced by the QEP to the curriculum of the science program was the introduction of technology education—to prepare students for modern society [3,4]. In fact, all of the compulsory science programs from Secondary One through Secondary Four are now named "Science and Technology". The QEP emphasizes that science and technology are intimately intertwined in the modern world and due to their intricate connections, it is not easy to draw concrete boundaries between the two domains [3] (p. 1).

Incorporating technical education into general education was part of a world-wide trend through the 1980s and 90s, supported by United Nations Educational, Scientific and Cultural Organization (UNESCO). Both the Canadian Council of Ministers of Education (CMEC) in their Common Framework of Science Learning Outcomes K to 12 as well as the American Association for the Advancement of Science (AAAS) in their landmark publication, Project 2061, strongly influenced the writing of the Science and Technology programs of the QEP. Prior to this movement, students who pursued technical education were directed to the workplace and those in general education, to higher education [4]. Using technology to teach science is well-researched—showing that technology-centered classrooms, can lead to effective science learning [5–10]. Engineering design is a key theme of QEP technology content [1]. Prior to the introduction of the QEP, all Secondary Three (grade nine) students took Introduction to Technology (ITT) [3]. Students worked in a woodworking lab developing engineering designs and building models. The QEP Science and Technology programs specifically integrated the essentials of ITT [11]. An integrated approach to teaching Science, Technology, Engineering, and Mathematics (STEM) is central to the QEP curriculum [12]. The STEM approach emphasizes the development of competencies related to mathematics, science, and engineering-based technology to develop students' scientific reasoning, critical thinking, and conceptual understanding by engaging in experimental inquiries [3]. Such inquiries encourage students to test their ideas by developing investigable questions, using organized observation, and devising procedures for their investigations. Through this process, they are expected to develop the skills to interpret and analyze their observations while drawing on logical arguments, when appropriate [3]. Furthermore, the STEM related competencies focus on "discerning patterns and relationships" in the data to understand the evidence that they collect.

The QEP highlights the relevance of science, technology, and mathematics to the evolving needs of society and the ways in which these fields have shaped modern society [5]. The QEP illuminates the common elements in these subject areas which focus on developing students' understanding, critical thinking, analytical reasoning, inquiry competency, and communication skills [3] (p. 186). Moreover, cultivating students' imagination, creativity and a desire to explore and discover is also emphasized as a significant element of STEM subjects. As explained in the QEP, scientific and technological literacy would enable youth to use scientific knowledge and skills appropriately and productively in their professional and personal lives. Schools are seen as key sites for developing students' abilities to achieve this key goal of public education in Canada [3].

The QEP Science and Technology program encompasses five scientific disciplines (chemistry, physics, biology, astronomy, and geology) and "various technological fields (e.g. mechanical design, medical, food and mining technology) studied in the context of cultural references" [3] (p. 225). This curriculum focuses on the following key competencies at the Secondary Cycle One level (grades seven and eight): (1) "Seeks answers or solutions to scientific or technological problems," (2) "Makes the most of his/her knowledge of science and technology," and (3) Communicates in the languages used in science and technology." The first competency focuses on developing students' inquiry skills as they actively engage in the process of asking questions and exploring possible solutions through "observations, hands-on activities, measurements, construction or experimentation, be it in a lab, in a workshop or in the real world" [3] (p. 226). The second competency focuses on the application of knowledge, particularly in real life situations. The students develop a deeper understanding of scientific concepts and technological models by analyzing how technical objects work [3]. The ability to effectively interpret and communicate scientific and technological knowledge using appropriate language is intimately connected to these competencies

Engineering-based technology provides a useful context for applying content knowledge as students engage in analyzing and designing complex systems [13–16]. Engineers are involved in such activities in real life settings when solving complex technological problems, improving manufacturing processes, building infrastructure, designing new devices (e.g., computers, electronic communication tools), and addressing socioenvironmental issues (e.g., waste and recycling management, public transit systems) [17] (pp. 370–371). The essential concepts and progression of learning goals for engineering-based technology in the QEP for Secondary Cycle One (grades seven and eight) focus on (a) graphical language, (b) mechanical engineering, (c) materials, and (d) manufacturing. Students are expected to learn and to represent the design of a technical object and its functional components. Graphical language focuses on explaining "the operation of a simple technical object by drawing a diagram illustrating the active forces and the resulting motion" [18]. Technical diagrams illustrate certain principles of simple machines (e.g., a lever or a wedge) and represent the construction of a technical object and the arrangement of its components.

Mechanical engineering for Secondary Cycle One focuses on forces and motion, technological systems, and engineering. Students are expected to learn about different types of motion, effects of a force, simple machines, different types of technological systems, key components of technological systems and their functions, and energy transformations in technological systems. Engineering includes basic mechanical functions of a technical object and motion transmission systems in technical objects.

In addition, students are expected to learn about different types of material resources, such as raw materials used in the industry, materials present in technical objects, the origins of these materials, and the tools that are used to manufacture technical objects. Understanding of the manufacturing process is also important for students at this level. For example, students should observe and critically analyze the structure of a technical object, the specifications involved in the design of that object, and its function in certain social, economic, and industrial environments. This process should enable the students to design and construct a prototype of a technical object or some components of that object [16]. Research suggests that developing a deeper and more meaningful understanding of students' scientific and technological concepts and processes requires an understanding of the conceptual models and resources that students bring to the science classroom. Below we discuss the literature on students' intuitive and alternative frameworks, and their role in science learning.

2. Students' Intuitive or Alternative Conceptions in Science

Researchers in all areas of science education have noted that students (and adults) often hold common sense beliefs that derive from their perceptual experiences and exploration of the physical world" [19–21]. Through a "continuous process of interaction between their cognitive system and the physical and cultural environment, human beings instinctively develop their explanations of natural phenomena" [22] (p. 553). Researchers argue that children's ideas are based on general abstractions from common experiences. They use this contextual knowledge to develop explanations in certain situations and in response to particular questions or problems in everyday life [23–26]. Children's intuitive or alternative conceptions tend to be very different from scientific conceptions and may often contradict the abstract scientific models [27–29]. Research shows that students' alternative explanations may persist even after students are exposed to the scientific models during formal instruction and continue to affect students' science learning [22,23,30–34]. Indeed, research indicates that deeply held intuitive or common-sense conceptions are fairly stable and cannot be completely replaced by the scientific conceptions through science instruction. Rather, alternative conceptions may co-exist with the scientific models [28,29,35]. Dawson (2014) argues that learners may construct a "conceptual profile" which encompasses their alternative conceptions along with the scientific models [35] (p. 389).

Ideas firmly held by students will directly impact science teaching and the ability of science instructors to help their students to develop a deeper understanding of accepted scientific models. At the same time, traditional science instruction tends to ignore students' own ideas and beliefs and is mostly unsuccessful in developing a robust understanding of accepted scientific models [36,37]. Recognizing students' common-sense ideas and the ways in which students use them to make sense of scientific and technological phenomena is of paramount importance in science education [13,38,39]. Therefore, eliciting and attending to students' alternative conceptions must be an integral component of science instruction.

Inquiry-based approaches to learning science encourage the learners to actively construct and apply scientific knowledge through problem-solving [40]. In this process, students construct new scientific knowledge by assimilation—adding ideas to their existing framework—or accommodation—restructuring their cognitive frameworks to make sense of and integrate the new concepts [41]. Thus, it is particularly important for students to examine and compare their own models vis-à-vis the accepted scientific models that they learn in school [28,29,35,38]. Scientific paradigms must be introduced carefully, especially in those instances where common sense beliefs are at odds with the scientific perspective [42,43]. As a consequence, it is vital that we provide teachers and curriculum developers with evidence of commonly held ideas. A variety of anthropological studies have attempted to develop an understanding of student viewpoints [44], as well as a clear picture of the intersection between alternative conceptions and instruction [45–48]. Science teachers need to understand the student perspective before attempting to teach new scientific ideas. Research suggests that the most effective instruction is based on initial consideration of students' prior conceptions, instructional goals, and careful alignment of pedagogical practice with those goals. Effectiveness of these instructional approaches can be determined through the use of conceptual assessment tools that are aligned to the instructional goals [46,49]. Eliciting students' thinking through formal diagnostic testing or open-ended verbal and pictorial student descriptions can provide very useful information to science teachers how to inform their instruction. In this paper, we share a collaborative project that brought together science and technology teachers and consultants from three school boards and university researchers in Québec to develop assessment tools for use in local schools.

With the implementation of the QEP science and technology programs, many science teachers found themselves unfamiliar with how to integrate technology into the science curriculum [50]. They needed ongoing professional training and support so that they could teach technology content and encourage their students to engage in technology and engineering design activities. The Québec Ministry of Education sponsored Centre de Developpement Pédagogique (CDP) and the English counterpart, Science and Technology Implementation Committee (STIC) provided teachers with activities so that students and teachers could work with technological objects that are familiar and relevant to students [51].

The authors were engaged in a collaborative professional development project to support science and technology teachers and to connect research in science education with professional practice in schools in Québec. This project was unique as it was collaboratively developed by science and technology education consultants and university faculty from Francophone and Anglophone sectors in response to science teachers' professional needs. Science teachers and consultants from three partner school boards (two Anglophone and one Francophone School Board) worked with faculty members from McGill and Université du Québec à Montréal over three years to achieve the following objectives: (1) Professional development of Secondary Cycle One (grades seven and eight) science and technology teachers to promote their students' conceptual development, technology skills, and problem-solving competencies and (2) Development of appropriate assessment questions to identify students' alternative conceptions related to science and technology concepts included in the QEP. The project team drew on current developments in science education research and practice to create assessment items and inquiry-based activities to foster students' engagement and learning. The assessment tools were developed in French and English for teachers from Francophone and Anglophone schools.

Science teachers worked together, in collaboration with the research team, to study and adapt existing assessment items from various sources, such as the American Advancement of Science (AAAS) and other conceptual inventories focusing on different science concepts for instructional purposes. Other practitioners and researchers can access the assessment item bank and the prevalent alternative conceptions in science available on the AAAS site. The assessment items were organized in accordance with the Progression of Learning goals and the four Worlds (i.e., the Material World, the Living World, Earth and Space, and the Technological World) in the QEP. The Ministry of Education has organized the learning content included in the QEP for each school subject. Progression of Learning goals guide teachers' instructional plans regarding the content that students are required to learn in a particular year. A distinctive feature of our project is that teachers and science education consultants from partner school boards played a key role in adapting existing, and developing new, assessment questions. The content validity of the questions was established by content experts in STEM disciplines. For example, scientists and engineers examined the questions relevant to their expertise in physics, chemistry, biology, technology, and earth and space science. Selected questions were also piloted by the teachers in their classrooms to elicit students' thinking about different natural phenomena, to ascertain the readability level, and to gather students' feedback on the clarity of the questions. The questions were further refined in light of this feedback. The questions were developed in French and English and addressed most of the essential concepts in science and technology included in the curriculum.

3. Methods

This paper presents selected technology assessment questions that teachers can to elicit their students' initial understandings of principles of engineering and technical design and to plan their instruction in response to students' alternative ideas. Notably, the development of technology items is an innovative contribution of this project. While the literature offers a vast amount of assessment items and conceptual inventories focusing on science (physics, chemistry, biology, geology, astronomy) concepts to diagnose students' misconceptions and to inform science instruction, there is a dearth of appropriate and efficient assessment tools to examine and track students' understanding of engineering and technology concepts. Science teachers often rely on rubrics to assess their students' technology skills during and after instruction. It is essential to gain an understanding of students' alternative ideas to effectively address their prior ideas through instruction. In this article, we share a set of questions related to specific technology concepts (e.g., forces and motion, simple machines, and technological systems) that were developed by practitioners and academics in science and technology education during our collaborative professional development model.

As noted earlier, the technology assessment items addressed common difficulties that the teachers and technology consultants had encountered while teaching technology concepts and skills to their students. More specifically, the distractors incorporated prevalent misconceptions of students which the teachers had discovered in their classrooms (all questions are in a multiple-choice format). The science teachers and consultants who participated in this collaborative project developed an efficient assessment tool using the multiple-choice format to elicit their students' intuitive notions. They can use assessment items creatively in their classrooms. For example, teachers could initiate a discussion in the classroom to encourage their students to further explain their reasoning and to become aware of the ideas that they bring to the classroom.

Engineering and technology experts reviewed these assessment items to establish content validity. Furthermore, the project team reviewed, revised, and refined these assessment questions in several face-to-face meetings, item by item, with the aim of achieving consensus about these questions. The technological concepts in these items were aligned with the Progression of Learning goals in the science and technology curriculum in the QEP. Afterwards, all items from the consensus version were translated from English into French by a native French bilingual speaker who was a doctoral student at the Faculty of Education Sciences, Université du Québec à Montréal. The translations were reviewed by two technology education experts who were also bilingual speakers and had extensive experience of teaching science and technology in primary and secondary schools in Québec. The final translations were reviewed once again by the third author to compare and check for any discrepancies in the French and English versions. When differences were noticed, the most appropriate wording for the Québec context was jointly agreed upon by the third author and the technology education experts. The final version was then given to the project team teachers to examine the clarity and appropriateness of these items for secondary students.

The questions that are presented in this paper cover the topics of forces and motion, manufacturing, technological systems, and engineering. These items were administrated to Secondary Cycle One students via GoogleForm in selected public Francophone and Anglophone schools in Quebec. In total, the questions were answered by 126 students in grades seven and eight (37 Francophone and 89 Anglophone students). The technology items and students' responses are presented below. Importantly, our analysis illuminates students' intuitive reasoning in relation to basic technology concepts and problems. If these intuitive ideas are not probed and addressed upfront in the classroom, they can continue to interfere with students' learning. We hope that science teachers and teacher educators can use these questions to elicit their students' intuitive understandings of technology, to inform their pedagogical decisions to address intuitive or alternative conceptions, and to examine changes in students' conceptions before and after instruction. These questions will also help teachers assess the ways in which students apply scientific concepts to solve technological problems.

4. Analysis of Students' Intuitive Conceptions of Technological Systems

Herein, we present responses to selected questions to illuminate students' conceptions of technology and technological systems. Students' responses reveal several areas that science and technology teachers need to focus on, when designing their lessons on technology, to foster a meaningful understanding of engineering-based technology in students.

4.1. Intuitive Notions of Technology and Technical Objects

The majority of the Secondary Cycle One students in our sample seemed to understand the difference between natural and designed objects (see Figure 1a). Around 90% of the students identified the natural objects which are not altered by human beings. However, a few still thought that a glass bottle and a granite countertop are made of materials that are not changed by humans. Students were also asked to identify the technical objects in the question below. Interestingly, only about a quarter of the students thought that a pencil, a knife, and a smart phone are technical objects (see Figure 1b). Approximately half of the students only considered a smart phone as a technical object. It seems that many students tend to think that complex electronic products are technical objects, whereas simple and commonly used technical objects are not considered as technological products.

Another question revealed students' notions about the characteristics of technical objects (see Figure 2a). Only about a quarter of the students thought that a technical object is conceived and manufactured by humans and meets one or more needs, where as many students thought that using electricity is an important characteristic of technical objects. Similarly, when asked what technology is, approximately 30% of the students associated electricity with technology (see Figure 2b). Only less than half of the students understood technology as a process used in making a technical object. More than 15% of the students also thought that technology means machines that are used for communication. Interestingly, some students perceived technology as the use of computers only. Students' intuitive understanding of technology seems to be influenced by the pervasive use of electronic devices, such as computers, tablets, smart phones, etc.

Assessment Item	Student Responses
Pick the group of objects that are made of materials which are not altered by human beings. A. Glass bottle, Granite countertop, Seashells B. Glass bottle, Sand, Pine cone C. Sand, Pine cone, Seashells D. Granite countertop, steel nail, Pine cone	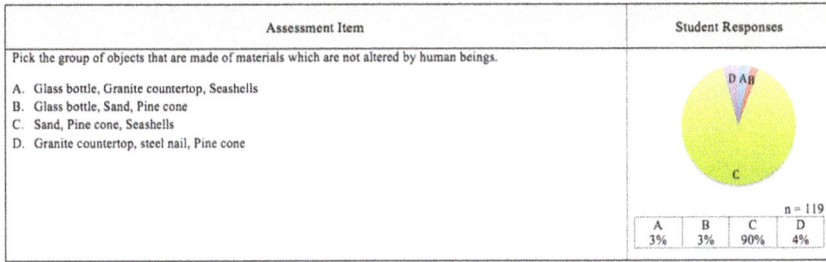 n = 119

A	B	C	D
3%	3%	90%	4%

(**a**)

Assessment Item	Student Responses
Which one of the following can be considered a technical object? I. a pencil II. a knife III. a smart phone A. I only. B. II only. C. III only. D. I and II. E. I, II and III.	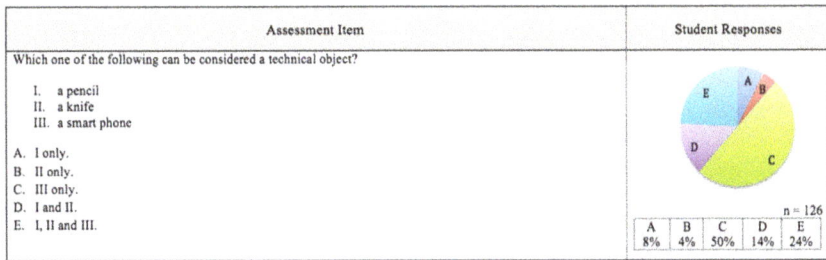 n = 126

A	B	C	D	E
8%	4%	50%	14%	24%

(**b**)

Figure 1. Students' Notions of Technical Objects. (**a**) Technical vs. Natural Objects; (**b**) Technical Objects.

Assessment Item	Student Responses
A technical object always has the following characteristics: I. Meets one or more needs II. Conceived by humans III. Uses electricity IV. Manufactured by humans V. Has two or more parts A. I and II B. III, IV and V C. I, II, and IV D. III and V E. II and IV	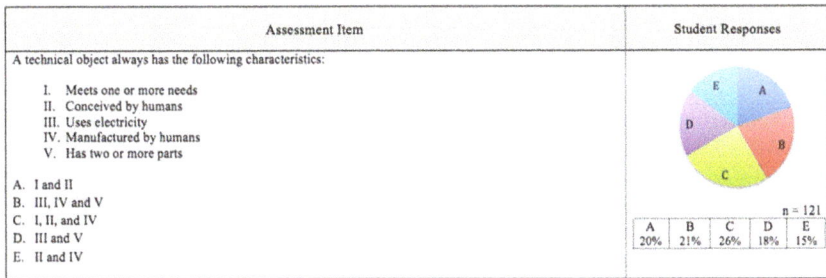 n = 121

A	B	C	D	E
20%	21%	26%	18%	15%

(**a**)

Assessment Item	Student Responses
What is technology? A. Something that uses electricity. B. A process used in making a technical object. C. The use of computers. D. Machines that communicate with each other.	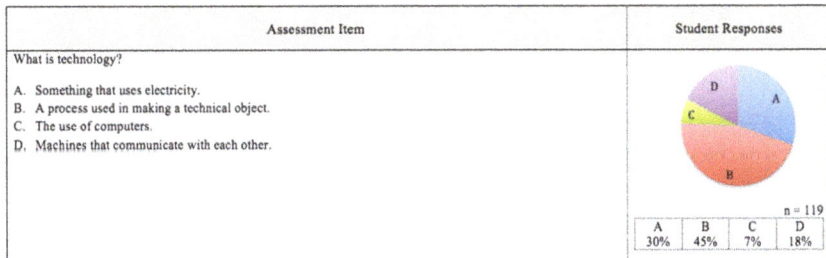 n = 119

A	B	C	D
30%	45%	7%	18%

(**b**)

Figure 2. Students' Notions of the Characteristics of Technical Objects. (**a**) Technical Objects and their Characteristics; (**b**) Technology.

4.2. Intuitive Notions of Simple Machines

While children's and adult's alternative conceptions about scientific phenomena have been well documented in the literature, a few studies have looked at children's mechanistic reasoning in relation to technological systems. Developing students' mechanistic and logical reasoning is central to K–12 STEM curricula (MELS, AAAS, NGSS). It is important to explore children's mechanistic reasoning as it illuminates how they understand the cause and effect relationships and underlying mechanisms in technological systems. In addition, mechanistic reasoning reveals how they make sense of the relationship between the structure and function of a technical object or a mechanical device. Simple machines, such as gears and pulley systems can serve as useful tools to explore children's mechanistic reasoning. A better understanding of children's reasoning about the mechanisms underlying these systems can help to develop a robust understanding of advanced concepts, such as mechanical advantage, torque, ratio in students [14,16]. Another advantage of gears and pulleys is that students can directly observe their arrangement and how they transmit motion. Furthermore, a thorough investigation of how these simple machines work can also foster the development of students' understanding of cause and effect relationships. The development of causal reasoning would enable students to understand more complex systems and their underlying mechanisms [14].

The majority of the students in this study (over 82%) correctly represented the motion of the gears in a gear system. Only about 18% had alternative ideas about the direction of the movement (see Figure 3). Similarly, when responding to the following two questions (see Figure 4a,b), 90% of the students correctly indicated the direction of movement in a simple gear system, which suggests that, based on their perceptual experiences, students are intuitively able to understand and make correct predictions about the motion of gears.

However, when asked about the rate of speed of gears with different number of teeth (and size), about two-thirds of the students demonstrated alternative conceptions about the rotational speed of a gear set (see Figure 5). On the other hand, one-third of the students had an intuitive understanding of how gear ratios work in terms of their speed of rotation. Calculating the gear ratio based on the number of teeth on a gear to predict an increase or reduction in the rotational speeds of gears in a system is a basic concept in mechanical engineering [52]. The pulley is an important simple machine. Pulleys serve to change the direction and decrease the amount of the force that is needed to move an object. Pulleys help in lifting heavy objects and are used in buildings, flagposts, boats, bicycle gears, elevators, cranes, etc.

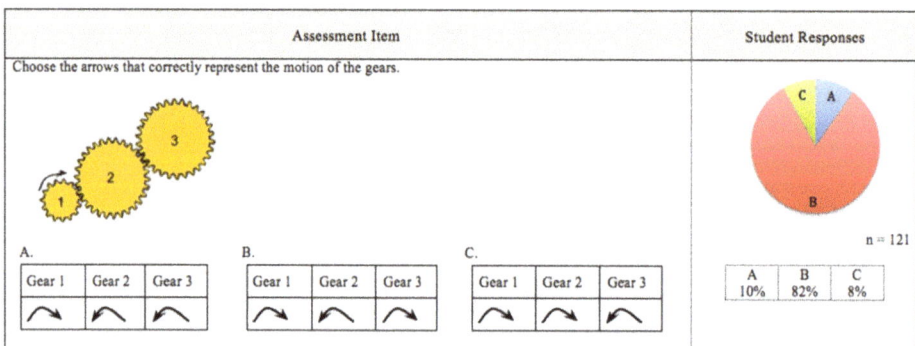

Figure 3. Students' Intuitive Notions of Simple Machines.

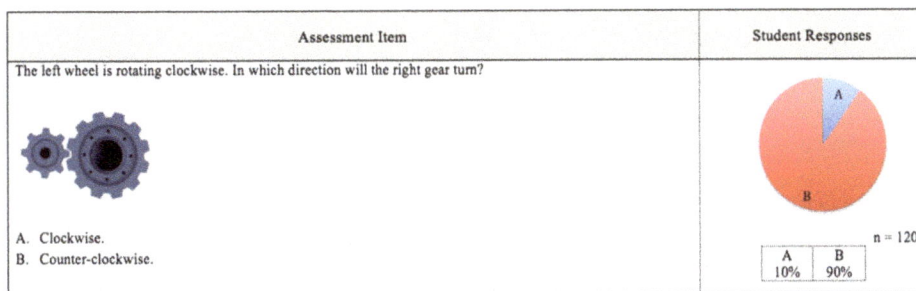

(a)

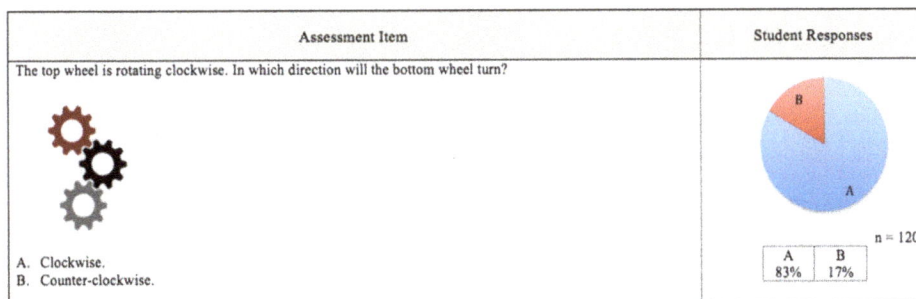

(b)

Figure 4. Students' Notions of the Motion of the Gears in a Gear System. (**a**) Direction of Movement in a Gear System; (**b**) Rotation in a Gear System.

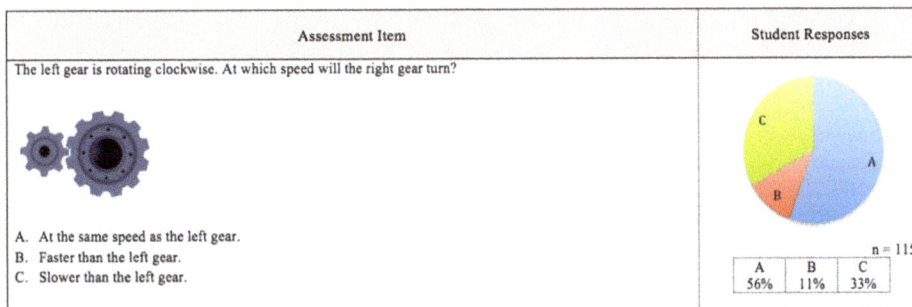

Figure 5. Students' Notions of the Rotational Speed of a Gear Set.

When asked to explain why the elastic band was crossed in a pulley system, approximately, 29% of the students said that it changes the direction of rotation (see Figure 6a). About 71% students, however, demonstrated their alternative conceptions while responding to this question. They thought that the elastic was crossed to add to tension to the elastic or to reduce the speed of the movement. In the same way, about 31% of the students intuitively explained that different sizes of pulleys are used in a pulley system to change the speed of the movement (see Figure 6b). The majority of the students, however, had alternative ideas about the function of size as they thought that different sizes of pulleys help in changing the tension or the direction of the movement.

Assessment Item	Student Responses
Why was the elastic crossed in the following pulley system: A. To add tension. B. To reduce speed. C. To change the direction of rotation. D. To solidify the system.	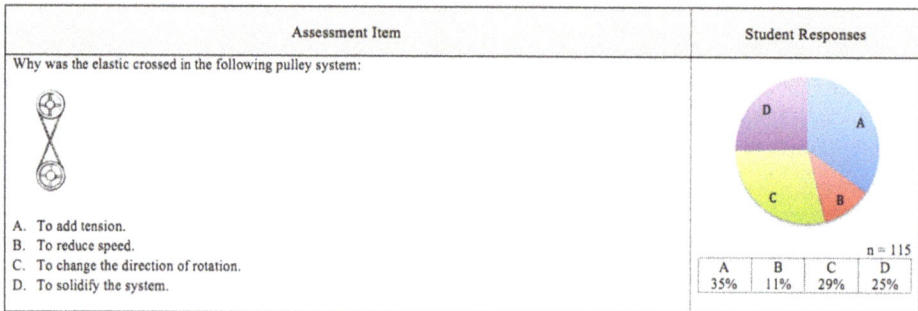 n = 115 A 35% | B 11% | C 29% | D 25%

(a)

Assessment Item	Student Responses
Why are pulleys of different sizes used in a pulley system? A. because they are the only ones available. B. to change the tension. C. to change the direction of the rotation. D. to change the speed of the movement.	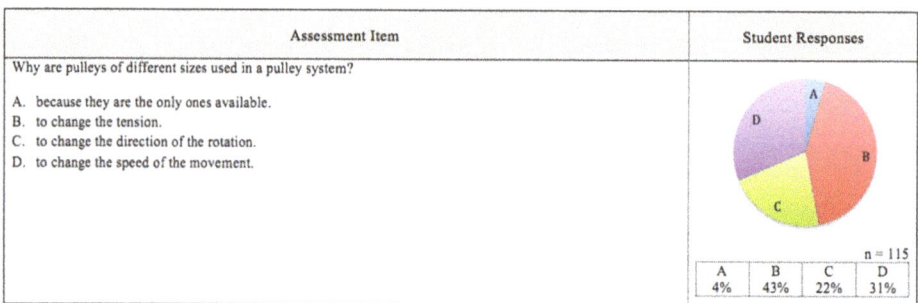 n = 115 A 4% | B 43% | C 22% | D 31%

(b)

Figure 6. Students' Notions of a Pulley System. (**a**) Arrangement of a Pulley System; (**b**) Pulley Size.

4.3. Intuitive Notions of Force and Motion in Technological Design

The QEP science and technology curriculum seeks to develop students' understanding of the effects of forces on simple machines and the "mechanisms that transmit motion (e.g. gears, pulleys, endless screw) and those that bring about a change in motion (e.g. cams, connecting rods)" [5] (p. 247). Learning about forces and different types of motion would enable students to understand how simple machines work. We used the following items to elicit students' initial ideas about forces and motion in relation to technical objects and simple machines.

One item asked the students to identify the forces applied by the user when using pliers (see Figure 7a). The majority of the students (85%) correctly identified the forces that are used on the pliers. Students own experiences with scissors and pliers may have contributed to their understanding. Students were also asked to identify the path of a tip when closing the pliers (see Figure 7b). Students' responses revealed their struggle with identifying the path of the tip as shown below. Only one-fourth of the students were able to visualize the curved path of the tip.

Secondary students in grades seven and eight are expected to develop a qualitative understanding of the concept of mechanical advantage that different simple machines offer (see Figure 8). The following question asked students to determine the set-up that would provide the best mechanical advantage. Less than one-half of the students responded correctly. Additionally, students' responses to items focusing on different types of motion elicited their alternative ideas. For example, when asked to identity rectilinear/translation motion in some real-life situations, some students (17%) thought that a child on a swing is moving in a straight line (see Figure 9). It is also interesting that 33% of the students did not think that the movement of an elevator is in a straight line.

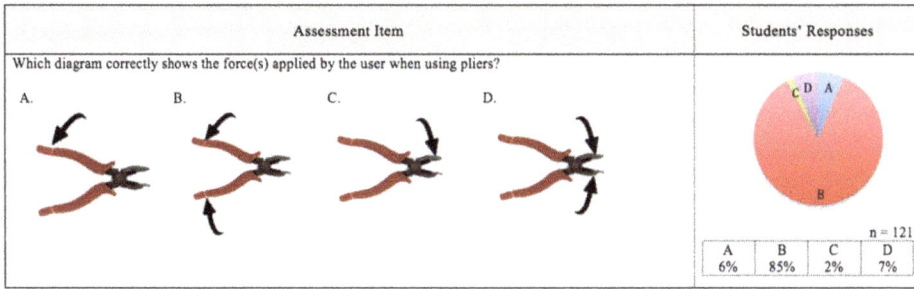

(a)

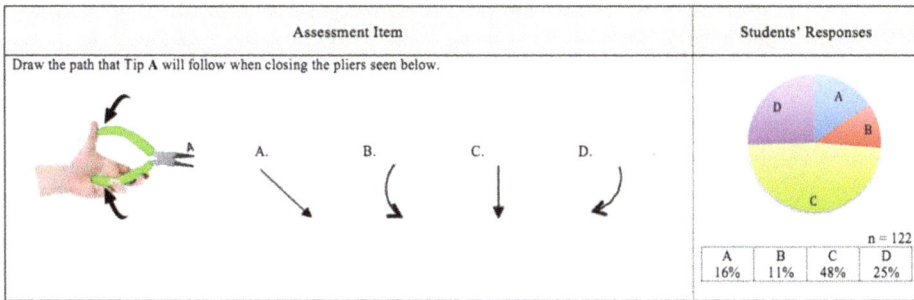

(b)

Figure 7. Students' Notions of Force and Motion in Technological Design. (**a**) Forces Acting on Pliers; (**b**) Direction of Movement in a Plier System.

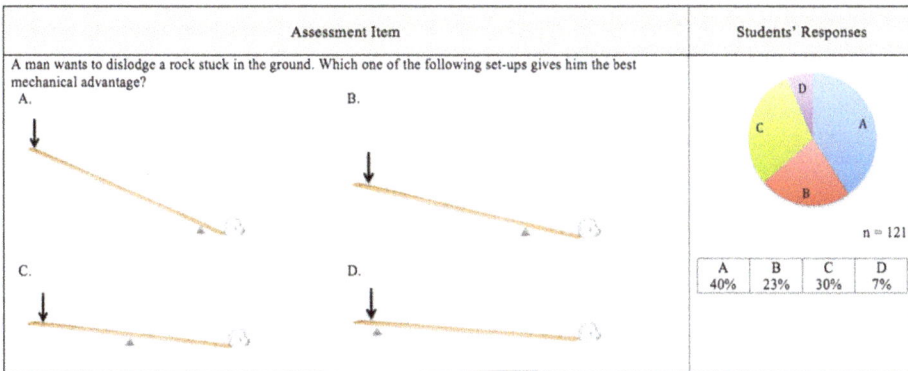

Figure 8. Students' Notions of Mechanical Advantage in Technological Design.

Assessment Item	Students' Responses
Which situation is an example of the motion that the object is moving along a straight line (rectilinear/translational motion)? I. A bowling ball rolling in the gutter II. A child swinging on a swing III. An elevator moving up to the 3rd floor A. I only. B. II only. C. III only. D. I and II. E. I and III.	 n = 119

A	B	C	D	E
16%	9%	30%	8%	37%

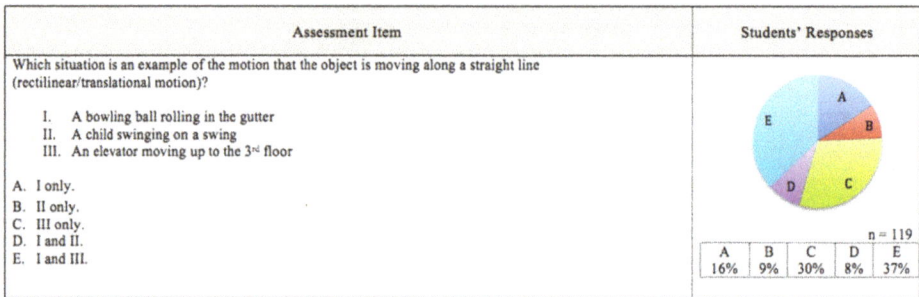

Figure 9. Students' Notions of Rectilinear/Translation Motion.

When asked to indicate an example of rotational motion, 23% of the students thought that a child sliding down a hill is exhibiting rotational motion (see Figure 10). Although approximately one-half of the students identified the Ferris Wheel as an example of rotational motion, many students (70%), did not think of the motion of a swing as rotational motion. While 36% of the students identified the movement of a bicycle's frame as translational motion, approximately 64% described it as only rotational or helicoidal motion (see Figure 11). A bicycle is a complex technological system and teachers can use it to elicit their students' understanding of the movement of different parts of a bicycle.

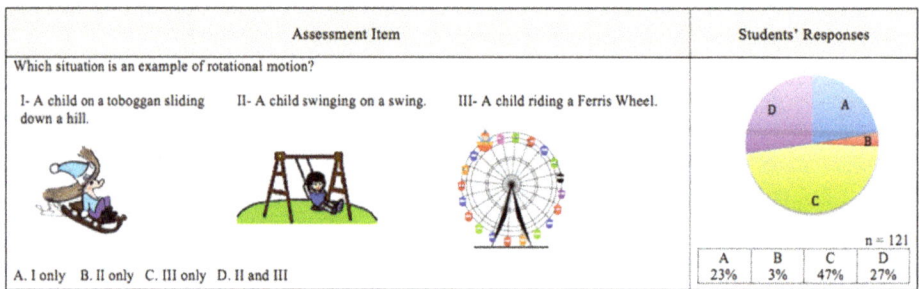

Assessment Item	Students' Responses
Which situation is an example of rotational motion? I- A child on a toboggan sliding down a hill. II- A child swinging on a swing. III- A child riding a Ferris Wheel. A. I only B. II only C. III only D. II and III	 n = 121

A	B	C	D
23%	3%	47%	27%

Figure 10. Students' Notions of Rotational Motion.

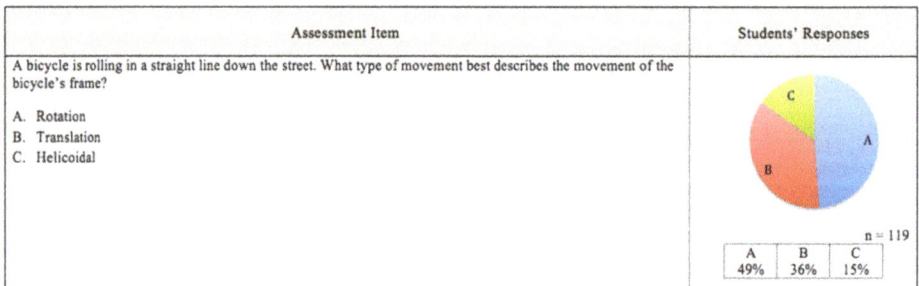

Assessment Item	Students' Responses
A bicycle is rolling in a straight line down the street. What type of movement best describes the movement of the bicycle's frame? A. Rotation B. Translation C. Helicoidal	 n = 119

A	B	C
49%	36%	15%

Figure 11. Students' Notions of Motion in Technological Design.

5. Discussion and Implications for Pedagogy

Our analysis revealed that students had a number of alternative ideas about basic concepts of technology. For example, some students did not understand the difference between the objects that exist naturally and those that are designed by human beings. Furthermore, many students thought that only electronic devices, such as a smart phone, are technical objects, whereas commonly used technical objects in our daily lives are not considered technological products. It seems that students' intuitive perception of technology is influenced by the pervasive use of electronic devices, as many students believed that technical objects need electricity. The majority of these students were intuitively able to understand and make correct predictions about the motion of gears. However, many students had alternative conceptions about the rotational speed of a gear set. While less than one-third of the students understood that the purpose of using different sizes of pulleys in a pulley system is to change the speed of the movement. Nevertheless, the majority of the students were not able understand the relationship between the pulley size and speed. At the same time, many students had alternative conceptions about the concept of mechanical advantage. The findings also suggest that students had difficulties in identifying the differences between different types of motion, such as rectilinear/translation motion and rotational motion. Science and technology teachers need to carefully consider these alternative conceptions while designing and teaching their lessons.

As noted earlier, based on the vast literature on children's intuitive conceptions and conceptual change approach to science teaching, it is critically important for science educators to elicit and carefully consider the intuitive ideas and conceptual resources that their students bring to learning situations to construct meaningful science learning experiences for students. As diSessa points out, ignoring students' conceptions and "sense of mechanism in instruction" creates an unwarranted wall between prior knowledge and scientific understanding," which may lead to alienation of students [23] (p. 206).

As discussed earlier, students' existing conceptions seem to be fairly stable and may co-exist with the scientific models that they learn through formal science instruction. Mounting evidence for the co-existence of alternative and scientific conceptions suggests that "abandoning or altering initial conceptions might not necessarily happen during conceptual learning" [38] (p. 57). Thus, instead of using the "conceptual replacement" approach, science educators need to focus on strengthening students' understanding of accepted scientific models and supporting students in carefully considering and choosing contextually appropriate models to solve problems [35] (p. 389). Dawson suggests that developing learners' "metacognitive abilities" is key to this process [35]. As Dawson explains:

> . . . learners must be made aware that different interpretations of a situation may be possible. They then actively contrast different views by deciding what each would say about a set of phenomena, comparing these predictions and, where possible, testing them against actual outcomes. Importantly, this step is aimed at keeping the views differentiated, with the sphere of application of each being explored and practised. This step aims to develop the metacognitive abilities to select the appropriate view for the context, and inhibit any others, for, as Duschl and Hamilton (1998) concluded from their review of literature, from both the history and philosophy of science and from psychological perspectives, context is fundamental when one is considering new learning and its application. [35] (p. 410)

The conceptual change model proposed by Posner and colleagues [53,54] also recognizes the resilience of children's prior conceptions and focuses on meaningful changes in their prior conceptions by testing them while solving problems, thereby assessing the strengths and limitations of their intuitive conceptions in terms of learning the scientific conceptions, and applying the concepts to comprehend and solve problems. Thus, students must be consciously aware of their intuitive conceptions in the face of complex problem-solving challenges, and use the scientific models to explain, predict, and solve problems [28,34].

Building on this approach, Windschitl and colleagues recommend the model-based inquiry (MBI) approach to engage learners in sharing, testing, and revising their intuitive explanatory models through scientific inquiries [55] (p. 941). The model-based inquiry approach focuses on encouraging students to examine their explanatory models based on evidence, assessing their models in terms of their explanatory adequacy and predictive power, evaluating these models using criteria such as accuracy and plausibility, refining and modifying the explanatory models, and using them to solve new problems [55,56]. Importantly, the model-based inquiry approach emphasizes deep connections between scientific models and processes and the nature of science [57] (p. 42). Engaging students to deeply reflect on their intuitive understandings in relation to accepted scientific concepts may facilitate conceptual change. More specifically, during scientific investigations, students should be encouraged to challenge their intuitive ideas by testing their hypotheses, developing evidence-based explanations by carefully considering the data that they have collected, and deliberatively engaging with their explanations in relation to the accepted models [58–60]. As such, authentic scientific and technology inquiries in school science can facilitate active construction and application of scientific knowledge, and also promote a meaningful "understanding of the nature of science" [55] (pp. 944–945).

Several instructional strategies to promote conceptual change have been reported in the literature, such as discrepant events to expose the limitations of students' existing models, problem-based learning approaches, and inquiry-based activities to foster student engagement in the active construction of their knowledge [28,34,59]. Evidence suggests that active engagement of students in problem-based STEM inquiries is crucial for developing a deeper understanding of accepted scientific and technological models through inquiry, exploration, and application of knowledge [37,46,61–64]. Sanger and Greenbow (2000) conducted a study with introductory college chemistry students using the conceptual change model developed by Posner and colleagues to look at the impact of this instructional approach on students' alternative conceptions about the flow of electrons in aqueous solutions of electrochemical cells [65]. Students in the conceptual change instruction group were given the opportunity to discuss and test some prevalent alternative explanations about these concepts as well as the scientifically accepted explanation using experimental demonstrations. This study showed that the conceptual change instruction was effective in addressing students' intuitive notions. Similarly, Weaver's (1998) study with elementary and secondary students showed that collaborative hands-on experiments combined with dialogue, discussion, and deep reflection on learning can promote conceptual change. K–12, and even college students, face difficulties in distinguishing between pure substances, heterogeneous mixtures, or homogeneous mixtures [66,67]. González-Gómez and colleagues (2017) carried out a study with elementary students to investigate the efficacy of conceptual change and laboratory instruction on these intuitive ideas. Students' intuitive models were elicited using a pre-test to inform subsequent instruction [66]. An interactive presentation on these concepts was followed by a hands-on lab session in which students worked in small groups to classify various materials, prepared different homogeneous or heterogeneous mixtures classify, and recorded their observations. The teacher guided the students to compare their initial knowledge with scientific explanations. In this process, students recognized that they needed to adapt their intuitive conceptions to develop a coherent scientific model to understand the composition of matter. The researchers argue that the conceptual change instructional approach is useful in promoting the construction and application of scientific models. Thus, teachers need to carefully select effective interventions that address students' alternative conceptions [28,63,64].

Based on this literature and our work with science and technology teachers during this project, we share the following steps that teachers can use to foster their students' engagement and learning in STEM. Teachers can use these assessment questions to inform instruction to facilitate the development of a deeper understanding of accepted scientific concepts in students. In particular, the intuitive conceptions that we discovered around technology, technical objects, and simple machines during this study provide useful information to teachers to develop and adapt specific activities to address their students' alternative conceptions about these foundational technology concepts.

- Elicit students' prior knowledge and initial ideas about natural and technological phenomena.
- Discuss students' responses with them and probe their ideas further to encourage them to articulate and share their explanatory frameworks.
- Encourage students to attend to each other's ideas and explanations.
- Choose appropriate inquiry-based activities to address students' alternative conceptions.
- Engage students in inquiries that encourage them to solve specific problems related to technological systems by asking questions, designing experiments to test their hypotheses, collecting data, and developing evidence-based explanations through making sense of data.

For example, teachers can encourage students to work with actual technical objects and simple machines to identify their functional components, represent the organization and operation of different components through visual diagrams, analyze the effects of forces acting on different parts of simple machines, and look at the mechanisms that transmit motion.

- Support students to compare their intuitive explanatory frameworks to accepted scientific and technological models.
- Provide a wide range of opportunities in different contexts to encourage students to apply their emerging understandings of scientific and technological models.

Given the paucity of research on alternative conceptions of technology, this study has explored middle school students' notions of basic technology concepts. Developing the assessment items to examine these foundational concepts entailed considerable effort on the part of the project team. Therefore, we were not able to explore advanced technology and engineering design related concepts. We only used the multiple-choice assessment questions in this study due to time and curricular constraints in science classrooms. Other creative assessment strategies, such as students' drawings, demonstrations, and think-aloud interviews with individual or small groups of students were not employed. It is important that future studies investigate the sophisticated and complex concepts included in the technology curriculum. Science educators and researchers can work collaboratively to develop a comprehensive tool using different assessment formats to explore students' ideas about all the technology concepts that are included in K–12 science curricula. Future research also needs to focus on the effectiveness of interventions that target technology and engineering concepts.

Author Contributions: A.A.'s contribution entailed conceptualization, literature review, funding acquisition, supervision, article writing and editing. Y.-S.H. assisted with data collection and analysis, literature review, and co-wrote the paper. K.E. contributed to the development of the assessment items, reviewed and wrote about the science and technology curriculum in Quebec and reviewed the drafts. Y.S. contributed to data analysis.

Funding: This research was funded by Ministère de l'Éducation et de l'Enseignement supérieur (MEES) Chantier 7 programme.

Acknowledgments: We thank our colleagues from Université du Québec à Montréal (UQAM) and McGill University who provided their insights and expertise that greatly assisted this work. We also thank Philip Ritchie and Jan Novak, members of the Science and Technology Implementation Committee (STIC) in Quebec, for assistance with the development of the items. We would also like to express our gratitude to the project team teachers and science consultants for sharing their pearls of wisdom with us during the course of this project.

Conflicts of Interest: The authors declare no conflict of interest. The funders had no role in the design of the study; in the collection, analyses, or interpretation of data; in the writing of the manuscript; or in the decision to publish the results.

References

1. Ministère de l'Éducation, du Loisir et du Sport. *Québec Education Program: Secondary Cycle Two*; Gouvernement du Québec, Bibliothèque et Archives nationales du Québec: Montréal, QC, Canada, 2007; ISBN 978-2-550-49674-8.

2. Ministère de l'Éducation, du Loisir et du Sport. *Québec Education Program*; Gouvernement du Québec, Bibliothèque nationales du Québec: Montréal, QC, Canada, 2001; ISBN 2-550-37958-6.

3. Charland, P.; Fournier, F.; Potvin, P. *Apprendre et Enseigner la Technologie*; MultiMondes: Montreal, QC, Canada, 2009.

4. Hasni, A.; Lenoir, Y.; Alessandra, F. Mandated interdisciplinarity in secondary school: The case of science, technology, and mathematics teachers in Quebec. *Issues Interdiscip. Stud.* **2015**, *33*, 144–180.

5. American Association for the Advcancement of Science. *Science for All Americans: Project 2061*; Oxford University Press: New York, NY, USA, 1993.

6. Council of Ministers of Education. *Canada Common Framework of Science Learning Outcomes K to 12: Pan-Canadian Protocol for Collaboration on School Curriculum*; Council of Ministers of Education: Toronto, ON, Canada, 1997.

7. DeCoito, I. STEM education in Canada: A knowledge synthesis. *Can. J. Sci. Math. Technol. Educ.* **2016**, *16*, 114–128. [CrossRef]
8. Roth, W.M. Learning science through technological design. *J. Res. Sci. Teach.* **2001**, *38*, 768–790. [CrossRef]
9. Tala, S. Unified view of science and technology for education: Technoscience and technoscience education. *Sci. Educ.* **2009**, *18*, 275–298. [CrossRef]
10. Waight, N.; Abd-El-Khalick, F. Nature of Technology: Implications for design, development, and enactment of technological tools in school science classrooms. *Int. J. Sci. Educ.* **2012**, *34*, 2875–2905. [CrossRef]
11. Barma, S.; Guilbert, L. *Different Visions de la Culture Scientifique et Technologique*; Gouvernement du Québec, Bibliothèque nationales du Québec: Montréal, QC, Canada, 2006; ISBN 2-550-41725-9.
12. Ministère de l'Éducation, du Loisir et du Sport. *Québec Education Program: Secondary Cycle Two*; Gouvernement du Québec, Bibliothèque nationales du Québec: Montréal, QC, Canada, 2004; ISBN 2-550-42071-3.
13. Bolger, M.S.; Kobiela, M.; Weinberg, P.J.; Lehrer, R. Children's mechanistic reasoning. *Cogn. Instr.* **2012**, *30*, 170–206. [CrossRef]
14. DiGironimo, N. What is technology? Investigating student conceptions about the nature of technology. *Int. J. Sci. Educ.* **2011**, *33*, 1337–1352. [CrossRef]
15. Lehrer, R.; Schauble, L. Reasoning about structure and function: Children's conceptions of gears. *J. Res. Sci. Teach.* **1998**, *35*, 3–25. [CrossRef]
16. Brophy, S.; Klein, S.; Portsmore, M.; Rogers, C. Advancing engineering education in P–12 classrooms. *J. Eng. Educ.* **2008**, *97*, 369–387. [CrossRef]
17. Progression of Learning in Secondary School. Available online: http://www1.education.gouv.qc.ca/progressionSecondaire/domaine_mathematique/science/index_en.asp?page=universTechnoligique (accessed on 15 November 2018).
18. Capobianco, B.M. Exploring a science teacher's uncertainty with integrating engineering design: An action research study. *J. Sci. Teach. Educ.* **2011**, *22*, 645–660. [CrossRef]
19. Driver, R. Students' conceptions and the learning of science. *Int. J. Sci. Educ.* **1989**, *11*, 481–490. [CrossRef]
20. Osborne, R.; Freyberg, P.S.; Bell, B. *Learning in Science: The Implications of Children's Science*; Heinemann: Auckland, New Zealand, 1985.
21. Yeo, S.; Zadnik, M. Introductory thermal concept evaluation: Assessing students' understanding. *Phys. Teach.* **2001**, *39*, 496–504. [CrossRef]
22. Babai, R.; Amsterdamer, A. The persistence of solid and liquid naive conceptions: A reaction time study. *Int. J. Sci. Educ. Technol.* **2008**, *17*, 553–559. [CrossRef]
23. DiSessa, A. Toward an epistemology of physics. *Cogn. Instr.* **1993**, *10*, 105–225. [CrossRef]
24. Driver, R.; Asoko, H.; Leach, J.; Scott, P.; Mortimer, E. Constructing scientific knowledge in the classroom. *Educ. Res.* **1994**, *23*, 5–12. [CrossRef]
25. Halloun, I.A.; Hestenes, D. The initial knowledge state of college physics students. *Am. J. Phys.* **1985**, *53*, 1043–1055. [CrossRef]
26. Peterson, R.F.; Treagust, D.F. Learning to teach primary science through problem-based learning. *Sci. Educ.* **1998**, *82*, 215–237. [CrossRef]
27. Baser, M. Fostering conceptual change by cognitive conflict based instruction on students' understanding of heat and temperature concepts. *Eurasia J. Math. Sci. Technol. Educ.* **2006**, *2*, 96–114. [CrossRef]
28. Potvin, P. Proposition for improving the classical models of conceptual change based on neuroeducational evidence: Conceptual prevalence. *Neuroeducation* **2013**, *1*, 16–43. [CrossRef]
29. Potvin, P.; Sauriol, É.; Riopel, M. Experimental evidence of the superiority of the prevalence model of conceptual change over the classical models and repetition. *J. Res. Sci. Teach.* **2015**, *52*, 1082–1108. [CrossRef]
30. Duit, R.; Treagust, D.F. Conceptual change: A powerful framework for improving science teaching and learning. *Int. J. Sci. Educ.* **2003**, *25*, 671–688. [CrossRef]
31. Gilbert, J.K.; Osborne, R.J.; Fensham, P.J. Children's science and its consequences for teaching. *Sci. Educ.* **1982**, *66*, 623–633. [CrossRef]
32. Liu, X.; Lesniak, K.M. Students' progression of understanding the matter concept from elementary to high school. *Sci. Educ.* **2005**, *89*, 433–450. [CrossRef]
33. Novak, J.D. Meaningful learning: The essential factor for conceptual change in limited or inappropriate propositional hierarchies leading to empowerment of learners. *Sci. Educ.* **2002**, *86*, 548–571. [CrossRef]

34. Kang, H.; Scharmann, L.C.; Kang, S.; Noh, T. Cognitive conflict and situational interest as factors influencing conceptual change. *Int. J. Environ. Sci. Educ.* **2010**, *5*, 383–405.
35. Dawson, C. Towards a conceptual profile: Rethinking conceptual mediation in the light of recent cognitive and neuroscientific findings. *Res. Sci. Educ.* **2014**, *44*, 389–414. [CrossRef]
36. Eryilmaz, A. Effects of conceptual assignments and conceptual change discussions on students' misconceptions and achievement regarding force and motion. *J. Res. Sci. Teach.* **2002**, *39*, 1001–1015. [CrossRef]
37. Libarkin, J.C.; Anderson, S.W. Assessment of learning in entry-level geoscience courses: Results from the Geoscience Concept Inventory. *J. Geosci. Educ.* **2005**, *53*, 394–401. [CrossRef]
38. Potvin, P. The Coexistence claim and its possible implications for success in teaching for conceptual "change". *Eur. J. Sci. Math. Educ.* **2017**, *5*, 55–66.
39. Caravita, S.; Halldén, O. Re-framing the problem of conceptual change. *Learn. Instr.* **1994**, *4*, 89–111. [CrossRef]
40. National Research Council. *Inquiry and the National Science Education Standards: A Guide for Teaching and Learning*; National Academies Press: Washington, DC, USA, 2000.
41. Piaget, J. Part I: Cognitive development in children: Piaget development and learning. *J. Res. Sci. Teach.* **1964**, *2*, 176–186. [CrossRef]
42. Driver, R. *Children's Ideas in Science*; McGraw-Hill Education: Maidenhead, UK, 1985.
43. Harlen, W. Primary school science: The foundation of science education. *Phys. Educ.* **1987**, *22*, 56–62. [CrossRef]
44. Brook, A.; Briggs, H.; Driver, R. *Aspects of Secondary Students' Understanding of the Particulate Nature of Matter*; Centre for Studies in Science and Mathematics Education, University of Leeds: Leeds, UK, 1984.
45. Solomon, J. Learning about energy: How pupils think in two domains. *Eur. J. Sci. Educ.* **1983**, *5*, 49–59. [CrossRef]
46. Libarkin, J.C.; Asghar, A.; Crockett, C.; Sadler, P. Invisible misconceptions: Student understanding of ultraviolet and infrared radiation. *Astron. Educ. Rev.* **2011**, *10*, 010105-1–010105-12. [CrossRef]
47. Asghar, A.; Libarkin, J.C. Gravity, magnetism, and "down": Non-physics college students' conceptions of gravity. *Sci. Educ.* **2010**, *19*, 42.
48. Fetherstonhaugh, T.; Treagust, D.F. Students' understanding of light and its properties: Teaching to engender conceptual change. *Sci. Educ.* **1992**, *76*, 653–672. [CrossRef]
49. Liou, P.Y. Developing an instrument for assessing students' concepts of the nature of technology. *Res. Sci. Technol. Educ.* **2015**, *33*, 162–181. [CrossRef]
50. Capobianco, B.M.; Feldman, A. Repositioning teacher action research in science teacher education. *J. Sci. Teach. Educ.* **2010**, *21*, 909–915. [CrossRef]
51. Loiselle, B. Actualiser l'enseignement des sciences par l'apprentissage de la technologie. In *Apprendre et Enseigner la Technologie: Regards Multiples*; Éditions MultiMondes: Montreal, QC, Canada, 2009.
52. Williams, K. *Gear Down for Speed*; Polytechnic Institute of NYUL: New York, NY, USA, 2009.
53. Posner, G.J.; Strike, K.A.; Hewson, P.W.; Gertzog, W.A. Accommodation of a scientific conception: Toward a theory of conceptual change. *Sci. Educ.* **1982**, *66*, 211–227. [CrossRef]
54. Strike, K.A.; Posner, G.J. A revisionist theory of conceptual change. In *Philosophy of Science, Cognitive Psychology, and Educational Theory and Practice*; State University of New York Press: Albany, NY, USA, 1992; pp. 176–185.
55. Windschitl, M.; Thompson, J.; Braaten, M. Beyond the scientific method: Model-based inquiry as a new paradigm of preference for school science investigations. *Sci. Educ.* **2008**, *92*, 941–967. [CrossRef]
56. Schwarz, C.V.; White, B.Y. Metamodeling knowledge: Developing students' understanding of scientific modeling. *Cogn. Instr.* **2005**, *23*, 165–205. [CrossRef]
57. Neilson, D.; Campbell, T.; Allred, B. Model-based inquiry. *Sci. Teach.* **2010**, *77*, 38.
58. Chinn, C.A.; Brewer, W.F. The role of anomalous data in knowledge acquisition: A theoretical framework and implications for science instruction. *Rev. Educ. Res.* **1993**, *63*, 1–49. [CrossRef]
59. Weaver, G.C. Strategies in K-12 science instruction to promote conceptual change. *Sci. Educ.* **1998**, *82*, 455–472. [CrossRef]
60. Windschitl, M.; Andre, T. Using computer simulations to enhance conceptual change: The roles of constructivist instruction and student epistemological beliefs. *J. Res. Sci. Teach.* **1998**, *35*, 145–160. [CrossRef]

61.   Millar, R. *Analysing Practical Science Activities to Assess and Improve Their Effectiveness*; Association for Science Education: Hatfield, UK, 2010.

62.   Tao, P.K.; Gunstone, R.F. The process of conceptual change in force and motion during computer-supported physics instruction. *J. Res. Sci. Teach.* **1999**, *36*, 859–882. [CrossRef]

63.   Harlen, W. *Primary Science: Taking the Plunge. How to Teach Science More Effectively for Ages 5 to 12*; Heinemann Publishing: Portsmouth, NH, USA, 2001.

64.   Asghar, A.; Bean, S.; O'Neill, W.; Alters, B. Biological evolution in Canadian science curricula. *Rep. Natl. Cent. Sci. Educ.* **2015**, *35*, 1.1–1.21.

65.   Sanger, M.J. Using particulate drawings to determine and improve students' conceptions of pure substances and mixtures. *J. Chem. Educ.* **2000**, *77*, 762–766. [CrossRef]

66.   González-Gómez, D.; Airado-Rodríguez, D.; Acedo, M.A.D.; Niño, L.V.M. Change in elementary school students' misconceptions on material systems after a theoretical-practical instruction. *Int. Electron. J. Elem. Educ.* **2017**, *9*, 499–510.

67.   Treagust, D.F.; Duit, R. Conceptual change: A discussion of theoretical, methodological and practical challenges for science education. *Cult. Stud. Sci. Educ.* **2008**, *3*, 297–328. [CrossRef]

education
sciences

MDPI

Article

Secondary Science Preservice Teachers' Perceptions of Engineering: A Learner Analysis

Trina J. Kilty [1],* and Andrea C. Burrows [2]

[1]   School of Counseling, Leadership, Advocacy, & Design, University of Wyoming, 1000 E. University Ave., Laramie, WY 82071, USA
[2]   School of Teacher Education, University of Wyoming, 1000 E University Ave, Laramie, WY 82071, USA; Andrea.Burrows@uwyo.edu
*   Correspondence: tkilty@uwyo.edu

Received: 30 November 2018; Accepted: 24 January 2019; Published: 29 January 2019

check for updates

Abstract: The purpose of this study was to describe how US secondary science preservice teachers, or those preparing to teach middle and high school science, at one university, perceive engineering and teaching engineering within an epistemological framework of required domain components pre- and post-instruction (intervention) as well as over three cohort years. Their perceptions reveal relevant prior beliefs helpful for designing instruction to address an external need to prepare secondary science teachers to teach disciplinary content ideas, cross-cutting concepts, and science and engineering practices to meet the Next Generation Science Standards. Questionnaires administered pre- and post-instruction (intervention), as well as over three years, asked participants to decide whether various scenarios qualified as engineering and then to provide reasoning. Intervention instruction included whole-class discussions of engineering design practices. The responses to the questionnaire were analyzed for thematic content. The results indicate that the secondary science preservice teachers (n = 43) have a novice understanding of engineering and teaching engineering. They gain an emerging understanding during the secondary science methods courses, consistent in all three years with expanding perspectives from narrow discipline views. As their perceptions are refined, however, there are risks of oversimplification, which may lead to forming misconceptions. The recommendations for designing instruction such as secondary science methods courses and early career professional development include creating opportunities for preservice and early career teachers to explore and challenge their perceptions of engineering design practices integrated within science and engineering practices.

Keywords: engineering education; preservice teacher beliefs; perceptions; secondary science; NGSS; learner analysis; K-12 teachers

1. Introduction

Science teaching in United States (US) K-12 schools is undergoing a change. With many states adopting the Next Generation Science Standards (NGSS) [1], most science teachers need to teach science and engineering practices (SEP) as well as cross-cutting concepts, in addition to disciplinary core ideas and concepts [1]. This change represents an *innovation*, something that is new to science teachers [2]. Science teachers should incorporate engineering design practices as the NGSS are implemented. Engineering design, however, differs from science inquiry practices [3]. A working definition of *engineering design practices* (EDP) has been described as "(a) defining and delimiting engineering problems; (b) designing solutions to engineering problems; and (c) optimizing the design solution" [1] (p. A2). EDP differs from SEP in that SEP typically investigates a natural phenomenon, while EDP focuses on designing and building systems [1]. The two share a teaching goal of hands-on practices to deepen and apply knowledge of scientific principles. In order to design and develop instruction for secondary science preservice teachers to prepare them to teach incorporating the NGSS in their science classrooms, it is important for researchers to describe what perceptions are held toward engineering. In this study, preservice teachers are students seeking teaching certification, and some have obtained previous science, technology, engineering, and mathematics (STEM) degrees. The *innovation* in this study is defined as the use of the NGSS, SEP section, which asks teachers to integrate EDP with science when planning, implementing, and assessing student learning. Implementation of the NGSS establishes an external need for instruction regarding teaching engineering [4]. An innovation may provide a need to design instruction [5]. Instruction may provide learners logical and compelling reasons to adopt the innovation [2]. Understanding learners, or *learner analysis*, is the first step towards designing instruction to address the innovation [5]. The participants in this study are the subject of the learner analysis and, for clarity, will be referred to as participants or secondary science preservice teachers rather than learners. The participants in this study are defined as three secondary science preservice teacher cohort groups from 2015–2017 (*n* = 43). *Instruction* in this study is defined as coursework, including secondary science teaching methods and professional development, that encompasses a variety of learning strategies and learner-centered activities. Secondary science teaching methods are two courses that are considered capstone courses, along with student teaching residency, before gaining teaching certification. The *learner context* setting is secondary science methods courses implemented at a research university in the Rocky Mountains of the US. Figure 1 showcases how this study fits within an instructional design innovation model.

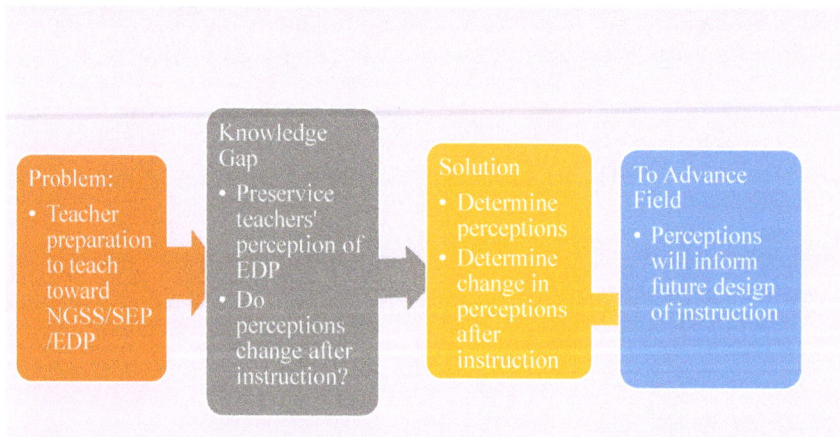

Figure 1. Overview of this study from statement of the problem and knowledge gap to the solution and advancement of the education field.

The purpose of this study was to describe how US secondary science preservice teachers, or those about to be certified to teach middle and high school science, at one university, perceive engineering and teaching engineering within an epistemological framework of required domain components pre- and post-instruction (intervention) as well as over three cohort years. An instructional design framework was used to place this study in terms of *learner analysis* and *need for instruction* [5]. This study describes perceptions, based on prior knowledge and beliefs that are refined after instruction, that are useful for designing instruction including methods courses and early in-service professional development for teachers.

1.1. Background

Like engineering, instructional design ideally begins with a problem that may be solved. In this case, the problem is how to effectively prepare secondary science preservice teachers to teach EDP. Instructional designers try to solve the problem by developing instruction to fill a gap in knowledge. One of the first steps in designing instruction is to know the audience, in other words, the characteristics of the learners within their context. Learner characteristics may be classified by similarities and differences in participants and whether those similarities and differences are stable or change over time [5]. Values, beliefs, motivations, and interests are considered to be changing differences among participants, influenced and shaped by experiences [5]. Perceptions toward engineering and toward teaching engineering may fit best into a changing difference, as perceptions are influenced by experience in life and in coursework. Secondary science preservice teachers craft these perceptions into a *belief* about what engineering is and how it is defined. This may be considered an *epistemological* belief about a disciplinary field and what knowledge that field encompasses. Their beliefs may exert some influence on how they will teach EDP. Figure 2 displays the study situated in an instructional design problem and solution.

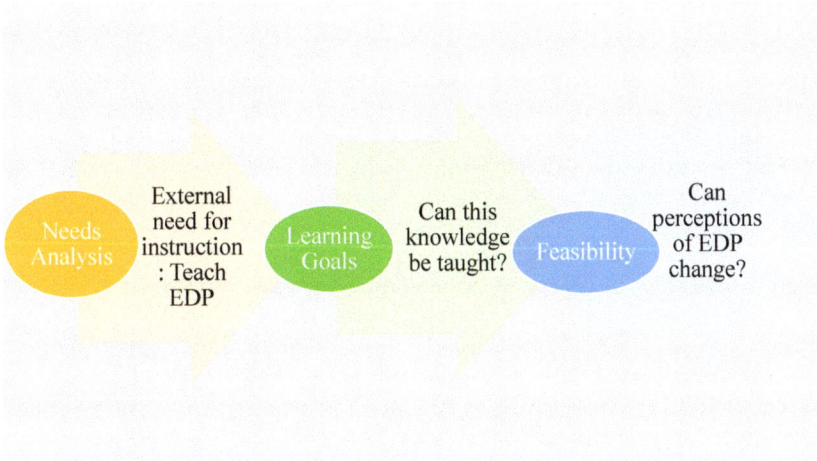

Figure 2. Innovation needs analysis model and the situation of this study within it [5].

The EDP domain and teaching engineering may be something secondary science preservice teachers never thought they would need to teach. However, the context of engineering education can be traced back to *Science for All Americans: Project 2061*, which explained the importance of a scientifically literate population able to make informed decisions based on familiarity with science and engineering practices [6]. The NGSS formally combined science with engineering into the SEP [1]. STEM communities are writing engineering and computer science standards in several states with implementation to follow shortly [1]. Because of these standards, it is important for preservice science teachers to prepare to incorporate engineering instruction and raise awareness of engineering career opportunities, which can also include computer science instruction.

Research communities have debated whether to incorporate standalone engineering standards for K-12 or to integrate engineering into science standards. Prior to the NGSS, several states included EDP in their science curriculum [7]. Some researchers proposed a framework for including standalone engineering courses that complemented a firm foundation in math and science [8], but others proposed a framework in which engineering was integrated into existing STEM courses [9]. Some have criticized the NGSS as only including EDP in the standards, not providing a complete picture of the engineering domain or focusing on the nature of engineering [10]. The NGSS do not include engineering disciplinary core ideas in the standards, but rather focus on integrating EDP into SEP. Integrated STEM classes should align with the NGSS, as the SEP portion of the NGSS combines science and engineering as one integrated process [1]. Although adoption of the NGSS and its integrated curriculum may settle the matter in some states, not all states have adopted the standards, or a variation of the standards [11]. Researchers have recommended the integration of engineering with other STEM disciplines in teacher training, primarily because teachers "differed widely on what they considered engineering to be" and "how they implemented engineering concepts" [12] (p. 9). One plan for science teacher preparation is to focus on the integration of engineering within existing STEM classes, especially science and technology, as opposed to planning to teach standalone engineering courses [13]. This plan allows preservice teachers to gain familiarity with the NGSS science and engineering integration framework as they prepare to begin teaching.

Thus, professional development for in-service teachers is important and needed to teach the NGSS integration skills. Throughout the US, professional development (PD) opportunities at all teaching career levels have been offered to facilitate implementation of the NGSS (i.e., encourage adoption of the innovation) and prepare teachers to teach EDP. Although the purpose of many professional developments is the adoption of an innovation, actual behavior change—changing practices in the classroom—must occur, and this is not always the case [14]. Professional development (PD) in teaching engineering for in-service teachers often includes instruction on fundamental content knowledge, essential pedagogical principles, and challenges for implementation [15]. The focus on content may come at the expense of emphasizing process and at the expense of developing strategies for adopting an innovation. Interpersonal skills, pedagogical applications of engineering, and reflective discussion have historically been rare activities in engineering professional development [15]. In recent years, however, progress has been made towards incorporating these activities [16–18]. These activities may be incorporated into secondary science methods courses to help secondary science preservice teachers socially construct their beliefs with peer support before entering their first classroom to teach. A preemptive approach of addressing the innovation earlier, such as in secondary science methods courses, may help adoption by refining perceptions before teachers begin teaching.

1.1.1. Epistemology of Engineering Design Practices

Secondary science preservice teachers' beliefs about engineering and teaching engineering are part of an overarching epistemological belief about knowledge and knowing about engineering as a discipline and how it relates to other disciplines. Epistemological knowledge of a domain such as engineering may encompass beliefs, perceptions, and ways of knowing to shape understanding [19]. Domain knowledge consists of declarative, procedural, and conditional knowing [19]. The researchers of this study asked participants to use procedural knowledge of the engineering domain to determine if a given scenario fits into an engineering domain and to explain their reasoning. Procedural knowledge is an intellectual skill learned in part through the *spread of activation* such as reminding the participant of prior knowledge, prior experience, or of acquaintances [20]. The spread of activation may cause secondary science preservice teachers to relate EDP to a science content domain with which they are more familiar.

Secondary science preservice teachers' prior experiences and domain knowledge in other content areas may influence their epistemological beliefs and practice regarding EDP. In one study, in-service teachers who began teaching after a career in science attached importance to aspects of science that were valued at their previous careers [21]. For example, a former lab technician prioritized precision in data collection, analysis, and interpretation during classroom activities. Ways of knowing about a knowledge domain, namely engineering, may relate to one's domains of expertise, or major content area, but precisely how epistemological knowledge of a familiar domain influences beliefs of a less familiar domain has not been explored in detail [19]. Data analysis, for example, is one area where prior knowledge in a science domain may affect reasoning [22]. Content domain knowledge in a science or mathematics discipline influences how a person interprets evidence [22]. Further research is needed to explore post-baccalaureate preservice teacher perceptions of teaching science and engineering in the classroom [21]. The authors believe that the participants of this study, because more than half in each cohort year were post-baccalaureates, present a sample that are in keeping with the research recommendations of Antink-Meyer and Brown [21]. Perceptions regarding data analysis represent another avenue deserving of study.

Knowledge of EDP as a domain is a prerequisite skill needed for lower, novice stages of learning before the expert (mastery) stage [20]. In this study, demonstration of novice to expert learning may be the recognition of different facets of the EDP domain by reasoning through examples and nonexamples. One characteristic of expert, as opposed to novice, is that knowledge is "the recognition of meaningful patterns of information . . . organized around core concepts" [23] (p. 36). Researchers characterize experts as having an "elaborateness of understandings" while novices may use recall to reason through a problem requiring knowledge domain [23] (p. 41). Instruction during a college course may facilitate progress toward mastery by helping preservice teachers organize their knowledge in meaningful patterns and apply general components of engineering to specific teaching and learning scenarios they will encounter during teaching.

The path to expert knowledge, however, is full of pitfalls. There is a danger that preservice teachers may develop misconceptions about EDP and teaching engineering and bring the misconceptions into the classroom. Four misconceptions held by teachers about engineering were identified in a previous study: (a) research methods in engineering are defined by long-term implications or outcomes, (b) science and engineering is hierarchal, (c) creativity is appropriate only in the design/planning phase, and (d) an engineering process cannot be a research outcome [24]. Because preservice teachers may not have prior coursework in engineering and may be unfamiliar with engineering, they may already hold or may develop a number of misconceptions about epistemology of engineering, such as the four previously mentioned here. In keeping with identified areas of need in the literature, Jones and Carter [25] specifically call for research studies that address individuals' patterns of reasoning that differ across content domains.

1.1.2. Instruments to Measure Perceptions

Advances have been made to address the knowledge gap of epistemological beliefs toward engineering. An instrument, entitled Conceptions of Teaching Engineering, was developed from the Conceptions of Teaching Science task [26,27]. Researchers interviewed in-service teachers and identified initial conceptions of the required components of engineering and teaching engineering [27]. Researchers prepared a list of engineering components to include (a) applications to the real-world; (b) creating or designing a model or product; (c) experimentation and gathering data; (d) conducting background research; (e) revising or optimizing the solution; (f) confronting a challenging, multi-step problem with multiple possible solutions; (g) brainstorming; and (h) communication within the team and to a wider audience [27]. The study explained in this article extends and builds on that work by determining if the identified engineering components replicate in a different group of participants.

Researchers have completed work exploring beliefs and conceptions that teachers hold about engineering. The Design, Engineering, and Technology (DET) instrument asks about items along many constructs, including (a) perceptions of familiarity, self-efficacy, motivation and desire to teach DET; (b) perceived importance of DET to the curriculum and barriers to teaching; (c) perceptions of a typical engineer; and (d) personal characteristics best suited for engineering [28]. The DET instrument was administered to elementary preservice teachers pre- and post-short-course on engineering design [29]. The preservice teachers gained a novice level of procedural knowledge [30]. The researchers in this study did not use the DET instrument because the constructs did not specifically address perceptions of what EDP is and is not.

Teachers need to effectively communicate to their students what a career in engineering entails, and this requires that they form a comprehensive understanding of the engineering field. In a prior study, an instrument was developed to measure in-service teachers' beliefs about students' aptitude for a career in engineering [31]. Although findings revealed teachers placed importance on attributes such as high GPA and advanced math skills, it was not determined what teachers thought was fundamentally required to classify activities as engineering. The recommendations to address this gap included raising awareness among teachers about what engineering is and what engineers do [32]. The aforementioned study focused on in-service teachers; and currently preservice teachers' views are poorly understood.

Other instruments have been developed to approach the problem from different angles. Researchers have asked elementary and middle school students to explain their perceptions of engineering and technology in an instrument containing pictures and images as well as open-ended questions about engineering and technology as defined by the participant [33,34]. While a comparison of perceptions from teacher and student perspectives is outside the scope of this study, it further illustrates the gap in the literature about secondary science preservice teachers' perspectives.

This study examined the domain perceptions that participants held outside of their major focus of study. Examining secondary science preservice teachers' beliefs about engineering partially addresses a recommendation from other researchers that future research determine "epistemological assumptions and patterns of reasoning [that] may differ for individuals across content domains" [25] (Future Research, para. 1). On the basis of this recommendation, the authors of this study identified a gap in the literature regarding how prior knowledge, or knowledge applied from other domains, may influence secondary science preservice teachers' beliefs and future classroom behaviors regarding engineering and teaching engineering. The participants in this study hold or are seeking degrees in science, mathematics, and education and their knowledge has been shaped by various previous knowledge, careers, and experiences.

Using the aforementioned literature gap in *patterns of reasoning*, this study begins to address previous researchers' recommendations by describing secondary science preservice teachers' perceptions of engineering and teaching engineering, many of whom hold degrees outside of the engineering domain. To probe the *patterns of reasoning*, the authors of this study administered a questionnaire to secondary science preservice teachers. The questionnaire items provided a framework for analyzing the participants' responses and formulating the research questions. The authors of this study administered the questionnaire over a period of three years to examine how perceptions may differ over time in different cohorts. Finally, this study placed perceptions of engineering into a *need for instruction* and *learner analysis* portion of an overall instructional design context. The questionnaire was administered both pre- and post-methods instruction to gauge if instruction was effective in changing perceptions and is therefore needed. To address Antink-Meyer and Brown's [21] and Jones and Carter's [25] recommendations, as well as determine if the findings of a previous study would replicate [27], the following research questions were created and examined:

1. How do secondary science preservice teachers describe their perceptions of engineering and teaching engineering within an epistemological framework of required domain components?
2. How do secondary science preservice teachers show changing understanding of engineering and teaching engineering from pre-instruction to post-instruction of secondary science methods course?
3. How do secondary science preservice teachers' perceptions of engineering and teaching engineering trend over three cohort years?

2. Materials and Methods

2.1. Theoretical Framework and Methodology

This study utilized qualitative research to answer the research questions. The framework is of an interpretivist, constructivism theoretical perspective [35]. This study used a subjectivist lens to describe individuals' beliefs and perspectives about a knowledge domain. The methods included the purposeful sampling of a homogeneous group of secondary science preservice teachers taking a capstone course entitled secondary science methods. Data were collected by open-ended written questionnaires and analyzed by textural analysis. The researcher's role was detached, as no conversations occurred while the participants completed the questionnaire. Participants produced the data individually on the questionnaire but had opportunities to discuss and plan for secondary science engineering lessons in the course. This study offers pragmatic validity [35], and readers might find pragmatic validity by determining if the results apply to other learners in other contexts. *Learner analysis* fits into a general instructional design paradigm termed *ADDIE*, which stands for Analysis, Design, Development, Implementation, and Evaluation. Instructional design models follow this overarching paradigm, illustrated in Figure 3 [36]. This study fits into the early stages (A, or analysis) of the instructional design process. Participants described perceptions relevant to their epistemology (learner analysis) and prior knowledge and beliefs (task analysis), which is based on experiences and conceptions regarding EDP and teaching engineering [5]. This study determined if a *need for instruction* existed for teaching engineering and if instruction was effective at changing participants' perceptions. By examining and decomposing prior knowledge and beliefs about EDP and teaching engineering, designers may analyze nuances and changes in understanding, which could focus and direct instruction more effectively [5]. The results from this study can help inform future steps of the instructional design process.

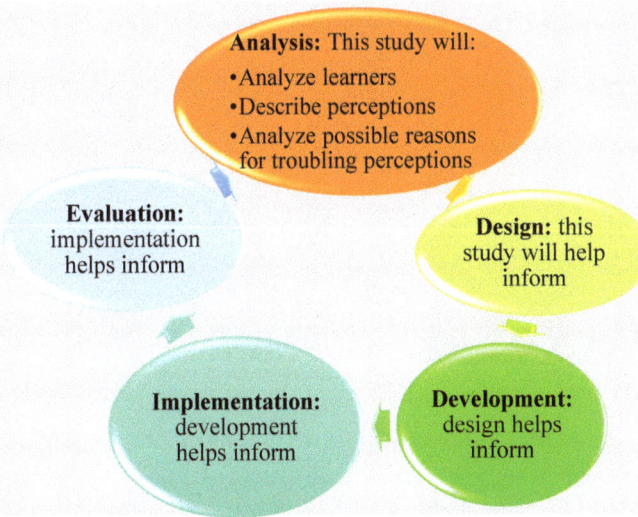

Figure 3. This study fits into the Analysis stage of the general instructional design Analysis, Design, Development, Implementation, and Evaluation (ADDIE) paradigm [36].

Within the general ADDIE paradigm lies an instructional design model to address an innovation and also one to design for motivation. This study fits into the initial stage of designing instruction, the Analysis stage [36]. This study helps inform design for motivation, which would focus on initial stages of relevance through describing prior knowledge and perceptions [20]. The findings gleaned during the analysis stage help inform the next stage of design, which in turn helps inform implementation and evaluation of the instruction, and analysis begins again after examining the evaluation. In this sense, instructional design is an iterative process of optimizing instruction and learning. The goal of informed design is for instruction to be effective. In this case, secondary science preservice teachers would adopt the innovation of teaching engineering design practices integrated with science practices.

2.2. Methods

2.2.1. Participants

The participants were a cohort of secondary science preservice teachers in two secondary science methods courses grouped in academic years for 2015, 2016, and 2017 (three years total). Secondary science preservice teachers typically took secondary science methods courses the semester (fall) before they student taught (spring). After that, they graduated and secured science teaching certification and teaching positions. The two methods courses are a capstone for secondary science education. In this study, each year is considered a cohort where secondary science preservice teachers completed the engineering scenario questionnaire, henceforth referred to as the pre-test, at the beginning of the semester. The same cohort then completed the same engineering scenario questionnaire, henceforth referred to as the post-test, upon conclusion of the courses at the end of the fall semester. All of the participants completed two secondary science education methods courses. Therefore, two required secondary science methods courses, taken concurrently, functioned as the intervention. Table 1 displays the learner characteristics of the participants by cohort year. Not all of the experiences add up to the *n* for each year because many participants held more than one degree conferred in different years, double-majored and/or pursued multiple minors, and/or both substitute-taught and tutored.

Table 1. Participant experiences, 2015–2017, by year.

Year	*n*	Science Degree(s) Held	Science Major(s) and Minor(s)	Years since Degree Conferred	Teaching and/or Tutoring Experience	Informal Teaching Experience	Non-Teaching Work Experience
2017	11	None (4) BS (7) MS (1)	Life Science (4) Physical Sci. (3) Earth Science (6) Math (1)	N/A (4) < 5 (6) 5–10 (1)	None (4) Substitute Teaching (1) Tutoring (6)	Yes (9) No (2)	Yes (10) No (1)
2016	15	None (5) AS (1) BS (11)	Life Science (9) Physical Sci. (4) Earth Science (6) Engineering (1)	N/A (5) < 5 (7) 5–10 (3)	None (8) Substitute teaching (2) Tutoring (5)	Yes (13) No (2)	Yes (15)
2015	17	None (11) AS (2) BS (4) MS (1)	Life Science (15) Physical Sci. (3) Earth Science (4) Math (1)	N/A (11) < 5 (6)	None (9) Substitute Teaching (5) Tutoring (3)	Yes (14) No (3)	Yes (15) No (2)
Total	43						

Overall, 43 secondary science preservice teachers participated in the study. The number of participants each year ranged from 11 to 17. Of the participants, about 47% were undergraduates who would earn their first degree that next spring; 58% already held degrees ranging from associate degrees to master's degrees; and approximately 12% held two or more degrees. Science degrees, majors, minors, and endorsements were in the general areas of life sciences (65%, typically biology), earth sciences (37%, typically geology), and physical sciences (23%, typically chemistry). The percentages do not add up to 100 because some participants listed more than one major, minor, and/or endorsement. Only one of the 43 total participants held a degree in engineering. Only two participants in different cohorts indicated a double major or minor in mathematics. All participants held a substitute teaching permit, as required by the program, but no one in the three years held a full teaching license with classroom teaching experience. This is not surprising, as the objective of the program is to earn a secondary science teaching certification. Only substitute teaching in K-12 environment was counted as teaching. Experience as an undergraduate teaching assistant at the university was counted as tutoring. For comparison purposes, participants were treated as a homogeneous group by cohort year.

2.2.2. Instrumentation

Data were collected by use of a questionnaire. The instrument, entitled Conceptions of Teaching Engineering (CTE), was developed from the Conceptions of Teaching Science (CTS) task [26,27]. Part two of the questionnaire included six questions inspired by the work that developed a task analysis for determining science and teaching science [26]. While likely inspired by a similar source, the authors of this study were unable to locate the original source of the items in part one. While the scenarios in part one could easily fit into a scientific domain, there was the possibility that participants would articulate differentiation criteria between what appeared to be science and with what they perceived to be engineering. Scenarios were modified to address engineering design practices [27]. Box 1 displays the items on the questionnaire and protocol.

Box 1. Modified Conceptions of Teaching Engineering (CTE) questionnaire [27].

Questionnaire Prompt: The purpose of these scenarios is to determine your thoughts on what makes an activity one where teaching engineering is taking place or not. There are two sets of scenarios that you will be asked to decide and explain whether or not you think that the scenario is an example of "teaching engineering". There are no right or wrong answers.

1. If you cannot tell (MAYBE)—What would you need to know if this is teaching engineering?
2. If YES—What tells you that this is an example of teaching engineering?
3. If NO—What tells you that this is NOT an example of teaching engineering?

Scenario Descriptions: (Part One)

1. Students in a 7th grade mathematics class are working on graphing data. The teacher has student pairs measure their pulse each minute for 10 min while one student jogs in place.
2. Sixth grade science students are studying a unit on earthquakes. The teacher asks students to find the difference between two historical earthquakes using a table involving magnitudes according to the Richter scale.
3. A 4th grade class is doing a project on dinosaurs. A group of students makes a chart that compares the sizes of the five different dinosaurs showing their metric heights and weights.
4. Students are investigating ocean floor depths using data from sonar equipment. They are given the equation $D = 1/2T \times V$, where D = depth in m, T = time in s, V = the speed of sound in water (1535 m/s). The students are then asked to compute ocean floor depths given the time required for sound to be sent and return to an echo sounder.
5. During a unit on the solar system, the teacher asks the students to create a scale model that shows the relative size and distance between the Earth and two other planets.
6. Eighth grade students are investigating crystal formation as the liquid in different solutions evaporates. Students are asked to observe and describe various characteristics of the crystals formed when the liquids evaporate.

Scenario Descriptions: (Part Two)

1. Two students working on slope y-intercept problems for homework from their textbook.
2. A student making fudge.
3. A student is home watching a documentary about building the Hoover Dam in the 1930s.
4. A 10th grade class creates rapid composting columns. The teacher puts out a challenge to the students to create a plan for a community rapid composting plant.
5. In an 11th grade physics class, the students use a rocket kit to build a compressed air rocket.
6. After an accident in the school parking lot, the teacher for an after school enrichment project decides the group should develop a traffic regulation system.
7. After learning about plate tectonics, an 8th grade science teacher has students create toothpick and marshmallow structures then tests their strength on a shake table.
8. A class reads an article about genetically modified foods, and then debates the pros and cons of using technology in food production.
9. A math teacher has students measure the water use by a dripping faucet in a 10 min interval, and then create a linear equation to represent the data.
10. A class trip to an amusement park.
11. Two kids adjust and test their BMX bike seat height to figure out how to get maximum speed going into a jump ramp.

The CTE previously described utilized an interview protocol, and the researchers in the former study verbally interviewed participants and transcribed the interviews [27]. In this study, the authors replaced the interviews with a pencil-and-paper questionnaire. The questions were typed, leaving space for participants to circle yes, no, or maybe as a response and then use additional space to explain or justify their answer. The questionnaires were printed, and the participants hand-wrote their answers. The questionnaires were distributed during class shortly after the class began. In some years, it was as early as the first day that the secondary science methods courses met. The post-tests were administered on the last day methods courses met. The study's authors secured the university's Institutional Review Board approval. Participants gave consent for the study on a separate form and created a unique code to ensure confidentiality.

The participants used procedural knowledge of EDP and teaching engineering to read through the scenario, decide whether the activity met their criteria to classify the scenario as an example of engineering or teaching engineering, and justify their reasoning. Answering the questions called for domain-specific *if-then* intellectual skills, either prior knowledge for the pre-test or after methods class instruction intervention for the post-test [20]. For example, for scenario 9 (measuring water in 10-min intervals and creating a linear equation of the data) participants needed to determine: *if* data collection was sufficient to label it engineering, *then* the answer was yes; *if* the activity gave no further details, *then* what additional activity was necessary to elevate it sufficient to be called engineering; and *if* the activity also required creating an equation, *then* that made it sufficient to label the activity part of the engineering domain.

2.2.3. Intervention Description

Secondary science methods courses served as the instruction intervention for this study. The participants at the university took two methods courses concurrently as part of their capstone instruction. The methods courses were designed to meet the US InTASC standards and Standards for Science Teacher Preparation to include content knowledge and related pedagogy, safety skills, assessment of student learning, learning environments, and professional knowledge and skills [37,38]. The courses included many activities that encouraged the thoughtful integration of SEP including developing and presenting demonstrations, creating and peer-critiquing videotaped micro-teach lessons, creating a professional portfolio of work (edTPA) that incorporated SEP into every lesson, and developing a unit plan that included SEP. The multiple assignments and projects that specify secondary science preservice teachers apply and use SEP are frequently utilized when the participants teach. For example, in the courses, secondary science preservice teachers created learning centers that addressed a misconception in their content area. Middle school students from a nearby school participated in the learning center activity and provided the secondary science preservice teachers authentic feedback for consideration when used in future K-12 science classrooms.

Regarding EDP specifically, instruction and activities varied by cohort year. In year 2015, secondary science preservice teachers completed an activity that used EDP using *Lego Mindstorm Robotics* [4]. During every cohort year, secondary science preservice teachers discussed their own and their future students' perceptions of engineering and teaching engineering as a large group. The science educator presented a slideshow that included a definition of engineering but did not provide a handout of the material. Secondary science preservice teachers were not required to create a separate, standalone project using EDP. Although secondary science preservice teachers in all cohort years created lesson plans that incorporated SEP, most of their projects utilized the science domain. For this study, the intervention common to all three cohort years, which was secondary science methods courses, included large group discussion with embedded explanations of possible future implementation of EDP as well as direct instruction with slideshow visuals defining and explaining EDP.

2.3. Data Analysis

Responses to the questionnaire provided data for qualitative analysis. Participant responses were typed into a spreadsheet and organized pre and post by year. Responses of yes, no, or maybe were tallied from the questionnaire. Data were separated by year and by pre-tests and post-tests. Coding of data into themes were first determined year-by-year and pre/post separately. Next, the themes and numbers of responses in those themes were compared to each other pre and post to look for changes from pre to post in a single year. Finally, the pre and post were combined to compare year-by-year across three years to determine changes over time.

Open-ended reasoning responses were categorized using a priori codes. The codes were developed based on open coding from in-service teacher responses and supported by the work of focus groups composed of professional engineers [27]. Codes were used a priori rather than creating new codes, as the researchers wished to replicate the earlier study with a different group of learners [27]. Also, the researchers tentatively predicted the participants held novice-level knowledge about engineering, given their lack of experience with engineering and teaching engineering. Because the codes from the earlier study were developed from experienced in-service teachers and supported by professional engineers, the researchers considered the codes pragmatically valid [27,35]. Table 2 displays the codes used.

Table 2. Modified code set for the components of engineering [27].

Code Set of Components of Engineering
1. Application/Real-world context
2. Creating a product/design/model
3. Experimentation
4. Background research
5. Revision process
6. Challenge/multistep-problem
7. Brainstorming
8. Communication

The codes represent components of engineering and are not necessarily linear or hierarchal. Participants' *if* reasoning was deemed more informative than the eventual *then* yes, no, or maybe decision about whether the scenario was an example of EDP or teaching engineering. The components of engineering codes align with the NGSS SEP [1]. The unit of analysis was the shortest phrase that expressed a single idea. For example, "building" or "solving a problem" were both coded as *creating a product/design/model*. If the participant used *and* to join related ideas, the response was coded as a *challenge/multistep-problem*. For example, "If they use the chart to compare, or note cause effect, proportions, etc., it could be an engineering project" was coded as *challenge/multistep-problem*. The authors of this study independently coded the responses. Through discussion, the team came to agreement about the classification of data into the codes and emergent codes.

Additionally, a few important themes emerged. Constant comparison between the two researchers elevated these codes into emergent themes [39]. The researchers of this study agreed to specify the emergent themes pertaining to secondary science preservice teachers, namely *teacher role* and *discipline-specific* themes of reasoning. The emergent themes were not part of components of engineering and did not replicate the earlier study [27]. The emergent theme of *teacher role* has some relation to earlier work that analyzed responses in terms of both teacher and student roles in engineering [27]. In this study, responses indicated the teacher needed to play an active role in learning or guide learning, for example, "If the instructor actually explained the engineering of the park". The *discipline-specific* theme emerged based on student responses to why a scenario was or was not engineering. The responses were typically single-words such as "bioengineering" or short phrases such as "sounds more like chemistry to me" without further elaboration.

3. Results

The number of yes, no, and maybe responses were remarkably consistent over three cohort years. Figures 4–6 display the results from the pre-tests and post-tests for each of the three years. Not only did the responses change very little from pre- to post-test, but each year contains roughly the same distribution of responses—yes was answered most frequently, then maybe, then no was answered least frequently. The yes, no, and maybe responses are also consistent with each scenario pre- and post-test over the three cohort years. In other words, no specific scenario saw an appreciable change in yes, no, or maybe responses.

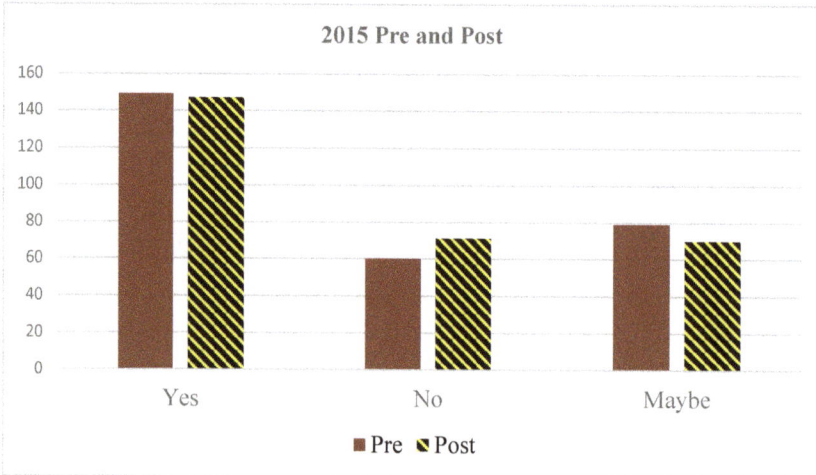

Figure 4. If answers (yes, no, and maybe) given for the scenarios, pre-test and post-test, 2015.

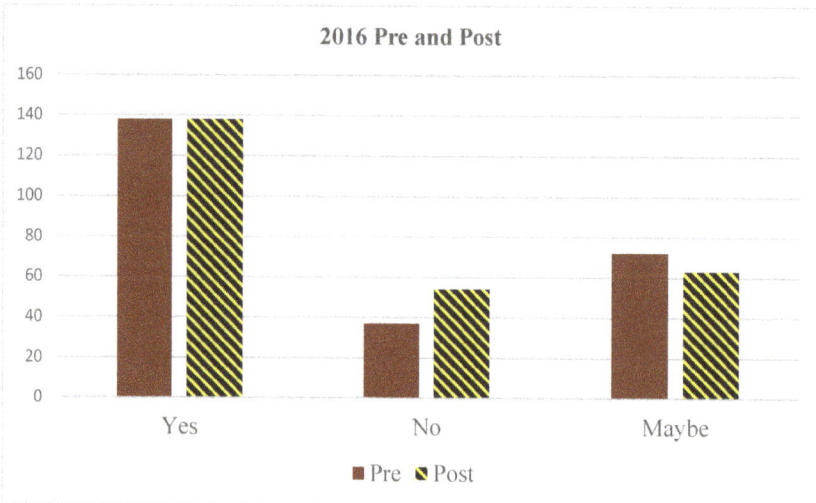

Figure 5. If answers (yes, no, and maybe) given for the scenarios, pre-test and post-test, 2016.

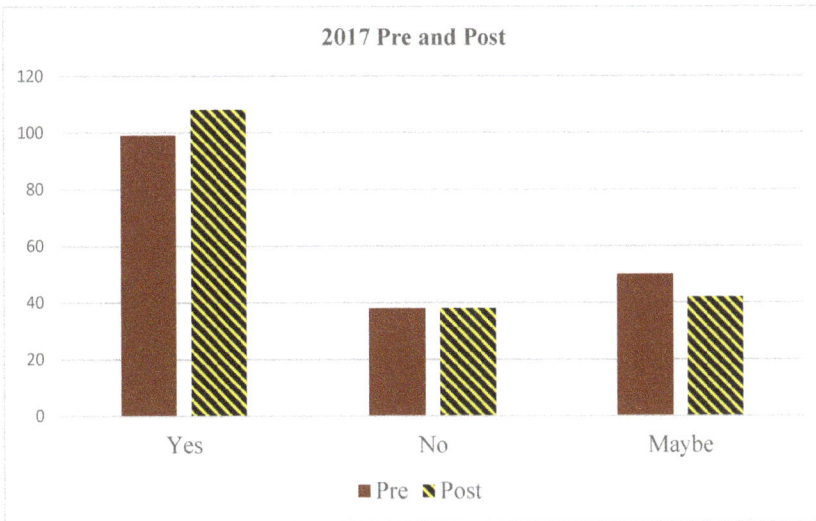

Figure 6. If answers (yes, no, and maybe) given for the scenarios, pre-test and post-test, 2017.

Open-ended reasoning responses were quantified by number of responses using reasoning that fit into one of the components of engineering or one of two emergent themes of reasoning. Overall, *creating a product/design/model* was the most often-used reasoning (554 total responses). The second most often-used reasoning was *challenge/multistep-problem* (312 total responses). The third most often-used reasoning was that engineering needed to have *application/real-world context* (260 total responses). Participants sometimes cited components such as *revision process* (90 total responses), *background research* (75 total responses), and *brainstorming* (42 total responses) as sufficient to be labeled engineering, although often tempered by the wish or constraint that these activities needed to produce something. Participants rarely used the components *experimentation* (28 total responses) and *communication* (19 total responses).

The authors created the aggregate trend column in Table 3 to showcase trends in responses from participants, pre- to post-test, over three cohort years. For example, the number of responses that used *application/real-world context* reasoning decreased from pre- to post-test in each year in all three years of the study. If there was no consistent trend from pre- to post-test in every year, no overall trend was reported.

The results showed a shift in reasoning from the pre-test to the post-test for certain reasonings. *Creating a product/design/model* increased from pre- to post-test over every cohort year and was also the reasoning with the highest total number of responses overall. Participants tended to cite *application/real-world context*, *background research*, and *brainstorming* as components sufficient to classify the activity as engineering less often after methods course completion. However, these decreases were offset by an increase in participants using the reasoning *creating a product/design/model* to solve a problem as a sufficient and necessary component of engineering. Figures 7–9 display the pre-test and post-test reasoning by cohort year.

Table 3. Results of a priori themes and the number of responses, pre-test and post-test, by cohort year.

Theme	Pre	Post	Pre/Post Cohort Trend
Application/Real-world context	57 (2015) 55 (2016) 16 (2017)	44 (2015) 43 (2016) 15 (2017)	Decrease
Creating a product/design/model	83 (2015) 50 (2016) 43 (2017)	121 (2015) 126 (2016) 66 (2017)	Increase
Experimentation	4 (2015) 2 (2016) 7 (2017)	4 (2015) 4 (2016) 2 (2017)	No overall trend
Background research	13 (2015) 9 (2016) 21 (2017)	7 (2015) 9 (2015) 12 (2017)	Decrease
Revision process	24 (2015) 7 (2016) 7 (2017)	16 (2015) 8 (2016) 11 (2017)	No overall trend
Challenge/multistep-problem	43 (2015) 53 (2016) 51 (2017)	45 (2015) 36 (2016) 59 (2017)	No overall trend
Brainstorming	8 (2015) 7 (2016) 9(2017)	5 (2015) 1 (2016) 7 (2017)	Decrease
Communication	6 (2015) 0 (2016) 8 (2017)	2 (2015) 2 (2016) 1 (2017)	No overall trend

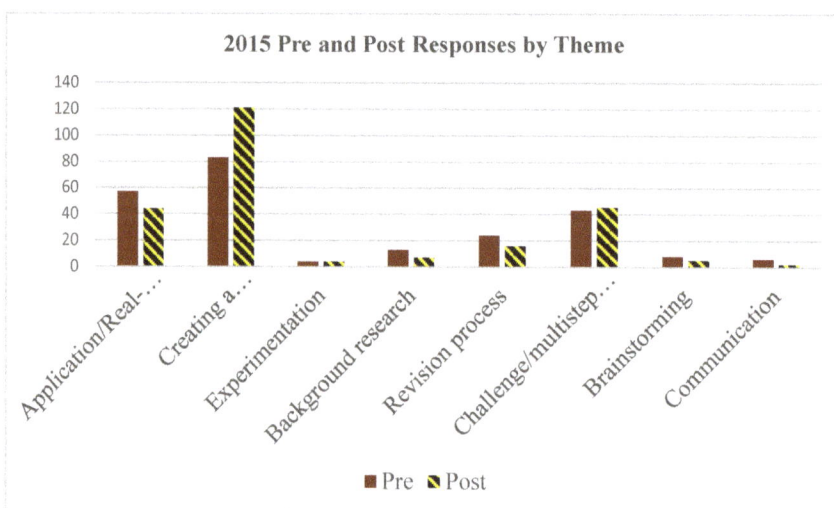

Figure 7. Pre-test and post-test results of the 2015 cohort.

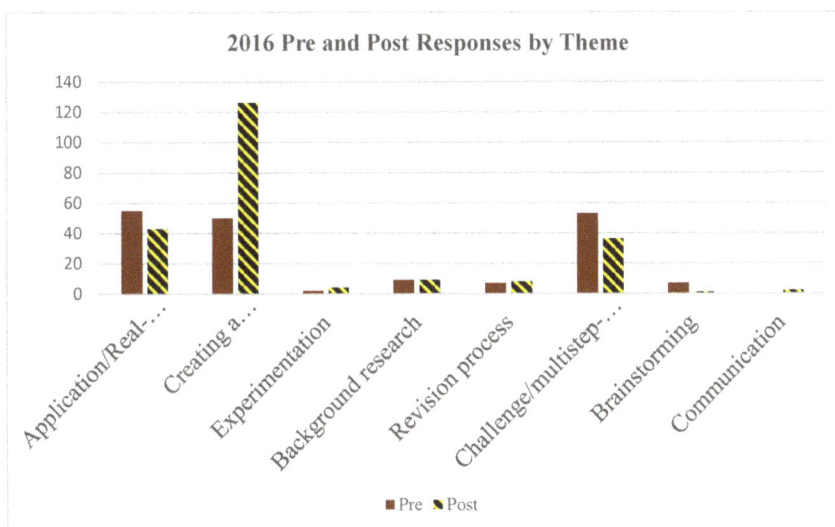

Figure 8. Pre-test and post-test of the 2016 cohort.

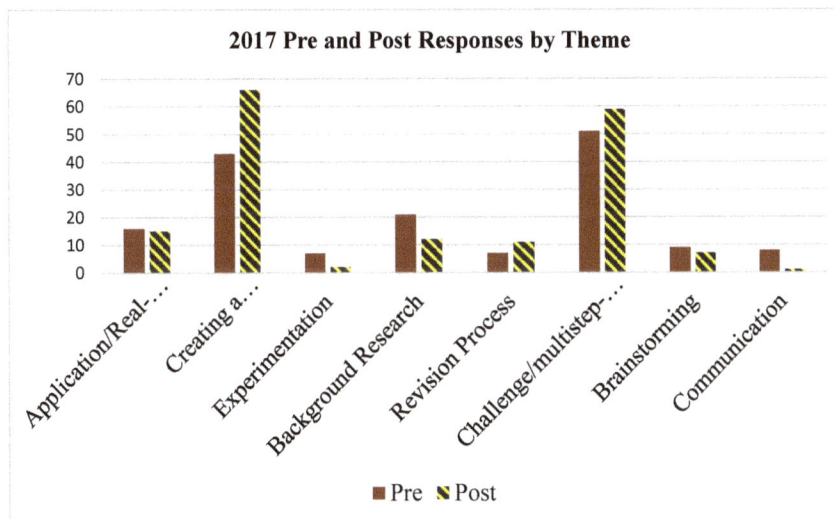

Figure 9. Pre-test and post-test of the 2017 cohort.

Given the high number of *challenge/multistep-problem* reasoning, participants seemed to perceive engineering as a multistep process that involves refining a best solution or design from several possibilities or iterations. Participants were satisfied that if the scenario called for a multistep process, especially if that process involved mathematical reasoning or solving equations, then it was engineering. Participants appeared to rationalize that although planning, data collection, and background research were an integral part of EDP, those components alone were not sufficient to call the activity engineering or an example of teaching engineering.

On the other hand, several participants across cohort years indicated that, in several scenarios, data analysis alone was sufficient for the activity to be considered engineering. There was no trend from pre- to post-test and no overall trend by cohort. As many participants described it, "Yes. Students must understand and interpret graphs" or "Yes. Analysis of data", represented a single necessary and sufficient component in terms of the scenario being classified as engineering. While some participants indicated that this step was one of many steps, others indicated that data analysis alone was considered sufficient to be classified as engineering.

Participants' reasoning was also examined in relation to the scenario questions, and a similar pattern of response to scenario was found consistently over time. One scenario, "A 4th grade class is doing a project on dinosaurs. A group of students makes a chart that compares the sizes of the five different dinosaurs showing their metric heights and weights" (1Q3) revealed that *challenge/multistep-problem* reasoning was used most often pre- to post-test in every cohort year. When participants changed their reasoning in the post-test, typically their responses changed to *creating a product/design/model*, which is consistent with the overall increase of use of that reasoning. Table 4 displays the most often-used reasoning by scenario, pre- to post-test, for each cohort year. The changes from pre- to post-test are highlighted with bar shading.

Table 4. Most often-cited reason given for each scenario by cohort year. Note: The numbers in parenthesis refer to the components of engineering found in Table 2, and the grey bars indicate a change pre- to post-test.

Scenario	Pre-test	Post-test
1Q1	2015: Challenge (#6) 2016: Challenge (#6) 2017: Challenge (#6)	2015: Challenge (#6) 2016: Creating product (#2) 2017: Challenge (#6)
1Q2	2015: Challenge (#6) 2016: Challenge (#6) 2017: Challenge (#6)	2015: Challenge (#6) 2016: Creating product (#2) 2017: Challenge (#6)
1Q3	2015: Challenge (#6) 2016: Challenge (#6) 2017: Challenge (#6)	2015: Challenge (#6) 2016: Challenge (#6) 2017: Challenge (#6)
1Q4	2015: Creating product (#2) 2016: Application (#1) 2017: Challenge (#6)	2015: Creating product (#2) 2016: Application (#1) 2017: Challenge (#6)
1Q5	2015: Creating product (#2) 2016: Creating product (#2) 2017: Creating product (#2)	2015: Creating product (#2) 2016: Creating product (#2) 2017: Creating product (#2)
1Q6	2015: Challenge (#6) 2016: Challenge (#6) 2017: Challenge (#6)	2015: Challenge (#6) 2016: Creating product (#2) 2017: Challenge (#6)
2Q1	2015: Application (#1) 2016: Challenge (#6) 2017: Challenge (#6)	2015: Challenge (#6) 2016: Creating product (#2) 2017: Challenge (#6)
2Q2	2015: Challenge (#6) 2016: Creating product (#2) 2017: Challenge (#6)	2015: Creating product (#2) 2016: Creating product (#2) 2017: Revision process (#5)
2Q3	2015: Background research (#4) 2016: Challenge (#6) 2017: Background research (#4)	2015: Background research (#4) 2016: Creating product (#2) 2017: Challenge (#6)
2Q4	2015: Creating product (#2) 2016: Creating product (#2) 2017: Creating product (#2)	2015: Creating product (#2) 2016: Creating product (#2) 2017: Creating product (#2)
2Q5	2015: Creating product (#2) 2016: Creating product (#2) 2017: Creating product (#2)	2015: Creating product (#2) 2016: Creating product (#2) 2017: Creating product (#2)

Table 4. *Cont.*

Scenario	Pre-test	Post-test
2Q6	2015: Creating product (#2) 2016: Application (#1) 2017: Creating product (#2)	2015: Creating product (#2) 2016: Creating product (#2) 2017: Creating product (#2)
2Q7	2015: Creating product (#2) 2016: Creating product (#2) 2017: Creating product (#2)	2015: Creating product (#2) 2016: Creating product (#2) 2017: Creating product (#2)
2Q8	2015: Application (#1) 2016: Challenge (#6) 2017: Communication (#8)	2015: Creating product (#2) 2016: Creating product (#2) 2017: Creating product (#2)
2Q9	2015: Creating product (#2) 2016: Challenge (#6) 2017: Challenge (#6)	2015: Application (#1) 2016: Creating product (#2) 2017: Creating product (#2)
2Q10	2015: Teacher role (no #) 2016: Application (#1) 2017: Teacher role (no #)	2015: Creating product (#2) 2016: Application (#1) 2017: Teacher role (no #)
2Q11	2015: Revision process (#5) 2016: Revision process (#5) 2017: Revision process (#5)	2015: Revision process (#5) 2016: Creating product (#2) 2017: Revision process (#5)

Overall, when reasoning changed, it changed to *creating a product/design/model*. However, this happened only in some scenarios; for example, in the debate on the pros and cons of genetically modified food (2Q8). Other scenarios gathered remarkably consistent reasoning, such as students building a compressed air rocket from a kit (2Q5) and students building a scale model of the solar system (1Q5). Participants gave consistent reasoning in scenarios that used words common in engineering, such as *scale*, *model*, and *rocket*.

Several participants in all three cohort years changed their reasoning in two scenarios. The two scenarios were the debate about the pros and cons of genetically modified foods (2Q8) and the math teacher who had students measure dripping water and then create a linear equation of the data (2Q9). For the genetically modified food debate, several participants in all three cohort years used *creating a product/solution/model* reasoning in the post-test. Reasoning included, "Not problem solving", and "They are not designing a solution to a need or problem" which is interesting to consider that the participant did not use *communication* reasoning as offering a solution to a problem. For the data collection and graphing of a dripping faucet, pre-test reasoning was that the scenario was too simplistic, "No, just graphing", while the reasoning on the post-test used phrases such as "No problem no product".

Several participants in two of the three years changed their reasoning in three scenarios. The three scenarios included two students working on an assigned slope y-intercept problem for homework from their textbook (2Q1), a student making fudge (2Q2), and a student at home watching a TV documentary about the building of the Hoover Dam in the 1930s (2Q3). While the slope y-intercept problem remained primarily "no", the reasoning changed from that it had no real-world application to that it did not create a product to solve a problem. The reasoning that it was too simple and did not offer a *challenge/multistep-problem* was used in both years. For the scenario of a student making fudge, there was an increase in reasoning that the activity could employ EDP to create or improve the product. This was in contrast to the pre-test, in which some participants viewed the activity as "cooking". Some participants changed their reasoning about the student watching the Hoover Dam documentary scenario, but in both the pre-test and post-test, the reasoning revolved around the activity as the students "not doing anything" or "No problem and no product".

Emergent Reasoning Themes of Secondary Science Preservice Teachers

A line of reasoning emerged during data analysis as that of the *teacher role*. Two reasoning themes that emerged in this study are displayed in Table 5. Several participants indicated that the teacher needed to emphasize the application to the real-world or guide students' thinking, for example, "Maybe. If the instructor can relate the rollercoaster design" and "Maybe. How does the teacher encourage their kids to think about the engineering/design process?" and "Maybe. As long as the teacher doesn't handle everything or make cookie-cutter plans". Others reasoned that a teacher needed to actively ensure learning, such as, "Maybe. If teaching actually occurs". Participants used the *teacher role* reasoning somewhat often (31 total responses) and most often as a response to one scenario, a class trip to an amusement park (2Q9). Use of the *teacher role* theme showed no overall trend over time.

Table 5. Emergent themes pre-test and post-test across cohort groups 2015–2017.

Emergent Reasoning Theme	Pre	Post	Pre/Post and Cohort Year Aggregate Trend
Teacher role	4 (2015) 0 (2016) 13 (2017)	4 (2015) 3 (2016) 4 (2017)	No overall trend
Discipline-specific	28 (2015) 12 (2016) 10 (2017) 3 (2018)	11 (2015) 4 (2016) 4 (2017)	Decrease

Another emergent theme of reasoning was *discipline-specific* connections, indicated by stating a particular discipline as reasoning with little further elaboration. As with the *teacher role* reasoning theme, a connection to other disciplines was not considered a component of engineering but rather a theme of reasoning why a scenario was or was not engineering. Some examples were, "No. Because fudge is more chemistry based than engineering", or "Yes. Focused in Civil Engineering", or "physics is taught here". This reasoning occurred moderately often compared to other responses (72 total responses) in every scenario with no strong correspondence to any scenario in particular. Use of this reasoning decreased from pre-test to post-test for every cohort year. For example, simple rationale such as, "Civil engineering" or "Bioengineering" decreased pre- to post-test and was often replaced by more descriptive reasoning, such as, "Yes. They have to make observations, measure, are creating something" for the scenario of a student making fudge.

Several participants, as rationale for their decision to categorize the activity as not engineering, claimed it "sounds more like chemistry" or "No, Cooking is hardly engineering". This represents novice understanding, where participants viewed academic disciplines as rigid and well-defined. As mentioned previously, such reasoning was more common in the pre-tests. The participants failed to see applications of other disciplines as pertinent to engineering. Most of the time these missed applications were other STEM disciplines, although one participant indicated that the debate about the pros and cons of genetically modified foods sounded, "more agricultural and social-political". The domain of mathematics was cited in various scenarios as rationale for considering the scenario engineering, "Maybe. If we discuss math behind this" and as rationale for considering the scenario as not engineering, "No. No math". Although several participants wrote that mathematics was necessary component of engineering, others indicated that it was part of background research, a skill building component, or that it needed to have multiple, complex steps and/or solutions and not just "plug and chug".

4. Discussion

This study builds on earlier work by replicating among preservice teachers many of the themes identified by in-service teachers in another study. The in-service teachers gave similar reasoning for required components of engineering or teaching engineering [27]. In-service teachers described

Application/Real-world context, creating a product/design/model, and *challenge/multistep-problem* most often as necessary components of engineering [27]. In this study, secondary science preservice teachers described the same three themes most often, although the exact ranking differed, most likely due to the difference in participants between that study ($n = 16$) and this one ($n = 43$). In light of the consistent results, the authors of this work believe that this study establishes replicability and pragmatic validity of the instrument.

The important themes of reasoning that emerged, namely *teacher role* and *discipline-specific*, pertain to the novice stage at which participants conceptualized engineering and teaching engineering and how those conceptions changed after instruction. This was most evident in the pre- to post-test change in *discipline-specific* reasoning. If science educators ask preservice teachers to integrate SEP into science lessons, then, the preservice teachers need to recognize that science, technology, engineering, and mathematics (STEM) disciplines are not mutually exclusive, and science educators must explicitly deliver this instruction. A model of integrated STEM courses has been proposed, which aligns with the NGSS [13]. Making explicit connections between disciplines and the integration of EDP into various science and mathematics domains may help move teachers from novice to expert levels [23,30]. A focus on the integration of STEM including activities such as lesson plans that encourage secondary science preservice teachers to integrate EDP into SEP may also be helpful.

Moving past a narrowly-defined concept of the boundaries of academic disciplines (or silos) is necessary if secondary science teachers aim to raise awareness of engineering careers in their students. One of the outcomes of an engineering PD for in-service teachers was fostering an awareness of engineering as a possible future career for their students [32], and this type of explicit instruction is beneficial and necessary. If secondary science teachers plan to instill an understanding of engineering in their student populations, then, they need to recognize that engineering is integrated among many STEM disciplines and moreover, that many STEM disciplines incorporate aspects of the engineering design process into discipline-specific practices. The fact that participants decreased the use of *discipline-specific* justifications as sufficient to exclude the scenario from engineering from pre- to post-test shows that participants may have recognized these cognitive contradictions and thought through how to resolve the issues [30]. Therefore, secondary science teachers could raise awareness of engineering careers in their classrooms by incorporating a more integrated, multidisciplinary, collaborative epistemological perspective of the engineering domain.

Many secondary science preservice teachers have an emerging understanding of the role the teacher should play in learning, particularly EDP. The responses that fit the *teacher role* theme used third-person rather than first-person. On the basis of textural analysis of the responses, the authors think use of this reasoning indicates an emerging perception of effective teaching in a general sense, not specific to teaching engineering domain. Because no participant indicated actual classroom teaching experience, no one drew a response from previous experience. Participants' *teacher role* responses may reflect emerging ideas about the role of the teacher in learning and the impact of student-centered learning. Secondary science preservice teachers' concepts of how teachers influence learning may need authentic experience to fully crystallize.

A novice level of understanding also became apparent by the number of responses that cited an over-simplified short phrase representing the *creating a product/design/model* theme as a component of engineering. This 'product for a problem' theme represented the most-often cited reason for categorizing the activity as engineering and was also the only theme that increased from pre-test to post-test in every cohort year. Novice knowledge does not entail the rich, multiple connections with other knowledge domains that is characteristic of expert knowledge [30]. Moreover, novices are less able to recognize subtle but important patterns and the significance of those patterns [23,30]. By applying an oversimplified, easy-to-remember phrase to many scenarios, participants revealed their inexperience with nuances and considerations that each scenario brings to bear. It is noteworthy to add that the science educator might have proliferated this participant response by repeating the phrase during the science methods coursework.

During the secondary science methods course discussion of EDP, providing a definition of engineering, and planning and implementing EDP in SEP, the science educator mentioned that engineering was a solution to a problem, provided a benefit to society, or was a process leading to a product realized by creating or building something. Many secondary science preservice teachers condensed these discussion points down to soundbite-size definitions that varied by cohort year. They tended to repeat the short phrase definition for almost all of the scenarios offered in the post-test. Almost all of the phrases dealt with a product, solution, or model. For example, a few phrases were: "Solving a problem", "Not creating anything", "No. No problem, no product", and "Starts with a problem, ends with a product". This style of reasoning most likely accounts for the slight drops in other components of engineering, namely *background research, brainstorming*, and *communication*, and the increase of defining engineering as *creating a product/design/model*. As participants internalized a new definition, in this case classification of the engineering domain, they tended to oversimplify and overgeneralize [23]. Hence, science educators should take caution and speak explicitly about what belongs in science and engineering practices.

Although the results represent progress in the sense that secondary science preservice teachers refined their epistemological knowledge of the EDP domain, opportunities exist for developing misconceptions. In recognizing that EDP involves creating of a model, product, or solving a problem, participants may have progressed from novice to "competent beginners" [23] (p. 37). Yet there is a danger for misconceptions to form. As mentioned previously, researchers in a prior study identified four misconceptions about engineering: (a) that research methods are defined by long-term implications or outcomes, (b) that science and engineering is hierarchal, (c) that creativity is appropriate only in the design/planning phase, and (d) that an engineering process cannot be a research outcome [24]. Any of those misconceptions could arise from early-career teachers simply applying the basic short phrase definition when planning future classroom curriculum.

4.1. Limitations

A limitation to this study is that although the results are compared to the themes generated in an earlier study, the methods of collecting data differed. Researchers in the earlier study collected data by verbal interview, which provided an opportunity to clarify questions, ask for clarification in responses, or ask follow-up questions [27]. A limitation of the written questionnaire is the inability to follow-up to the participants' responses. On the other hand, participants were free to expand on their reasoning and in fact, prompted to do so, limited only by how much they chose to write. One advantage of a written questionnaire is the reduction of interviewer bias and greater participant confidentiality. In this study, participants completed the questionnaires individually, and did not discuss their answers with their peers during questionnaire administration, which might have led to more honest answers. Participants were assured confidentiality to perhaps a greater extent than they would in-person interviews due to reaction of the interviewer, nonverbal language, prior acquaintance, etc. Participants were also assured of confidentiality because they generated a four-digit code for the pre- and post-questionnaires. They did not use their names anywhere other than the separate consent form.

This study was also limited by the learner context. Because all of the participants attended the same university and moved through the same secondary teacher education program over three years, the learner context did not appreciably differ by cohort year. While this encouraged reduction of variables, it also limited generalizability and multiple perspectives. Another limitation is that the researchers did not ask how many engineering courses participants had taken. It is not a requirement at the university where the study took place for students pursuing a secondary science education degree to take engineering courses. Other than the sole engineering major, it is unlikely that any of the participants had taken courses in engineering content.

This study used a subjectivist lens to describe individuals' beliefs and perspectives about a knowledge domain. In light of the modest cohort size (n = 43), no practical significance from year to year, and qualitative methodology the study is not generalizable to a larger population. The overall qualitative research framework using an interpretivist, constructivism theoretical perspective does not lend itself to quantitative analysis of the yes, no, and maybe questionnaire responses [35]. General trends were described to find practical significance [35]. Readers might find pragmatic validity to this study by determining if the results apply to other learners in other contexts.

4.2. Recommendations

From an instructional design vantage point, this study indicates a *need for instruction*. There is a clear need for this type of instruction if secondary science preservice teachers are providing novice-level reasoning as rationale for their answers to the scenario questions [5]. For example, several participants began with narrowly defined views of discipline areas, such as civil engineering or biology. Those participants did not view engineering as multidisciplinary endeavor, or, alternatively, that other disciplines could integrate engineering. Although evidence of this reasoning decreased from pre- to post-test, it still indicates novice conceptualizations need to be explored in greater detail in early-career PD or incorporated into redesign of secondary science methods courses.

This study indicates that science educators of secondary science preservice methods courses should begin instruction from a point of novice student understanding. Standard learner analysis parameters in instructional design include prior beliefs, knowledge, and experience [5]. With baseline information provided by this study, namely that instruction does impact beliefs about the EDP domain, effective instruction may be designed that can assist teachers adopt an innovation of integrating EDP in the classroom. Additionally, instructional efforts should be directed at preventing misconceptions, examining each component of EDP, and integrating EDP into SEP as well as with other STEM disciplines.

Examining each component of EDP should include examining the component of data analysis. Authentic science projects emphasizing how components of EDP fit together may help further participant understanding [18]. Secondary science preservice teachers' perception that data analysis alone is sufficient for classification as engineering presents an area for further research. Some researchers have begun to address this issue through expanded lessons focusing on data interpretation as evidence [22]. There is a need for methods instruction that encourages secondary science preservice teachers to expand their epistemological knowledge about engineering and the role data analysis plays as one necessary, but not entirely sufficient, part of EDP.

5. Conclusions

This study contributed to an instructional design needs and learner analysis by describing perceptions of engineering and teaching engineering among secondary science preservice teachers. Specifically, the authors described participant perceptions of which engineering components were required to classify an activity as engineering. As stated earlier, participants can be analyzed by a description of changing learner characteristics [5]. Although yes, no, or maybe responses did not appreciably change from pre- to post-test in any year, participants' reasoning did appreciably change after methods courses instruction in all three cohort years. This indicates that instruction is an effective way to shape perceptions and epistemological beliefs about engineering and teaching engineering [5]. Thus, this study supports a *need for instruction* on an innovation, illustrated in Figure 2—knowledge can be taught, and perceptions can change, about an innovation.

While it is encouraging to see that cognitive shifts in thinking occurred after instruction intervention, this study also comes with a warning of the dangers of oversimplification. Participants gained an emergent understanding of engineering and teaching engineering after methods course intervention. During instruction, many secondary science preservice teachers absorbed a working definition of engineering that shortened to some version of a process leading to the creation of a product or solving a problem. Although these soundbite-size definitions helped many to conceptualize engineering in a more holistic way, opportunities exist for misconceptions to arise following a too-narrow definition. Caution should be taken to ensure that the opportunity to acquire these misconceptions is minimized. Recommendations for designers of secondary science methods courses and early-career PD include providing opportunities for teachers to refine their perceptions and deepen their understanding about engineering and teaching engineering. Ways this may be addressed include examining the role of data analysis in SEP and exploring how EDP may be integrated with other STEM disciplines.

Author Contributions: Conceptualization, A.C.B.; Data curation, T.J.K. and A.C.B.; Formal analysis, T.J.K.; Funding acquisition, A.C.B.; Investigation, A.C.B.; Methodology, T.J.K.; Project administration, A.C.B.; Supervision, A.C.B.; Validation, T.J.K. and A.C.B.; Writing—original draft, T.J.K.; Writing—revisions & editing, A.C.B.

Funding: This work was supported by a National Science Foundation Noyce grant [#1339853]. Any opinions, findings, conclusions, or recommendations expressed in this material are those of the authors and do not necessarily reflect the views of the National Science Foundation.

Conflicts of Interest: The authors declare no conflict of interest.

References

1. NGSS Lead States. *Next Generation Science Standards: For States, by States*; The National Academies Press: Washington, DC, USA, 2013.
2. Rogers, E.M. *Diffusion of Innovations*, 5th ed.; Free Press: New York, NY, USA, 2003; ISBN 978-0-7432-2209-9.
3. Vincenti, W.G. *What Engineers Know and How They Know It: Analytical Studies from Aeronautical History*; The Johns Hopkins University Press: Baltimore, MD, USA, 1990; ISBN 0-8018-4588-2.
4. French, D.A.; Burrows, A.C. Evidence of science and engineering practices in preservice secondary science teachers' instructional planning. *J. Sci. Educ. Technol.* **2018**. [CrossRef]
5. Smith, P.L.; Ragan, T.J. *Instructional Design*, 3rd ed.; John Wiley & Sons, Inc.: Hoboken, NJ, USA, 2005; ISBN 0-471-39353-3.
6. American Association for the Advancement of Science (AAAS). *Project 2061: Science for All Americans*; Oxford University Press: New York, NY, USA, 1990.
7. Moore, T.J.; Tank, K.M.; Glancy, A.W.; Kersten, J.A. NGSS and the landscape of engineering in K-12 state science standards. *J. Res. Sci. Teach.* **2015**, *52*, 296–318. [CrossRef]
8. Locke, E. Proposed model for a streamlined, cohesive, and optimized K-12 STEM curriculum with a focus on engineering. *J. Technol. Stud.* **2009**, *35*, 23–35. [CrossRef]
9. Carr, R.L.; Bennett, I.V.L.D.; Strobel, J. Engineering in the K-12 STEM standards of the 50 U.S. states: An analysis of presence and extent. *J. Eng. Educ.* **2012**, *101*, 539–564. [CrossRef]
10. Pleasants, J.; Olson, J.K. What is engineering? Elaborating the nature of engineering for K-12 education. *Sci. Educ.* **2018**, 1–22. [CrossRef]
11. Wyoming State Board of Education. *2016 State Standards*. Available online: https://edu.wyoming.gov/educators/standards/science (accessed on 10 November 2018).
12. Katehi, L.; Pearson, G.; Feder, M. *Engineering in K-12 Education: Understanding the Status and Improving the Prospects*; National Academies Press: Washington, DC, USA, 2009.
13. Burrows, A.; Slater, T. A proposed integrated STEM framework for contemporary teacher preparation. *Teach. Educ. Pract.* **2015**, *28*, 318–330.
14. Ebert-May, D.; Derting, T.L.; Hodder, J.; Momsen, J.L.; Long, T.M.; Jardeleza, S.E. What we say is not what we do: Effective evaluation of faculty professional development programs. *Bioscience* **2011**, *61*, 550–558. [CrossRef]
15. Daugherty, J.L.; Custer, R.L. Secondary level engineering professional development: Content, pedagogy, and challenges. *Int. J. Technol. Educ.* **2012**, *22*, 51–64. [CrossRef]
16. Burrows, A. Partnerships: A systemic study of two professional developments with university faculty and K-12 teachers of science, technology, engineering, and mathematics. *Probl. Educ. 21st Century* **2015**, *65*, 28–38.
17. Burrows, A.; Borowczak, M.; Slater, T.; Haynes, J. Teaching computer science & engineering through robotics: Science & art form. *Probl. Educ. 21st Century* **2012**, *47*, 6–15.
18. Burrows, A.C.; DiPompeo, M.; Myers, A.; Hickox, R.; Borowczak, M.; French, D.; Schwortz, A. Authentic science experiences: Pre-collegiate science teachers' successes and challenges during professional development. *Probl. Educ. 21st Century* **2016**, *70*, 59–73.

19. Hofer, B.K.; Pintrich, P.R. The development of epistemological theories: Beliefs about knowledge and knowing and their relation to learning. *Rev. Educ. Res.* **1997**, *67*, 88–140. [CrossRef]
20. Gagné, R.M.; Briggs, L.J.; Wager, W.W. *Principles of Instructional Design*, 4th ed.; Harcourt Brace Jovanovich College Publishers: Fort Worth, TX, USA, 1992; ISBN 0-03-034757-2.
21. Antink-Meyer, A.; Brown, R.A. Second-career science teachers' classroom conceptions of science and engineering practices examined through the lens of their professional histories. *Int. J. Sci. Educ.* **2017**, *39*, 1511–1528. [CrossRef]
22. Duncan, R.G.; Chinn, C.A.; Brazilai, S. Grasp of evidence: Problematizing and expanding the next generation science standards' conceptualization of evidence. *J. Res. Sci. Teach.* **2018**, *55*, 907–937. [CrossRef]
23. National Research Council. *How People Learn: Brain, Mind, Experience, and School*; National Academy Press: Washington, DC, USA, 2000.
24. Antink-Meyer, A.; Meyer, D.Z. Science teachers' misconceptions in science and engineering distinctions: Reflections on modern research examples. *J. Sci. Teach. Educ.* **2016**, *27*, 625–647. [CrossRef]
25. Jones, M.G.; Carter, G. Science teacher attitudes and beliefs. In *Handbook of Research on Science Education*; Abell, S.K., Lederman, N.G., Eds.; Routledge: New York, NY, USA, 2007.
26. Hewson, P.W.; Hewson, M.G.A.B. Analysis and use of a task for identifying conceptions of teaching science. *J. Educ. Teach.* **1989**, *15*, 191–209. [CrossRef]
27. Thatcher, W.; Meyer, H. Identifying initial conceptions of engineering and teaching engineering. *Educ. Sci.* **2017**, *7*, 88. [CrossRef]
28. Yasar, S.; Baker, D.; Robinson-Kurpius, S.; Krause, S.; Roberts, C. Development of a survey to assess K-12 teachers' perceptions of engineers and familiarity with teaching design, engineering, and technology. *J. Eng. Educ.* **2006**, *95*, 205–216. [CrossRef]
29. Tank, K.M.; Raman, D.R.; Lamm, M.H.; Sundararajan, S.; Estapa, A. Teaching educators about engineering. *Sci. Child.* **2017**, *55*, 74–79. [CrossRef]
30. Ambrose, S.A.; Bridges, M.W.; DiPietro, M.; Lovett, M.C.; Norman, M.K. *How Learning Works: Seven Research-Based Principles for Smart Teaching*; John Wiley & Sons: San Francisco, FL, USA, 2010; ISBN 978-0-470-48410-4.
31. Nathan, M.J.; Tran, N.A.; Atwood, A.K.; Prevost, A.; Phelps, A. Beliefs and expectations about engineering preparation exhibited by high school STEM teachers. *J. Eng. Educ.* **2010**, *99*, 409–426. [CrossRef]
32. Autenrieth, R.L.; Lewis, C.W.; Butler-Purry, K.L. Long-Term impact of the enrichment experiences in engineering (E³) summer teacher program. *J. STEM Educ.* **2017**, *18*, 25–31.
33. Hammack, R.; Ivey, T.A.; Utley, J.; High, K.A. Effect of an engineering camp on students' perceptions of engineering and technology. *J. Pre-College Eng. Educ. Res.* **2015**, *5*. [CrossRef]
34. Cunningham, C.M.; Lachapelle, C.; Lindgren-Streicher, A. Assessing elementary school students' conceptions of engineering and technology. In Proceedings of the 2005 American Society for Engineering Education Annual Conference & Exposition, Portland, OR, USA, 12–15 June 2005; Available online: https://peer.asee.org/14836 (accessed on 26 December 2018).
35. Koro-Ljungberg, M.; Yendol-Hoppey, D.; Smith, J.J.; Hayes, S.B. (E)pistemological awareness, instantiation of methods, and uninformed methodological ambiguity in qualitative research projects. *Educ. Res.* **2009**, *38*, 687–699. [CrossRef]
36. Branch, R.M.; Dousay, T.A. *Survey of Instructional Design Models*, 5th ed.; AECT: Bloomington, IN, USA, 2015; ISBN 9780997075502.
37. Council of Chief State School Officers. *Interstate Teacher Assessment and Support Consortium InTASC Model Core Teaching Standards and Learning Progressions for Teachers 1.0: A Resource for Ongoing Teacher Development*; CCSSO: Washington, DC, USA, 2013.
38. NSTA. Standards for Science Teacher Preparation. Available online: http://www.nsta.org/preservice/docs/2012NSTAPreserviceScienceStandards.pdf (accessed on 10 November 2018).
39. Merriam, S.B.; Tisdell, E.J. *Qualitative Research: A Guide to Design and Implementation*, 4th ed.; Jossey-Bass: San Francisco, CA, USA, 2016; ISBN 978-1-119-00361-8.

education sciences

MDPI

Article

Training Future Engineers to Be Ghostbusters: Hunting for the Spectral Environmental Radioactivity

Matteo Albéri [1,2,*], Marica Baldoncini [1,2], Carlo Bottardi [1,3], Enrico Chiarelli [1,2], Sheldon Landsberger [4], Kassandra Giulia Cristina Raptis [1,2], Andrea Serafini [1,3], Virginia Strati [1,3] and Fabio Mantovani [1,3]

[1] Department of Physics and Earth Sciences, University of Ferrara, Via Saragat 1, 44121 Ferrara, Italy; baldoncini@fe.infn.it (M.B.); bottardi@fe.infn.it (C.B.); enrico.chiarelli@student.unife.it (E.C); kassandra.raptis@lnl.infn.it (K.G.C.R); serafini@fe.infn.it (A.S.); strati@fe.infn.it (V.S.); mantovani@fe.infn.it (F.M.)
[2] INFN, Legnaro National Laboratories, Viale dell'Università, 2, 35020 Legnaro, Padua, Italy
[3] INFN, Ferrara Section, Via Saragat 1, 44121 Ferrara, Italy
[4] Nuclear Engineering Teaching Lab, University of Texas, Pickle Research Campus R-9000, Austin, TX 78712, USA; s.landsberger@mail.utexas.edu
* Correspondence: alberi@fe.infn.it; Tel.: +39-329-0715-328

Received: 12 November 2018; Accepted: 11 January 2019; Published: 15 January 2019

check for updates

Abstract: Although environmental radioactivity is all around us, the collective public imagination often associates a negative feeling to this natural phenomenon. To increase the familiarity with this phenomenon we have designed, implemented, and tested an interdisciplinary educational activity for pre-collegiate students in which nuclear engineering and computer science are ancillary to the comprehension of basic physics concepts. Teaching and training experiences are performed by using a 4" × 4" NaI(Tl) detector for in-situ and laboratory γ-ray spectroscopy measurements. Students are asked to directly assemble the experimental setup and to manage the data-taking with a dedicated Android app, which exploits a client-server system that is based on the Bluetooth communication protocol. The acquired γ-ray spectra and the experimental results are analyzed using a multiple-platform software environment and they are finally shared on an open access Web-GIS service. These all-round activities combining theoretical background, hands-on setup operations, data analysis, and critical synthesis of the results were demonstrated to be effective in increasing students' awareness in quantitatively investigating environmental radioactivity. Supporting information to the basic physics concepts provided in this article can be found at http://www.fe.infn.it/radioactivity/educational.

Keywords: physics education; laboratory activity; environmental radioactivity; nuclear engineering experiment; Web-GIS platform; scintillator detector; Android app; in-situ measurements; computer science application; γ-ray spectroscopy

1. Introduction

In the last decade, various educational approaches have been developed by different scientists and teachers with the aim of giving a clear picture about radiation issues [1,2]. In the public domain, radioactivity can evoke negative feelings that are associated to nuclear accidents or radioactive waste management or diseases [3,4]. In this perspective, one of the missions of traditional radiation physics lectures is to make students aware that radiation from the ground and from the sky is all around us, with much of it passing through us constantly and that even food and our bodies are radioactive, to a degree. In this paper, we present two educational activities for pre-collegiate students, which adopt a mixed method that is based on applying nuclear engineering concepts and computer science tools to explore in-situ environmental radioactivity.

The two teaching and training activities are addressed to a group of 5–8 students and they are conceived as 4-h hands-on experiments (Table 1) involving the use of multiplatform software (Android, Windows) for the gamma spectra acquisition and analysis and for ad-hoc Web-GIS applications. A 4″ × 4″ thallium-activated sodium iodide (NaI(Tl)) scintillation detector, a relatively accessible and affordable instrument is employed in both experiments. Its high detection efficiency and the fact that it works at room temperature given the possibility of performing quick and reliable measurements in different experimental conditions, as typically requested in the case of educational experiences [5–7]. The experimental setup also consists of wireless dedicated nuclear electronics for the digitization of the signal, which integrates data storage as well as a data-taking programming capability in terms of main experimental parameters (acquisition time, operating voltage, etc.).

The indoor experiment is designed as a propaedeutic experience for the comprehension of the nature of gamma photons and of the main features characterizing a gamma-ray spectrum acquired with a scintillation detector. The outdoor experiment is structured in multiple in-situ measurements over different ground coverage types. This activity is intended to familiarize the students with the range of radioactivity levels that are present in the environment and to aid their critical understanding of the measurement of spatial resolution and of the spatial distribution of radioactivity in the investigated area.

Table 1. The supplies (equipment and software) used for the two experiments carried out during the educational activities, together with the corresponding educational aims. In both cases, the measurements are performed with a 4″ × 4″ thallium-activated sodium iodide (NaI(Tl)) detector and a MultiChannel Analyzer (MCA) γstream by CAEN.

	Equipment and Software	Educational Aims
Indoor experiment	• 4″ × 4″ NaI(Tl) detector with MultiChannel Analyzer (MCA) γstream by CAEN • Tablet or smartphone • GammaTOUCH app • Lead slabs • Point-like radioactive source (^{137}Cs) • Aluminum layers	• Assembling an experimental setup critically understanding the functioning of the components and the operation mode • Learning how to interpret a γ-ray spectrum acquired with a scintillation detector • Using an ad hoc Android app for gamma spectra analysis • Understanding of the high penetration capacity of gamma photons • Determination of linear attenuation coefficients of gamma radiation
Outdoor experiment	• 4″ × 4″ NaI(Tl) detector with MultiChannel Analyzer (MCA) γstream by CAEN • Tablet or smartphone • GammaTOUCH app • Google Maps • Google Earth	• Learning how to design and perform in-situ γ-ray spectrometry measurements • Exploiting the potentialities of a client-server system based on a Bluetooth communication protocol • Critical understanding of all unplanned factors making an in-situ γ-ray survey a complex issue • Adopting an open access Web-GIS platform to share and visualize the results through an interactive GUI

This educational path was tested preliminarily, involving pre-collegiate students and teachers of Italian high schools and improved in the framework of the Maymester "Concepts in Nuclear and Radiation Engineering" developed from an international cooperation between the University of Ferrara (Italy) and the Cockrell School of Engineering at the University of Texas at Austin (USA).

2. Theoretical Background

Radioactivity is a physical phenomenon occurring when an unstable nucleus undergoes a transition from one energy state to another and it is typically measured in becquerels, corresponding to one decay per second. Natural or artificial radiation sources can be found everywhere, starting from the first moments of life of our universe. Natural sources include the cosmogenic radionuclides, which are related to the interaction between cosmic rays and nuclei of atoms in the atmosphere, and the so-called primordial radionuclides existing since the Earth formed and that have not completely decayed due to their long half-life (~10^9 yr and longer). The most common isotopes in the Earth responsible for the so called terrestrial radiation are ^{238}U, ^{232}Th, and ^{40}K, together with their multiple daughter products. Although ^{235}U is also present, it is not considered as its isotopic abundance is 0.72%, to be compared with the 99.28% isotopic abundance of ^{238}U. It is estimated that 80% of the average annual dose for the world's population comes from natural background radiation [8].

While ^{40}K undergoes one single decay, ^{238}U and ^{232}Th produce decay chains that comprise α, β, and/or γ decays. The γ decays, in contrast to α and β, do not change the atomic number of the nuclei: they occur when a nucleus in an excited state, which is often produced by a previous decay (typically alpha or beta), emits a photon, called a γ ray, in order to reach a more stable configuration [9]. γ rays have the same physical nature as visible light but belong to a region of the electromagnetic spectrum characterized by higher frequencies (i.e., higher energies, tens to thousands of keV): as a consequence, they are invisible to our eyes and a detector is needed in order to reveal them.

Uranium-238 has a half-life of 4.47×10^9 years and its decay chain comprises 18 unstable isotopes among which the main gamma emitters are ^{234m}Pa, ^{214}Pb, and ^{214}Bi. ^{232}Th has a half-life of 1.41×10^{10} years, its decay chain includes 12 unstable isotopes, among which the main gamma emitters are ^{228}Ac, ^{212}Pb, ^{212}Bi, and ^{208}Tl. Here, we measure ^{214}Bi and ^{208}Tl by monitoring gamma lines having an energy of 1764 keV and 2614 keV, respectively. In particular, the 2614 keV gamma emission from ^{208}Tl corresponds to the endpoint of the terrestrial γ-ray spectrum that is associated with the ^{232}Th decay chain. Argon-40, the daughter of ^{40}K decays, produces a gamma signal at 1460 keV, which is usually a distinctive feature of the environmental gamma spectrum.

A photon can interact with matter mainly via three processes: the photoelectric effect, the Compton scattering, and the pair production-annihilation [10]. Through these phenomena, the energy of the γ rays is deposited in a given material in the form of kinetic energy of electrons. The photoelectric effect is predominant for low energies and it arises from the absorption of a photon by an atom and the ejection of an electron from one of the atomic bound shells. Compton scattering is the main interaction mechanism of terrestrial gamma photons, as it dominates at intermediate energies (~1 MeV). It is the process by which a photon scatters from a nearly free atomic electron, resulting in a less energetic photon and a scattered electron carrying the energy lost by the photon. The energy that is gathered by the scattered electron (and finally deposited in the detector) is a continuous function of the scattering angle and it is what gives rise in a measured spectrum to the Compton continuum (Figure 1b). The maximum energy transferable to the electron in a single collision is obtained for backscattered photon and it is at the origin of the formation of the so called Compton edge (Figure 1b). The pair production process corresponds to the conversion of a γ ray into an electron-positron pair and it occurs only if the gamma has a minimum energy equal to the mass of the particle pair ($2 m_e c^2 = 1022$ keV).

If one considers a gamma beam propagating in matter in the direction x and if N_0 corresponds to the initial number of gammas, due to the interplay of the three attenuating processes described before, the beam loses a number of photons ΔN. The relative photon loss $\Delta N/N$ is proportional to the covered distance Δx:

$$\frac{\Delta N}{N} = -\mu_{mass}\rho\Delta x, \tag{1}$$

with μ_{mass} in cm^2/g being the mass attenuation coefficient of the traversed material [11]. Figure 1a shows the overall μ_{mass} for aluminum as a function of the gamma energy, together with the relative contributions of the three interaction mechanisms. The linear attenuation coefficient μ represents the inverse of the distance at which the number of photons is reduced by a factor *1/e*, as can be inferred by the following equation [12]:

$$N = N_0 e^{-\mu x}, \tag{2}$$

where μ in cm^{-1} is obtained by multiplying μ_{mass} times the material density ρ in g/cm^3. In order to experimentally test this theory, a monoenergetic photon beam can be produced by surrounding a point-like radioactive source that is characterized by a single gamma emission with a lead box having a small hole on one side, which is meant to produce a collimating effect.

The experiments are performed by using a 4″ × 4″ (NaI(Tl)) detector that can acquire a γ-ray spectrum (see Section 3), i.e., a histogram of events classified according to the energy deposited inside the detector itself. A typical feature that can be observed in a γ-ray spectrum is the so-called photopeak, which is populated by those events in which a gamma photon, having energy that is equal to the one of the decay, impinges on the scintillator depositing its full energy in the active detector volume (Figure 1b).

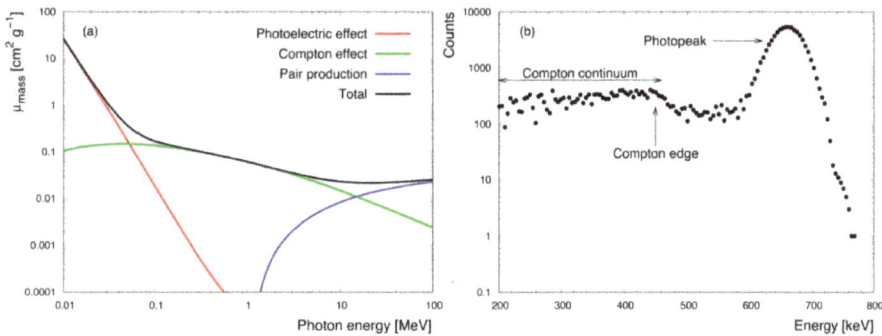

Figure 1. (a) Mass attenuation coefficient (μ_{mass}) for aluminum as function of the photon energy (source: https://physics.nist.gov): the three contributions due to the photoelectric, Compton and pair production interactions are separately displayed. (b) Example of a gamma spectrum acquired by juxtaposing a ^{137}Cs point-like source to a non-shielded NaI(Tl) detector in which the photopeak shape centered at 661.7 keV is clearly visible, together with the lower energy Compton continuum and the structure of the Compton edge.

Equation (2) is the key for understanding the lateral horizon of in-situ γ-ray spectroscopy. The horizontal field of view of a γ-ray detector expresses the relative contribution to the total signal that is produced within a given radial distance from the detector vertical axis. The lateral horizon depends on the height of the detector: for instance, a spectrometer that was placed at ground level receives 90% of the signal from a radius of ~0.5 m (Figure 2); at a height of 0.5 m, 90% of the signal come from a radius of ~8 m (Figure 2 of [11]).

Supporting information to the basic concepts that are provided in this section can be found at http://www.fe.infn.it/radioactivity/educational, a website designed for teachers and students who want to deal with the topic of environmental gamma radioactivity using the didactic approach that is described in this paper.

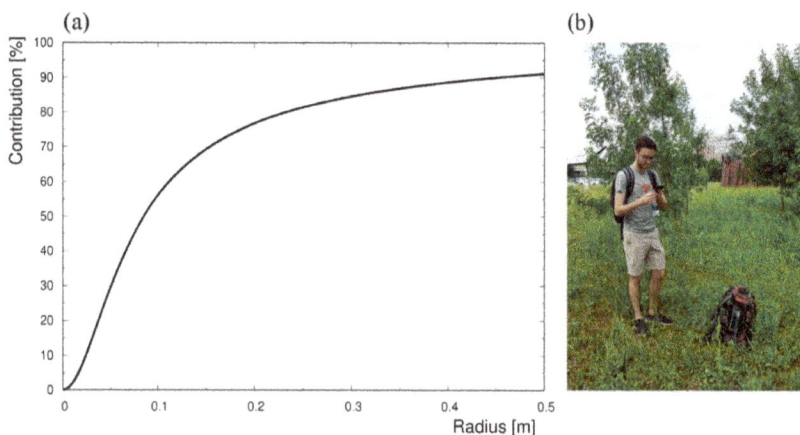

Figure 2. (**a**) Cumulative percentage contribution to the 1460 keV (⁴⁰K) unscattered γ signal as function of the radial distance from the vertical symmetry axis of the detector placed at 5 cm above the ground, assuming a homogeneous radioactive content of the soil. (**b**) A student performing an in-situ measurement with the backpack placed on the ground.

3. Indoor Experiment

The indoor experiment functions as preparatory training for the outdoor experiment depicted in Section 4. By assembling an experimental setup in the laboratory, students learn about the mode of operation of a detector during an environmental γ-ray spectroscopy measurement. Using an ad-hoc Android app, the students learn to handle the measurements and visualize the acquired spectra. Finally, by retrieving the counting statistics information, students are able to determine the linear attenuation coefficient of a given material [13]. This educational experience has the aim of enhancing the knowledge about radioactivity in terms of both natural and artificial sources as well as making the students gain experience of the high level of penetration of γ-rays in matter, which makes γ-ray spectroscopy an effective in-situ monitoring technique.

The experimental setup consists in a 4″ × 4″ NaI(Tl) detector, a PhotoMultiplier Tube (PMT) and a digital MultiChannel Analyzer (MCA, γstream by CAEN) (Figure 3).

Figure 3. Experimental setup for the indoor experiment: on the left the tablet showing the graphical interface of the GammaTOUCH app during the acquisition, on the right the 4″ × 4″ NaI(Tl) detector and the lead box.

During an acquisition, the detector produces an amount of scintillation light proportional to the energy that is deposited in the NaI(Tl) crystal by the incident γ-ray. By coupling the NaI(Tl) to a PMT, scintillation light is converted to an amplified electric pulse that is proportional to the gamma energy. This signal is in turn digitized by a MCA, allowing for one to obtain recorded events classified according to the deposited energy and therefore to populate an energy spectrum. Since the NaI(Tl) crystals are characterized by a relatively high scintillation efficiency, the detector is usually able to collect sufficient statistics in a short time, also yielding an energy resolution of a level to enable radionuclide identification. The γstream can be operated via the Android app GammaTOUCH, which uses the Bluetooth communication protocol: this app allows the user to set the operating voltage, specify the acquisition time, and start the measurement. The measurements of this experiment are performed while using a collimated point-like ^{137}Cs source that emits monochromatic gamma photons at 662 keV.

3.1. Energy Calibration of the Gamma Spectrum

In the first part of the experiment, students start an acquisition, setting the γstream operating voltage to 850 V and the acquisition time to 800 s. The graphic interface of the GammaTOUCH app continuously updates the histogram shape by showing the cumulative number of events over time. This preliminary step helps the students to identify the main photopeaks and to distinguish them from local fluctuations, as well as to start decrypting the information that was encoded in the different energy ranges. When the acquisition ends, the spectrum is saved in an ASCII file that lists, in a single column, the number of events for each channel and that can be opened and manipulated in an Excel spreadsheet.

A dedicated Android app performs the energy calibration of the spectrum (Figure 4), which converts the acquisition channels into energy deposited inside the detector according to the following equation:

$$E = m \cdot ch + q, \tag{3}$$

where E is the energy in keV corresponding to the channel ch, m is the gain in keV/ch (i.e., the width of a single acquisition channel), and q is the intercept in keV, corresponding to the energy of the first channel (Figure 4b).

The energy calibration procedure is based on the reconstruction of the Gaussian shapes of the [40]K and [208]Tl photopeaks corresponding, respectively, to the 1460 keV and 2614 keV gamma emissions. Knowing the energies of the gamma emission and the channels corresponding to the Gaussian means, the slope, and intercept of the linear relation given by (3) are calculated, as shown in the app graphical user interface (Figure 4a) and subsequently used by the students to integrate the counts of measured spectra in the energy windows of interest (Figure 5).

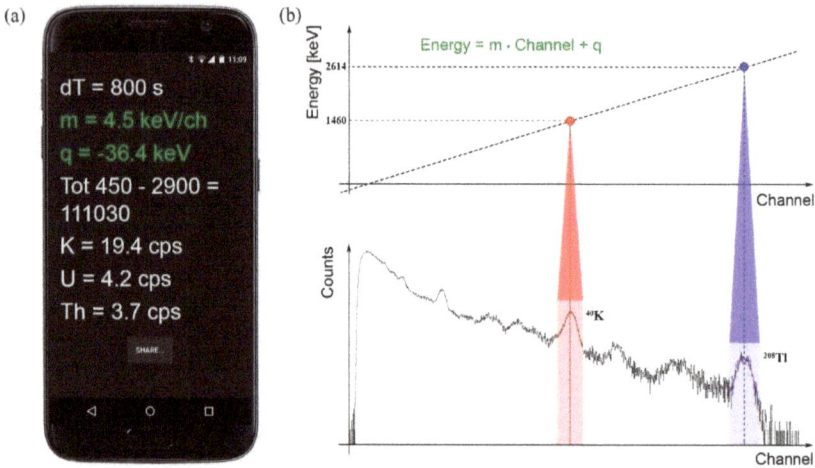

Figure 4. (**a**) Screenshot of the output of the Android app performing the energy calibration of the gamma spectrum: m and q represent respectively the slope and the intercept of the linear function determined on the base of the Gaussian reconstruction of the ^{40}K and ^{208}Tl photopeaks at 1460 keV and 2614 keV (**b**).

The integrated number of occurrences N for each of the four energy windows of interest [14] (Figure 5) is obtained by summing the number of counts N_i recorded in all of the energy channels belonging to the specific window. The count rate n is then directly calculated by normalizing for the acquisition time T as $n = \frac{N}{T}$. At the end of this procedure, the students measured the count rate in the ^{137}Cs photopeak energy window in the absence of any ^{137}Cs source. This measurement represents the environmental background acquisition determining the background count rate $n_{Cs\text{-}bkg}$.

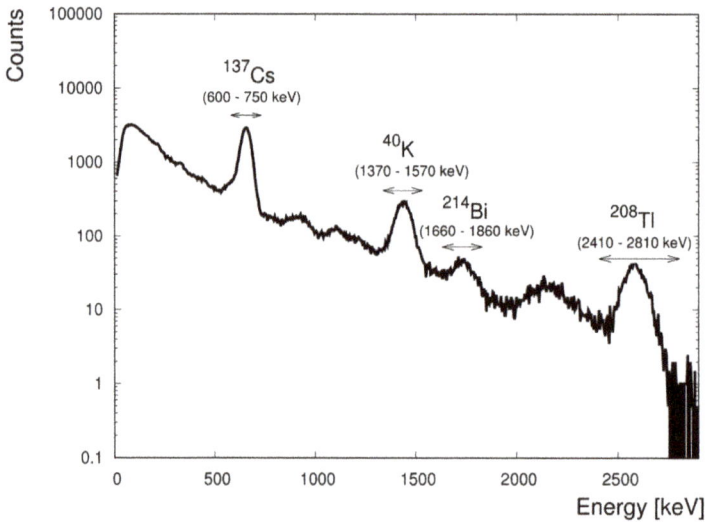

Figure 5. A γ-ray spectrum acquired in laboratory with a 4″ × 4″ NaI(Tl) detector in presence of a ^{137}Cs point-like source for an acquisition time of 360 s. The most prominent photopeaks of ^{137}Cs, ^{40}K, ^{214}Bi (^{238}U daughter) and ^{208}Tl (^{232}Th daughter) are highlighted, together with the energy windows of interest in keV used for the count rate integration.

3.2. Linear Attenuation Coefficient Derivation

The goal of the second part of the experiment is to derive the linear attenuation coefficient of aluminum by using the ^{137}Cs point-like source and 16 aluminum layers, each one having a thickness of 2.9 mm. The source is located inside a lead shielding box at a distance of 46.4 mm from the crystal bottom, which corresponds to the full thickness of all the aluminum attenuating layers (Figure 6a). The lead box has a 0.5 cm diameter hole, which allows the collimation of the gamma radiation in order to reproduce the mono-directional boundary condition described in Section 2 (see Equations (1) and (2)).

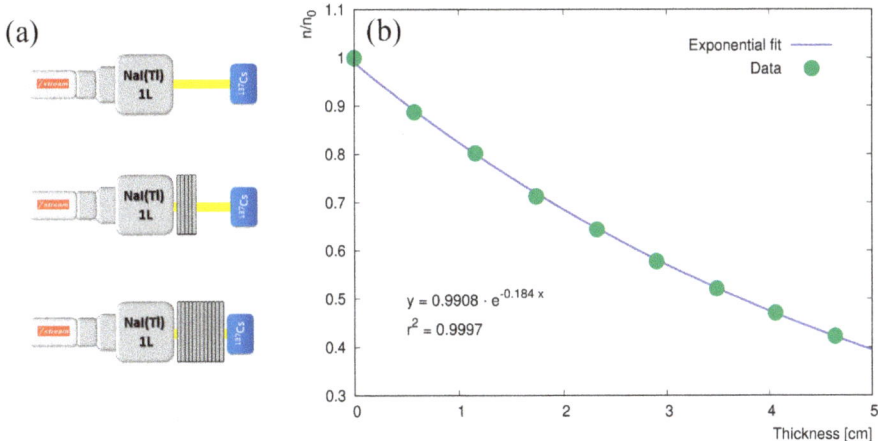

Figure 6. (a) A scheme of the different experimental configuration designed for the determination of the aluminum linear attenuation coefficient μ. The students perform consecutive acquisitions by adding two aluminum layers each time, until the space between the detector and the ^{137}Cs point-like source is completely filled. (b) The green points represent the experimental values of the ratio $\frac{n}{n_0}$ where n_0 and n are, respectively, the net count rates recorded in the ^{137}Cs photopeak in the absence and in the presence of aluminum attenuating layers of given thickness. The blue curve is the exponential fit function from which the experimental μ of aluminum (0.184 cm^{-1}) is retrieved.

Once the experimental setup is ready, the first 360 s acquisition is started in the absence of any attenuating layer. Then, the eight successive 360 s acquisitions are performed by adding each time two aluminum layers. Finally in the last measurement, the space between the detector and the source is completely filled (Figure 6a).

The net count rate in the ^{137}Cs photopeak n is obtained by subtracting to the total count rate n_{total}, measured in presence of a given aluminum thickness, the background count rate n_{Cs-bkg}, measured during the environmental background acquisition in the first part of the experiment. The net count rate that was measured in the absence of any attenuating material n_0 is used as the normalization factor for each measurement performed in the presence of aluminum layers. Indeed, for each configuration, the ratio $\frac{n}{n_0}$ is plotted versus the layer thickness (Figure 6b). The Excel fitting tool is employed in order to reconstruct the exponential trend of the ratio $\frac{n}{n_0}$ as a function of the total thickness of aluminum layers, retrieving the value of the aluminum linear attenuation coefficient μ (as in Equation (2)).

The obtained result (0.184 cm^{-1}) is converted into a mass attenuation coefficient $\mu_{mass} = 0.0681$ cm^2/g by dividing for the 2.70 g/cm^3 aluminum density. The students compare the result that is obtained with the reference value of 0.0747 cm^2/g taken from the National Institute of Standards and Technology (NIST) database (https://physics.nist.gov). The students are stimulated to critically discuss the result, trying to justify the differences between the experimental and the reference value, due, for instance, to the presence of the stainless steel crystal housing or to the imperfect collimating effect of the hole in the lead shielding box. By checking the μ_{mass} value on the NIST database the students can appreciate from a numerical and graphical point of view its energy dependence and discuss the dominating interactions in different energy ranges.

Finally, the students are asked to make a further comparison between the experimental μ of aluminum and the NIST database value of μ for air (9.52×10^{-5} cm^{-1}). The discussion raised from this further comparison is functional in making the students master, through a joint and interdisciplinary approach, the concepts of the highly penetrating nature of the gamma radiation and of the dependence of the linear attenuation coefficient on the type of attenuating material.

4. Outdoor Experiment

The outdoor experiment is dedicated to the design and the realization of in-situ γ-ray spectrometry measurements during which the potentialities of a client-server system are exploited. This hand-on experiment lets the students familiarize themselves with the factors affecting the different levels of terrestrial gamma radiation in the environment. Unlike a laboratory experience, in the outside environment, it is impossible to manage all of the parameters characterizing the experimental conditions. In the specific case of in-situ γ-ray spectroscopy, there are many variables that could interfere with the measurement, such as the presence of vegetation or buildings and the morphology of the area affecting the field of view of the spectrometer (Figure 2a) [15,16]. In addition, soil humidity has an attenuating effect on gamma radiation and sources having weak intensities need longer acquisition times. In order to compensate for these potential nuisances, a well-designed measurement procedure could help in minimizing the effects of outdoor factors. In this sense, students are stimulated to carefully adhere to the acquisition procedure, which comprises taking notes of all the relevant experimental conditions, especially in terms of their potential impact on the experimental outcomes. Finally, the results of the measurements are translated in a thematic map that can be visualized and then shared, together with the input data, on an open access Web-GIS platform via an interactive GUI.

The same detector (4" × 4" NaI(Tl)) described for the indoor experiment is employed for the outdoor survey, just arranged inside a backpack for portability. As the protagonists of the Ghostbusters movie, the students wear a backpack that makes them able to capture γ-ray spectra, which, like ghosts, are invisible to the eye. In outdoor campaigns, the potential of the instrument is fully exploited, as performing the measurement with just the use of an Android tablet simplifies and quickens the data taking operations.

4.1. In-Situ Gamma-Ray Survey

The in-situ survey is planned keeping in mind the spatial resolution of the desired information. The adopted strategy consists in choosing the sampling points in order to cover the surveyed area comprehensively for the different types of ground coverage, like asphalt, grass, or brick (Figure 7). A map of the measurement points located in and around the area is previously loaded in the Google Maps app of a smartphone. For each measurement point, the students perform a 180 s acquisition, take a picture of the area surrounding the detector, and compile the measurement sheet with GPS coordinates, type of ground coverage, and the measurement ID provided by the GammaTOUCH app. Knowing the detector field of view (Figure 2a), the students place the backpack at a sufficient distance from vertical structures (e.g., walls, trees) and avoiding standing close to the instrument during the acquisition. In this way, both the attenuation and the radiation emission effects of their bodies are minimized. During the data acquisition, the students are encouraged to make questions and assumptions, i.e., about the effects that a change in atmospheric conditions or soil humidity or about the type of ground coverage that would be the most or least abundant in natural radioactivity and to explain why, in order to support their views.

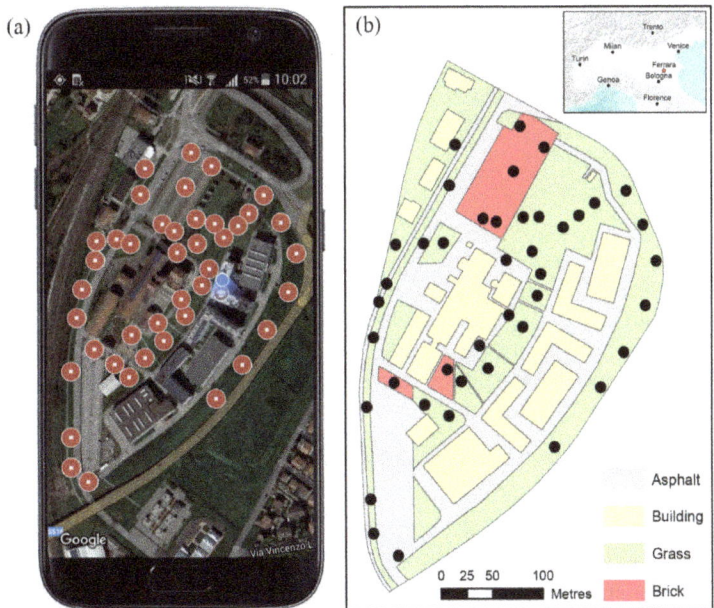

Figure 7. (**a**) Planned measurement points (red dots) reported in the Google Maps app; (**b**) Simplified map of the campus and the superimposed measurement points (black dots). The background colors indicate different types of ground coverage.

4.2. From Counts to Radioelements Concentrations

After the survey, the experimental results are organized in an Excel file, together with the information that is related to the data taking conditions. The Android app that is described in Section 4 is used for the energy calibration of the gamma spectra and for retrieving the total counts in the ^{40}K, ^{214}Bi, and ^{208}Tl energy windows of interest (Figure 5) applying the Window Analysis Method [14]. The *K*, *U*, and *Th* concentrations (*C*) are determined by essentially applying the expression:

$$C = \frac{N}{S},\qquad(4)$$

where *N* is the net count rate in the photopeak associated to the investigated element and *S* is the sensitivity coefficient determined from the calibration measurements on the ground at natural sites [17].

The total specific activity *A*, measured in becquerel per kilogram (Bq/kg) due to the terrestrial radionuclides radiation is then determined as [14]:

$$A = 313 \cdot C_K + 12.35 \cdot C_U + 4.06 \cdot C_{Th},\qquad(5)$$

where C_K is the potassium concentration in 10^{-2} g/g and C_U and C_{Th} are the uranium and thorium concentration in μg/g. More details about the analysis method as well as on the conversion from mass abundance to specific activity are provided in http://www.fe.infn.it/radioactivity/educational.

The results of the in-situ γ-ray measurements that were performed during the 2017 Maymester "Concepts in Nuclear and Radiation Engineering" are reported in Table 2 in terms of *K*, *U*, and *Th* concentrations.

Table 2. Mean and standard deviation of the *K*, *U*, and *Th* concentrations that were obtained from the in-situ γ-ray measurements distinguished according to the different ground coverage types. The measurements were performed during the 2017 Maymester.

Ground Coverage	Number of Measurements	K [10^{-2} g/g]	U [μg/g]	Th [μg/g]
Brick	7	0.82 ± 0.19	1.8 ± 0.5	4.1 ± 1.0
Grass	28	2.08 ± 0.32	1.7 ± 0.4	9.5 ± 1.8
Asphalt	7	1.20 ± 0.10	1.9 ± 0.4	5.1 ± 0.7

Adopting a Web-GIS platform, a kml file, a Google Earth supported format that is suitable for open access on-line publication, is created. The kml file reports the measurement points, each one assigned with the corresponding total specific activity and a picture of the acquisition location (Figure 8a). By easily inspecting the data reported in the kml file, the students are able to discuss the results, understand how radioactivity is spatially distributed, and how it relates to the ground coverage type.

4.3. From Measurements to Map

The measurements performed during the outdoor experiment are used to create the map of the natural radioactivity expressed in total specific activity in Bq/kg of the investigated area and a kml file for open access on-line publication (Figure 8b). The data spatialization is performed by adopting a multivariate geostatistical interpolator, the Collocated CoKriging [18] (CCoK). The CCoK is applied in order to predict the total specific activity, the under-sampled primary variable, using as constraint a secondary variable known in each location, i.e., the type of ground coverage. A continuous grid is created for the investigated area and a pseudo-random value is assigned to each type of coverage in order to obtain a normal distribution. The radiometric measurements are spatially conjoined to the coverage grid and a multivariate point dataset is obtained. The CCoK interpolation models are obtained by calculating experimental semi-variograms and experimental cross-semivariograms. Finally, the spatial interpolation is performed using a homogenous grid with a 10 m resolution. The students are encouraged to take under consideration the spatial resolution and distribution of γ-ray spectroscopy measurements.

The map of the natural radioactivity of the area investigated during the Maymester can be downloaded at http://www.fe.infn.it/radioactivity/educational (Mapping section), together with the kml files.

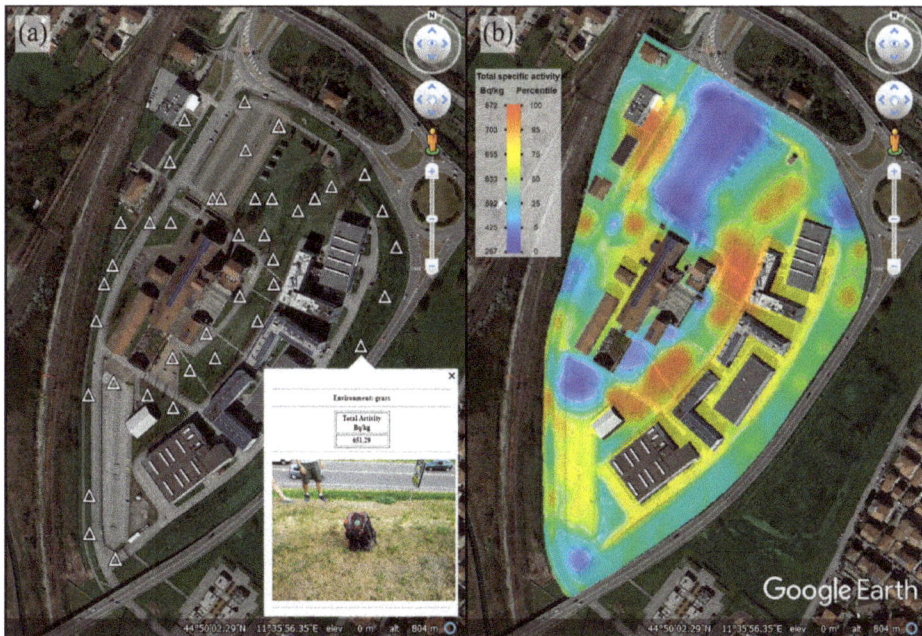

Figure 8. (**a**) Web-GIS tool for visualizing the measurement points (triangles) of natural radioactivity in the area investigated during the Maymester. By clicking on them a box containing the information gathered by the students shows up. (**b**) Map of the total specific activity in Bq/kg obtained from the spatial interpolation of the 42 in-situ γ-ray measurements.

5. Conclusions

The presented educational activities addressed to pre-collegiate students provide a successful example of the effectiveness of a mixed approach based on the use of engineering and computer science tools for conveying basic physics concepts that are related to the environmental radioactivity in-situ measurement. By reproducing these practical lectures, teachers are able to provide by means of a coherent multidisciplinary approach a method that is focused on a problem-solving attitude and consisting in analysis design, critical thinking, communication, and teamwork. The hands-on experiments are an opportunity for pre-collegiate students to break out of the traditional learning approach and to concretely tackle the challenges that a professional engineer could face.

By carrying out the indoor and the outdoor experiments, the students learnt how to perform a γ-ray spectroscopy measurement from the point of view of both hardware assembling and of software data taking and analysis. The gamma radiometric acquisition was discussed in all the relevant aspects, from the interpretation of the distinct features of the spectrum to the critical inspection of the experimental conditions that can potentially affect the outcome of the measurements. In the elaboration of the experimental data, the students are asked to work collaboratively in teams in order to extract from the acquired spectra quantitative information on the attenuating properties of a given material or to assess the radioactive content of different types of ground coverage.

During the indoor experiment, the students gather propaedeutic knowledge that is related to the interpretation of a γ-ray spectrum by identifying the distinct spectral features of the Compton continuum and of the photopeaks. Furthermore, the students quantitatively assess the high penetration nature of gamma radiation by estimating the linear attenuation coefficient of aluminum and by comparing it with the reference value and with that of air.

A total of 42 outdoor measurements were performed on brick, grass, and asphalt by using an Android app both for the managing of the experimental set up and for the retrieving of the net count rates in the natural radionuclide main photopeaks. The results that were obtained during the outdoor experiment in terms of total activity originating from *K*, *U*, and *Th* are visualized and published by means of a Google Earth kml file on an open access platform and they are synthetized in the natural radioactivity map of the investigated area.

Finally, the course assessment questionnaires were demonstrated to be an excellent source of feedback from the students regarding the educational content of the activities as well as the teaching methodologies.

Author Contributions: Conceptualization, M.A., M.B., S.L., V.S. and F.M.; Investigation, M.A., M.B., E.C., K.G.C.R. and F.M.; Methodology, M.A., M.B., E.C., K.G.C.R. and F.M.; Resources, M.A., M.B., E.C., K.G.C.R. and F.M.; Software, M.A., M.B. and E.C.; Writing—original draft, M.A., M.B., C.B., E.C., S.L., K.G.C.R., V.S. and F.M.; Writing—review & editing, M.A., M.B., S.L., K.G.C.R., A.S., V.S. and F.M.

Funding: This work was partially founded by the National Institute of Nuclear Physics (INFN) through the ITALian RADioactivity project (ITALRAD) and by the Theoretical Astroparticle Physics (TAsP) research network. The co-authors would like to acknowledge the support of the Geological and Seismic Survey of the Umbria Region (UMBRIARAD), of the University of Ferrara (Fondo di Ateneo per la Ricerca scientifica FAR 2017–2018).

Acknowledgments: The authors would like to thank the staff of Consorzio Futuro in Ricerca, CAEN Spa and GeoExplorer Impresa sociale s.r.l. for their support and Sandro Bardelli, Roberto Calabrese, Ivan Callegari, Giovanni Di Domenico, Adam Drescher, Adriano Duatti, Giovanni Fiorentini, Michele Montuschi, Andrea Motti, Ferruccio Petrucci, Barbara Ricci, Raffaele Tripiccione and Gerti Xhixha. We are indebted to the University of Texas Cockrell School of Engineering and Ellen Aoki, Senior Academic Program Coordinator, and the Study Abroad Program in the International Office for organizing the one month course in 2016, 2017 and 2018.

Conflicts of Interest: The authors declare no conflict of interest.

References

1. Siegel, P. Gamma spectroscopy of environmental samples. *Am. J. Phys.* **2013**, *81*, 381–388. [CrossRef]
2. Pilakouta, M.; Savidou, A.; Vasileiadou, S. A laboratory activity for teaching natural radioactivity. *Eur. J. Phys.* **2016**, *38*, 015801. [CrossRef]
3. Prather, E. Students' beliefs about the role of atoms in radioactive decay and half-life. *J. Geosci. Educ.* **2005**, *53*, 345–354. [CrossRef]
4. Neumann, S.; Hopf, M. Students' conceptions about 'radiation': Results from an explorative interview study of 9th grade students. *J. Sci. Educ. Technol.* **2012**, *21*, 826–834. [CrossRef]
5. Anjos, R.; Okuno, E.; Gomes, P.; Veiga, R.; Estellita, L.; Mangia, L.; Uzeda, D.; Soares, T.; Facure, A.; Brage, J. Radioecology teaching: evaluation of the background radiation levels from areas with high concentrations of radionuclides in soil. *Eur. J. Phys.* **2003**, *25*, 133. [CrossRef]
6. Anjos, R. Radioecology teaching: response to a nuclear or radiological emergency. *Eur. J. Phys.* **2006**, *27*, 243. [CrossRef]
7. Peralta, L. Measuring the activity of a radioactive source in the classroom. *Eur. J. Phys.* **2004**, *25*, 211. [CrossRef]
8. UNSCEAR. *Sources and effects of ionizing radiation. Volume I: Sources Report to the General Assembly, with Scientific Annexes*; United Nations Publications: Herndon, VA, USA, 2000.
9. Kocher, D.C. *Radioactive decay data tables*; Oak Ridge National Lab.: Oak Ridge, TN, USA, 1981.
10. Tsoulfanidis, N.; Landsberger, S. *Measurement and detection of radiation*, 4th ed.; Group, T.F., Ed.; CRC Press: Boca Raton, FL, USA, 2015.
11. Baldoncini, M.; Albéri, M.; Bottardi, C.; Chiarelli, E.; Raptis, K.G.C.; Strati, V.; Mantovani, F. Investigating the potentialities of Monte Carlo simulation for assessing soil water content via proximal gamma-ray spectroscopy. *J. Environ. Radioact.* **2018**, *192*, 105–116. [CrossRef] [PubMed]
12. Kucuk, N.; Tumsavas, Z.; Cakir, M. Determining photon energy absorption parameters for different soil samples. *J. Radiat. Res.* **2012**, *54*, 578–586. [CrossRef] [PubMed]
13. Adamides, E.; Koutroubas, S.; Moshonas, N.; Yiasemides, K. Gamma-ray attenuation measurements as a laboratory experiment: Some remarks. *Phys. Educ.* **2011**, *46*, 398. [CrossRef]

14. IAEA. *Guidelines for Radioelement Mapping Using Gamma Ray Spectrometry Data*; Technical Report Series No. 323; International Atomic Energy Agency: Vienna, Austria, 2003.

15. Xhixha, M.K.; Albèri, M.; Baldoncini, M.; Bezzon, G.; Buso, G.; Callegari, I.; Casini, L.; Cuccuru, S.; Fiorentini, G.; Guastaldi, E. Uranium distribution in the Variscan Basement of Northeastern Sardinia. *J. Maps* **2016**, *12*, 1029–1036. [CrossRef]

16. Baldoncini, M.; Albèri, M.; Bottardi, C.; Chiarelli, E.; Raptis, K.G.C.; Strati, V.; Mantovani, F. Biomass water content effect in soil water content assessment via proximal gamma-ray spectroscopy. *Geoderma* **2019**, *335*, 69–77. [CrossRef]

17. Caciolli, A.; Baldoncini, M.; Bezzon, G.; Broggini, C.; Buso, G.; Callegari, I.; Colonna, T.; Fiorentini, G.; Guastaldi, E.; Mantovani, F. A new FSA approach for in situ γ ray spectroscopy. *Sci. Total Environ.* **2012**, *414*, 639–645. [CrossRef] [PubMed]

18. Guastaldi, E.; Baldoncini, M.; Bezzon, G.; Broggini, C.; Buso, G.; Caciolli, A.; Carmignani, L.; Callegari, I.; Colonna, T.; Dule, K. A multivariate spatial interpolation of airborne γ-ray data using the geological constraints. *Remote Sens. Environ.* **2013**, *137*, 1–11. [CrossRef]

MDPI

St. Alban-Anlage 66

4052 Basel

Switzerland

Tel. +41 61 683 77 34

Fax +41 61 302 89 18

www.mdpi.com

Education Sciences Editorial Office

E-mail: education@mdpi.com

www.mdpi.com/journal/education

www.ingramcontent.com/pod-product-compliance
Lightning Source LLC
Chambersburg PA
CBHW051315020426
42333CB00028B/3355